Succeeding in College
with Asperger Syndrome

of related interest

The Complete Guide to Asperger's Syndrome
Tony Attwood
ISBN 978 1 84310 495 7

The Autism Spectrum and Further Education
A Guide to Practice
Christine Breakey
ISBN 978 1 84310 382 0

A Self-Determined Future with Asperger Syndrome
Solution Focused Approaches
E. Veronica Bliss and Genevieve Edmonds
ISBN 978 1 84310 513 8

Career Training and Personal Planning for Students
with Autism Spectrum Disorders
A Practical Resource for Schools
Vicki Lundine and Catherine Smith
ISBN 978 1 84310 440 7

Asperger Syndrome and Employment DVD
A Personal Guide to Succeeding at Work
Nick Dubin with Gail Hawkins
ISBN 978 1 84310 849 8

Asperger Syndrome and Long-Term Relationships
Ashley Standford
ISBN 978 1 84310 734 7

Coming Out Asperger
Diagnosis, Disclosure and Self-Confidence
Edited by Dinah Murray
ISBN 978 1 84310 240 3

Counselling People on the Autism Spectrum
A Practical Manual
Katherine Paxton and Irene A. Estay
ISBN 978 1 84310 552 7

Succeeding in College with Asperger Syndrome

A student guide

John Harpur, Maria Lawlor and Michael Fitzgerald

Jessica Kingsley Publishers
London and Philadelphia

Extract from *A Guide to Asperger Syndrome* by Christopher Gillberg
reproduced with permission. Copyright © 2002 Cambridge University Press.

First published in the United Kingdom in 2004

Reproduced with permission
by Jessica Kingsley Publishers
116 Pentonville Road
London N1 9JB, UK
and
400 Market Street, Suite 400
Philadelphia, PA 19106, USA

www.jkp.com

Library of Congress Cataloging in Publication Data
Harpur, John, 1958-
    Succeeding in college with Asperger syndrome : a student guide / John Harpur, Maria Lawlor, and
Michael Fitzgerald.
        p. cm.
    Includes bibliographical references and index.
        ISBN 1-84310-201-3 (pbk.)
        1. Autistic children—Education (Higher) 2. Asperger's syndrome—Patients—Education (Higher)
3. College student orientation.
        I. Lawlor, Maria, 1959- II. Fitzgerald, Michael, 1946- III. Title.
        LC4717.5.H37 2004

                                                                        2003026948

British Library Cataloguing in Publication Data
A CIP catalogue record for this book is available from the British Library

ISBN 978 1 84310 201 4

Printed and bound in the United States by
Thomson-Shore, Inc.

Contents

Acknowledgements

The authors would like to acknowledge the support of the following groups during the preparation of this manuscript. Intel (Ireland) generously sponsored the early part of this work. We gratefully acknowledge the tremendous efforts made on our behalf by Evelyn Pender and Frank Turpin of Intel. Microsoft (Ireland) has given us software to keep our machines up to date. The Irish Autism Alliance and the North Eastern Autism Support Group contributed towards video production efforts as a precursor to this work. Ornaigh Malone of ASPIRE, the national Irish Asperger organization, provided contacts and assistance.

JH would like to thank the Department of Rural and Community Affairs, and the Higher Education Authority for providing grants to the authors to develop multimedia supports for AS students. The Minister for Education, Noel Dempsey, has provided much encouragement and good -will. We are immensely grateful for his support. Ann, Trisha and Aidan have assisted many students with social impairments through the Access Office in Maynooth College. The staff of the Child and Family Centre in the North Eastern Health Board commented on various sections of the manuscript. ML thanks them for their patience and the anonymous parents of several patients for their assistance. MF would like to thank his anonymous patients and postgraduate registrars for useful insights and bursts of humour. A special debt is owed to Gert Job who drew on his 25 years in sexuality education with learning disabled people to assist us with the sections on AS and relationship formation. In addition, the authors wish to acknowledge the comments of David Jordan on this work for a very special reason. David is currently completing his PhD in geology but in between his studies he has found time to establish a social skills club for students. On top of that David was diagnosed with AS several years ago. Vivienne Foley, Principal Speech and Language Therapist at the Beechpark Centre for Autism, provided feedback on interviews with AS individuals which was useful in the early planning stages of this project.

Finally, we acknowledge the many unfortunates within our families and among our colleagues who were pinned down to read and advise on sections of the manuscript. Any remaining impairments are entirely due to the authors' inability to do without sleep.

Introduction

If you ask anyone with a college qualification what they recall about their first few days in college it will probably be their sense of excitement, wonder and anxiety. It is quite natural to feel a little intimidated by moving from high-school education on to college. Larger buildings set into larger landscapes with greater numbers of people than ever encountered before will intimidate even the best of us at times. As a new student, you're an explorer in large unfamiliar territory. Even if your chosen college is right next door, stepping through its gates or onto its campus in your official capacity of undergraduate student brings new challenges. Eventually, the 'newness' of the environment gives way to familiarity. New friendships are made. New obligations are accepted, and a new set of responsibilities for oneself is discovered. Attending college is one particular type of transition from the stricter monitoring of the school environment to the looser, more independent environment of early adulthood.

It must be emphasized that the college environment is primarily a learning environment. Students come to college to study, pass their exams and move on to a career. How one behaves and what choices one makes socially can impact on performance. Like it or not, this new environment brings with it choices, expectations and obligations that require the exercise of a range of coping skills. Some of these skills are intellectual: *Can I cope with the workload in my chosen subject areas?* Some are simply focused around preserving one's personal health: *What do I do if I feel ill?* Others are predominantly social: *How do I make friends?* A large range of skills is required. Your personal capacity to use existing skills and develop new skills is constantly tested. Every student will experience problems coping with college from time to time, but those with different social skills from their peers may find their experiences more complicated. Students with Asperger syndrome (AS) will find that surviving college requires more of their coping resources than before. Consequently the student with AS requires more assistance in managing his or her daily routines in college.

Over the past decade public awareness of conditions on the autistic spectrum such as AS has increased remarkably. Yet there is still a formidable lack of resources to directly assist those with AS move along chosen career paths. Despite the growing public profile of AS, the establishment of robust support systems in educational institutions is some time away. Most students with AS therefore have to rely on existing student support services that, through no fault of their own, may not have planned for their arrival, or are just developing a service. Moreover, people with AS tend to be highly individualized. This poses a challenge to support services that are usually only resourced to provide 'one size fits all' responses. However, drawing on their intellectual strengths, students with AS typically may be expected to accept self-help measures more readily than other categories of students with 'disabilities'. One of the great virtues of the AS student is his or her intellectual capabilities. These gifts can be harnessed in various ways to improve the quality of life. Part of the motivation behind this book is to indicate just how this is possible.

In this book, we concentrate on recommendations for organizing one's life in college, managing one's academic commitments, making friends and generally developing useful self-monitoring skills. We outline specific strategies for developing conversations and communication skills. Most of these strategies are best described as guiding rules to facilitate communication, to negotiate the social environment. These can range from using simple reminders on personal hygiene, addressing someone appropriately, and assembling progress reports for the support services, through to establishing a student society to assist AS students support one another. Attending lectures, studying and exam preparation are the main activities that define the academic commitments of students. We have a range of practical suggestions to help with stress management and hopefully overall performance. Many of the observations and recommendations are drawn from first-hand interviews with AS students and parents, coupled with over 80 person-years of professional and clinical experiences among the authors.

Given its importance to human satisfaction and pleasure, we devote a chapter to contact with the opposite sex. Sexuality and its expression are extremely challenging behaviours for many with AS. The boundaries between acceptable, inappropriate, abusive and even dangerous behaviour must be acknowledged and carefully described. One cannot write a prescription for each relationship, but certain conventional understandings between couples have proved themselves useful over the past few millennia.

The primary purpose of this book is to assist those with AS cope with the challenges that college life brings. We hope it will help students during all of their years in college and beyond. Hopefully the strategies and advice outlined in this text will help them complete their college career successfully. The book is also written to assist parents in understanding some of the hurdles that may confront their son or daughter, and what roles they might play in the process. Counsellors in student services and external therapists will also be interested in strategies for helping AS students with self-help. In line with these objectives we have tried to steer the book away from recounting current medical thinking on AS. Instead we have focused on developing a practical handbook to navigate the college terrain.

Many of those with AS coming to college will already have explored the literature in depth. This is a common and welcome reaction to the diagnosis. There are many excellent sources of information on research into the condition, and some of these are listed in the References at the end of the book. Frequently, we use the expressions 'student counsellor or external therapist' or 'student counsellor or your therapist' when suggesting who best to contact about a specific problem. A student counsellor is the counsellor for students attached to the student support services. These expressions are used to indicate that the student with AS has a choice when dealing with therapeutic professionals. Not all student counsellors (or therapists) will be equally well informed or sufficiently trained to meet the needs of people with AS. These are crucial qualities to look for, and demand, in anyone offering support.

We have made an effort to make the book as accessible as possible without avoiding certain difficult and discomfiting topics. It is well known that many people with AS experience social isolation, rejection, frustration and anxiety. These experiences can result in a number of symptoms, not among the least of which is academic failure. The development of depression and a sense of hopelessness are very worrying in a young person with AS. People with AS must learn to identify 'early warning' signs and seek help at an early stage. This can be difficult when one is away from home and in a strange environment. As a consequence we have included a chapter dealing with anxiety, depression and suicidal intentions. We would strongly recommend that the student reading this book would also ask his or her parents to read these sections as well.

1 Preparing for College

A Brief Preamble

Hello! If you have made it into college or are just preparing your application for college then we hope this book will prove of service to you. It is designed to be a practical guide to help students with AS progress successfully through college. Hopefully the skills described here will also serve you well after college. By the way, if you have made it into college, congratulations, and well done! You are now part of an academically successful group, and you should take a moment to congratulate yourself.

In this short opening chapter we are going to offer advice on getting ready for college. It's a big task in itself at the best of times, but if you have AS or know someone with AS then some extra requirements are worth considering. In the first place the high-school student with AS who is considering college is likely to be in the upper 30 per cent in his or her class. The student is academically above average, and college is a logical choice for someone with this ability and usually specialized interests or hobbies. If you have AS yourself, and you are reading this, then we haven't told you anything new about yourself yet. In the second place, AS will not 'go away' when you arrive in college, but college is one of the few places where it is likely to be less of a social impairment. Why? Because colleges respect bright people and what they have to offer. Your specialty or hobby suddenly becomes not just significant to you, but also to an assortment of other people interested in the same area and fired with equal levels of passion and enthusiasm. Without keenly passionate explorers of selective areas of science and technology, progress would grind to a halt. Many of the greatest scientific thinkers in western history have possessed strong AS traits, so you are in good company.

If you are already in college, this section will still be of use to you in your discussions with others preparing for college. However, if you are planning to go to college we suggest that you discuss the recommendations made throughout the book with your parents and career guidance teachers. You will be able to help them understand the challenges ahead more clearly.

Read me first: how to use this book

You can profit from this book in a number of ways. First, it is a handbook for you. However, your parents, counsellor and therapist will be able to give you more assistance if they also read it. Second, we recommend that you read each chapter quickly to get an overview and then go back and study the detail. We tend to repeat crucial pieces of advice from time to time to help your memory. When something is repeated, that means it is very important. Third, some parts of the book will require more attention, more of your time, than others. For instance, Chapter 6 deals with the tricky topic of conversation, and Chapter 7 builds on that to discuss relationships with the opposite sex. There is a lot in these chapters, so take your time. Finally, the skills and advice in the book will require implementation. That means practice. Your counsellor and social skills group will help practise a lot of what is here. If you join a support group, consider using this book to frame your agenda. Our final piece of advice is to proceed slowly and by small steps. Minimize frustration. One fundamental recommendation we have for students with AS is that they get a computer, preferably a laptop, as early as possible in their college years. The computer is a wonderful gadget for keeping diaries, schedules and appointment lists, not to mention helping prepare coursework. If a computer is too expensive, then try to find a good value electronic organizer.

A project: preparing for college

In this section we ask you to undertake a short but important project. The project could be called: 'My Preparation for Going to College'. The purpose of the project is to help you become better prepared for entering college, and that means better prepared for managing the routines and adjusting to the stresses. You need to ask yourself, before beginning the project: *Why do I want to go to college?* If your answer doesn't include something along the lines of *I enjoy learning*, then you might want to reconsider your choices. College is about learning. It is a learning environment, and if you are not interested in learning, college will be very nerve-racking. We will ask this question again in the next chapter.

Everyone coming to college will have some set of expectations, even if these are not plainly understood. They may have expectations about what it will be like to attend an academic class (a lecture), how the academic staff (professors, lecturers and tutors) will dress, what the social life will be like, how much time they will need to spend studying, and so on. An expectation is like an outlook on what things might be like. Let us have a look at how these common expectations arise. Many of these expectations, which we might define as images of what is to come, are based on reports from others and portrayals of college life in various media. The other people might be family members, teachers, relations, friends of the family, a counsellor (if you have one), past pupils, and brothers and sisters of classmates. Your school has had a tradition, probably, of encouraging students towards a set number of colleges, and that's a useful starting point for collecting information. Nevertheless, you need to carefully filter these reports over a period of months before reaching a decision on both the course and college you are targeting. We would recommend that you consider discussing what you have heard and learnt with your parents and teachers to get their comments.

At the stage of planning to go the college, it is always useful to learn about the experiences of other people who have been students in a college environment. Even if these people have not been in the college of your choice, their experiences of student life should be noted. It is also possible that your parents have a college education; your teachers certainly have, and their experiences may help you in your choice of course and college. You may ask: *What is the point in listening to other people's recol-*

lections of student life? The point is that you ask them to recall (1) their routines; (2) problems they encountered; (3) solutions they used. You do this as part of a quest to build up advance knowledge of what college life entails. If you were in the military, what you are doing would be described as an intelligence operation. However, getting people to give you the information requires them to set aside time for you out of their normal schedule. We suggest therefore that you limit the number of people involved to near family, brothers and sisters of classmates, and your teachers. You might consider agreeing a minimum and maximum number of people to question with your career guidance teacher. If that option is not available, try questioning at least two people who have been through college, but certainly no more than six. Just think of the time involved in analysing their responses. On practical grounds, you may find it easier to get responses from your teachers. The other reason for conferring with your teachers is that they at least have passed through college success-fully. They have emerged with their qualifications. Taking advice from someone who tried college but has been unsuccessful would not be wise. We present a typical list of questions to ask your teachers about college:

1. Can you describe your weekday routines in college?

2. Can you describe your weekend routines?

3. Where did you eat during the week in college?

4. Where did you eat during the weekends in college?

5. What kind of accommodation did you live in during your time in college?

6. Did you ever have any problems with other students and/or staff in college?

7. Did you ever have any problems managing money?

8. How did you solve any problems you had in college?

9. I want to be a success in college. What advice can you offer me?

This is not an exhaustive list, but the answers will be enough to give you an indication of the routines and choices that engage a typical college student's interest. You might consider asking your career guidance officer to be your partner in this project.

In addition to these questions, it would be useful to find someone with a college education in your chosen area. This may be less easy to achieve as there may be few people in your area with the relevant qualification. Colleges offer many different specialist courses. For example, if you are interested in a career in astrophysics, you may find a shortage of people in your locality with astrophysics degrees. If you do not directly know of someone with a qualification in your area of interest, then your career guidance teacher may be able to locate someone. However, in most cases you will find a teacher who has a qualification close to, if not the same as, your area of interest.

A final practical consideration is how you will collect all these answers together for this part of the project. If your school is farsighted, there may be a handbook already answering the questions. If there is not, then either pen and paper or a voice recorder (such as Dictaphone) could be considered. Our recommendation is that you use neither of these methods, but if possible use email to send out your questionnaire (better still, persuade your career guidance officer to get involved in the operation and he or she may email it around). Give the recipients at least two weeks to respond. When the responses come back, study them carefully. Given your analytical skills you will find it easy to separate the responses into what they have in common and where they are different. For instance a 'difference' under the accommodation question would be if one person stayed in the college dormitories while another lived at home with parents. To minimize the chances of misinterpreting a response, it is worthwhile asking your career guidance teacher (or your parents or counsellor) to look over them with you. Once you have completed this work, you will have some advance knowledge of the kind of routines that influence the daily college life of students. You will also have picked up a few tips on feeding yourself, managing money and resolving a few problems. All this information will become more valuable in the long term.

Sources of information

Depending on your jurisdiction, people with AS will have different legal entitlements to accommodation, support and care, for instance. Before coming to college inform yourself about your legal entitlements. An environment that has satisfied the needs of typical students may not entirely meet your needs. In many colleges, especially in the USA, student services for students with AS will be handled by the college disabilities office. Throughout this book, however, we stick with the less provocative phrase 'student support services' or 'student services'.

It is crucial that anyone with AS who is planning to attend college should have information on the range of student support services available in any college of interest. Do you really want to attend a college that is unfriendly or indifferent to AS? Knowing a good deal about the college in advance helps you get a better picture of how it operates, and what it has to offer you. In the education equation, you are the important factor. Advance knowledge is essential for proper organization and planning. Inform the student support services in advance of coming to college that you have AS. They will probably communicate that information to the relevant academic staff on your courses. If you are planning a preview of the college, then the staff will be better prepared for you if the services have briefed them on AS.

One thing is certain – most students will revise their expectations after their first term in college. This advice applies to everyone, but especially someone with AS; have an outlook that is not unrealistic. Even though you have a lot to offer, do not expect to be the centre of attention because of your intellectual abilities. Equally, do not expect college staff immediately to understand how best to communicate with you. You also need to accept that you are unlikely to meet a group of enthusiasts for your special area of interest straight away. These things take time to develop. In this book we describe strategies to help you make the most of your strengths and earn appropriate recognition.

There are many media sources of high quality information on colleges and their courses. Many national newspapers publish reports on activities in colleges. You should concentrate on collecting reports dealing with your subject of interest. There are several excellent technical publications giving overviews of research which are available in newsagents (for example, *New Scientist*). Furthermore, every college will have its own website with information on courses and departments. Once you have narrowed your focus to a selection of colleges, spend time browsing their websites. Try to get a sense of activity in the relevant departments offering the courses that interest you. However, at a certain point in time you must decide on which course to pursue and in which college to pursue it. Rank your choices of college, and for each one draw up a list of advantages and disadvantages. Do not forget to factor in financial constraints. You might consider discussing the list with both your career guidance teacher and your parents. Discuss each point on the list with them. Listen to what they have to say, and try not to become upset if your list of points is criticized. It is rare for anyone to produce an analysis that is beyond criticism. Remember that your parents and teachers are working with you to make the right choice.

Making the right choice for you

As someone with AS you may find yourself particularly influenced by the opinions of authority figures (or made anxious by the opinions of other people such as relations or classmates). Making the right choice of college and course can be difficult. Few potential students sift easily through the opinions and recommendations. Deciding that you will go to college X because the scientist that gave a lecture on television wore an interesting jacket would be unwise. On the other hand, if the scientist gave a stimulating lecture and his or her website looked particularly interesting, then applying to that college makes more sense.

Our recommendation is that you check out what attracts you to a particular college. Make sure that you are attracted to college X because it is the logical choice for someone with your interests and abilities. It is also important to accept that having an interest in an area and having both the ability and motivation to pursue its study in college may not coincide.

A few years back, Sarah came to study computer engineering in a particular college. Sarah has AS and has always been attracted to computers. In high school she became a wizard at using office software applications. Sarah had one session with a career guidance teacher and impressed upon the teacher her interest in computers. She thoroughly enjoyed producing reports and formatting documents. After a year in computer engineering, she realized that she really didn't want to study computers in that level of detail. She was interested in using computer applications rather than developing new ones. Subsequently, she transferred onto an accountancy based degree course and was much happier. She is now in the early stages of a successful accountancy career. Sarah's case is not that unusual. Every year a minority of students will switch courses after their exams. However, it is preferable and less stressful if the right choice is pursued from the beginning.

An educational psychologist can make an assessment of your skills and abilities. This may have already happened when you were in your late childhood or early teens. That's great! Hopefully it has helped you, your career guidance teacher and your parents discuss appropriate choices. If you have not had an educational assessment, persuade your parents to organize one. If you are living away from home and returning as a mature student to college, get an assessment, and make sure you understand the results. The value of an educational assessment is illustrated in the case described below.

Michael was a bright young man with an IQ of 130. He had been diagnosed with AS when he was 11 years old. At the age of 13 he had an educational assessment which indicated that his capacity to recognize patterns was below average (which was slightly surprising for someone with AS). The educational psychologist recommended that he avoid disciplines which required very good visualization skills. When he was completing his final year in high school, he expressed a strong interest in studying for a degree in structural engineering. He had a friend in his class who had decided on this degree course and Michael wanted to pursue the same course at the same college. Over a period of a few months, Michael was persuaded by his parents and teachers to move away from his choice of degree. He was also offered another educational assessment. On the basis of this assessment he chose a degree in mathematics. Michael made a very brave choice, but he made one that played to his strengths and that ensured his later success in college. He also listened to the advice of those trying to help him. Michael completed his degree and also a PhD in the USA. In conversation a few months afterwards, he said that he was grateful that his parents pursued the educational assessment. If he had pursued his interest in structural engineering it is likely that his college career would have been much more stressful and probably much less successful. He still admires strong forms in buildings, but has no interest in structural engineering any more.

Our advice is that you spend time with your career guidance teacher discussing your interests and your abilities. You should consider involving your parents in the process as well. As an emerging intelligent young adult, treat this exercise as a *partnership exercise* with your parents and teachers. In a partnership arrangement, no one member of the partnership dictates the agenda or dominates the discussion. Partnerships begin by identifying a common goal and then working to achieve it. Michael, in the case above, was in a partnership with his parents and guidance teacher. All three 'groups' identified the goal as being 'doing what was best for Michael educationally'. Partnership obviously worked in Michael's case.

We are going to have a lot more to say about partnership arrangements throughout this book. Partnership helps us formalize rules that define the 'give and take' required in certain situations. In other words, partnership can become a way of exhibiting reciprocity.

Previewing the college

Anyone with AS should put in extra preparation before making a choice. However, once you have made your choice and got the necessary grades in your final school exams, then you must commit to making a success of your time in college. In addition to the preparatory projects you completed in school, there are other very practical steps you can take to prepare yourself for entry to college.

In the first place, you should take a tour of the college well in advance of arriving there. You could go on your own but it will be more enjoyable and useful if you go with your parents or a friend. Possibly there are others from your school planning to attend the same college and a few family groups might go on the same day. Obviously, we are not suggesting that you jump in the car and drive off in a hurry. Visit the college's website a week or so in advance of the planned visit. Download and print off maps, course information and staff profiles. Make multiple copies for everyone going on the visit. Ideally, the visit should coincide with a lull period between summer and autumn exams when there are fewer people about. A college is relatively quiet during this period and it will give you (and the family) time to explore with less opportunities for drifting into anxiety provoking situations.

Once you have been accepted onto a course, the college will have sent you a bundle of information covering how courses are taught in the college, where they are given (the locations) and what is expected of each student. Keep these documents safely aside for reference. The key components of any college tour should include visiting the buildings that you will occupy for courses, noting the facilities within the buildings (be they vending machines or noticeboards), examining the necessary rooms such as lecture halls, toilets and locker areas, and especially arranging to meet staff who will lecture on the courses. A lot of information has to be gathered during the tour and you may find it helpful to have family members record some of the information.

Families should return from these visits with maps of the college, and spend time locating the relevant rooms on the maps using the academic course timetable. It is advisable to bring a digital camera to record key features and buildings. You could use the photos to 'map' locations around the college using the standard paper maps of the college. If you have access to a digital video camera, it will capture more of your experience of the college. There is no shortage of cheap software available to help you organize all this information into a useful project. You may like to bring this project up to college as a memory aid when you start your first college term. We further recommend that you take pictures of yourself in the various locations (use the time setting on a camera). This will give you a much more personal sense of yourself in the space. The photos will help make the space yours.

Organizing your own college tour will take a bit of time. Many colleges will set aside tour days for new students, but in our experience these days come too close to the beginning of term for students with AS. Generally, someone with AS will need an extra bit of planning time, so it is worthwhile arranging to have a tour earlier in the year during a vacation break. It is probably best if the school guidance teacher organizes the tour as he or she will have a good understanding of how to frame the request appropriately. In the spirit of partnership you should meet with your parents and guidance teacher (or therapist) to decide what you need to learn from the tour (the goal), and how best to organize it to achieve that goal. In particular you need to decide on the materials you will bring on the tour, and who best (if anyone) would be of most assistance to you, and should accompany you on the tour. As mentioned earlier, your school may well organize tours of local colleges. Go on these tours – they will be useful. However, we would recommend that anyone with AS also have a private tour where they will have more time to themselves to consider the environment. The drawback with 'bulk' tours is that the stimuli are flying by you so fast that you can become confused and actually come back from the tour with very little gained. People with AS have to work out what's right for them in these situations, and this may mean that a more individualized tour of the college is necessary.

Now to be honest, no one involved in teaching wants a stranger, let alone a whole family, to arrive in his or her office unexpectedly. Tour visits need a reasonable amount of planning. The best arrangement will involve you, probably with your family, meeting the teaching staff for your courses and outlining your concerns. The dates and times need to be agreed by all parties. Again, all of the times and dates will need to be coordinated in advance, and that's why we recommend working with your guidance teacher on the arrangements. Once you have met staff members, and if you feel comfortable, remain with the staff for a short private introduction. Meeting all the relevant staff may not be possible in the one day, so further visits could be arranged at mutually convenient times. What does a prospective Asperger student, let alone a family, say to staff in these circumstances? How do you talk to them? What questions do you ask?

Our advice is to keep the first meeting simple. You need to introduce yourself, state your area of interest in two sentences and make sure that the staff member knows you have AS.

Ask staff members for their names and how they prefer to be addressed. Let us assume that the staff member has a PhD in astrophysics and her name is Miriam Goldberg. The answer you need is whether to address her as Dr Goldberg or Miriam. At your introduction you will refer to her as Dr Goldberg. It's polite to do this. Each staff member may vary the rules for addressing them depending on how much contact they have with you. Do not worry about becoming confused. Every student becomes anxious over how to address the teaching staff. We'll return to this issue later. You will also want to check that this person is teaching you the courses listed. Sometimes the schedule may be changed and it can come as a surprise to turn up at a class with an unexpected staff member. It is also useful to ask about the coursework involved. The answer will help you estimate the time you will need to devote to coursework in an average college week. Undoubtedly each member of staff will give you an overview of their courses. Finally, we suggest you request the option of communicating with staff via email and using a voice recorder in your classes. These are relatively trivial requests in a modern college, but still it is better to make polite requests of staff. If everything has operated as planned, the college student support services should have provided information on AS to the staff. However, plans often go awry, so we suggest you bring along a few photocopies from a book on AS for the staff. Your guidance teacher or therapist will be able to provide these materials if you do not have any at home. We recommend that you keep your introductory meeting short and stick to the questions above. This will help minimize any stress.

In addition to the academic staff, you and your parents (if possible) must see the support services. Early notification to the support office that you have AS allows the support staff to prepare better for your induction. In addition, the support office should notify the relevant departments that you will be taking their courses. It is also likely that the support office will set up a schedule of regular meetings with you over the opening months of the first term to monitor your reactions to the changes. A difficulty that can arise here is when parents ask the support office to keep them informed of your progress. In most cases that is just not legally possible without your explicit consent. You may want to ensure that the support office can inform your parents if you are in ill health. That is a reasonable demand. Regarding other issues, we suggest you work out an agreement with the support office. Your rights to confidentiality will be zealously protected by the college. The staff will be familiar with this situation and will suggest sensible solutions. Nevertheless both your parents and you should be clear on what support will be offered to you and, most importantly, at what point outside agencies, such as psychiatric services, would be called in for an opinion.

Examining accommodation options

Outside the direct academic environment, the next most important inspection is of the proposed accommodation. Is the accommodation on campus or off campus? Is it self-catering or is there a kindly landlady? Accommodation is so important to maintaining general well-being that a section is devoted to it later in the book. You should note that for most parents, student accommodation rides alongside doubts about the hygiene practices that accompany single life. When you are looking over any proposed accommodation find out where (if at all) you can cook a meal. Look carefully over the quality of any cooker or food storage item. Does the cooker work? Is the refrigerator in good condition? Next examine the sleeping arrangements. If it is your first time sharing a dormitory or bedroom, you are bound to feel a bit uncomfortable. For the present, on your tour, just make sure the bed is in good condition and that you have somewhere to store your clothes. Finally, check out the bathroom facilities. Is everything clean and in working order? Make a note of anything defective for discussion later. If you have to rent private accommodation away from the college, you may find yourself doing this exercise several times before you find suitable accommodation. Our advice is to seek good quality accommodation. Substandard accommodation will only damage your morale in college.

At this point you have collected a fairly sizeable amount of information about your future college, its routines and your accommodation options. By the time you've digested and debated the advantages and disadvantages with your parents, therapist and guidance teacher you will be much better prepared to take on the challenge of college life.

Something for mature students

Our apologies, but if you are a mature student (over 25 years old) you are probably wondering when will they get around to me, to my needs? If you are planning to go to college as a mature student, you should consider completing the preparation project described above. Your experience in employment may enable you to take some shortcuts in your planning, but you still need to focus on getting the advance knowledge.

AS is usually more mellow in mature students than in those fresh from high school. This is a great advantage. As a mature student with AS, you will have a better ability to navigate social conventions. The other advantage is that when you slip up in interactions your student peers will put your mistakes down to your age. Comments such as *Do not mind him. He's older than us* are not uncommon and, to be fair, usually charitable. The other great benefit to you is that you are probably now doing what you always wished you could do but had postponed for various reasons. College is a very meaningful and important career choice; one that you did not just drift into because everyone else you knew was going to college.

One reason for treating mature students in a separate category is that they often come to college having left employment but with family responsibilities. The pressures on mature students outside the college environment are therefore different from those experienced by the average younger student. All mature students, whether they have AS or not, experience a degree of unease mixing with typical students that are often half or even a third their age. However, with AS you may find yourself less able to make allowances for the age gap compared to typical mature students. As one mature student said: *You need to let a lot of what the younger students say pass over your head.* The lesson to be drawn, especially if you have AS, is learning to ignore some of the challenging behaviours and comments of the students. While it is tempting to say *I know more about that than you, as I've been out working for ten years,* resist doing so. Remember there is always tomorrow to think about. Take decisions that minimize stress.

If you have difficulties managing family commitments and college, then discuss options with the support staff. Unfortunately, it isn't uncommon for mature students with AS to leave college prematurely. In most circumstances solutions can be arrived at that keep the mature student in college and allow family commitments to be kept. In employment the mature student with AS may have coped reasonably well by carving out a private work area and a routine within his or her workplace. These private work areas and routines are usually designed to minimize social interaction. College however demands greater participation and inevitably this requires social interaction. All of these new demands will be unsettling initially. Working on group projects requires that you build flexibility into your interactions. Our advice is that you ask about working a 'buddy' system with the student support office. In a buddy system someone will be assigned to meet with you regularly to discuss life in and out of college.

Most colleges that accept mature students will have *mature student coordinators* to help them understand and meet their academic commitments. The student support office will work with the coordinators who are usually members of the academic staff. In addition the support office will usually have a small team dedicated to supporting mature students. Make yourself known to these groups in the beginning, and work with them on formulating a *college life plan* for yourself. Many mature students, not just those with AS, complain about not being able to talk about their life outside college with the students. The experience gap is too wide between the groups. Mature students usually get around this by meeting each other and talking out their problems. They build up a social network involving other mature students. It may take time for a mature student with AS to find such a network or even to realize that one exists. On top of that, you may be very uncomfortable talking to a group of strangers about your home life and this option may be too stressful initially. At this point you should consider teasing out your difficulties with either a mature student coordinator or the support staff (in addition to any therapist you may have seen). If you are married and the demands of college are putting too much of a strain on your home obligations, then we suggest that you consider asking the support services to organize family therapy sessions. You may also have to take a temporary break from your studies to resolve any issues which arise. But do not despair. Many mature students with AS have completed college successfully. As we have emphasized throughout, proper preparation will help you to cope with the transition to college life.

Review and recommended reading

There are many excellent and accessible books available on AS. Luke Jackson (2002) has written a very cheerful and insightful book describing several common social hurdles in adolescence. One of the most accessible general texts is written by Tony Attwood (1998) and should be on your shelf. A book that you, your parents or partner will also find very useful is by Ozonoff, Dawson, *et al.* (2002). Finally, the renowned psychiatrist Christopher Gillberg (2002) presents an overview of technical issues which you may find valuable at a later stage in college.

In this chapter we outlined several general principles that you can use when planning your choice of college and course. The key element for students with AS is to be prepared in advance for any change. Obviously not every change is predictable, but a good logical approach to college planning will help you to cope with anxiety and stress. Equip yourself with notebooks, a camera, even a computer ideally, to help you organize the material into an intelligible picture of the college and course. Picture yourself in the relevant spaces in an attempt to make them yours.

We have also suggested that you adopt a partnership approach to college planning involving your parents, teachers and counsellor. Previewing your choice of college through a tour of the areas of interest will give you an understanding of routines and academic commitments. Once you have collected all the relevant information, then you are better prepared to make a final choice. If you are a mature student, then the same process is recommended. Above all else, get to know the support services. These will be your buddies in times of stress initially. Most of the recommendations in the rest of the book apply to all students with AS, irrespective of age. Let's move on.

2 Welcome to the Rest of Your Life

In this chapter we want to welcome you to your college life and discuss some of the commitments that flow from your choice. We reiterate that competent preparation for college in high school will pay dividends in college. The objective of this chapter is to present an overview of the rest of the book. Of necessity some of the points that we make here will be repeated in the relevant chapters.

Question: Why should someone with AS bother with college?

Answer: A college education provides an opportunity to spend time studying a subject that passionately interests you, which might be astronomy, computer science, engineering, geology, mathematics or physics. Your skills, your expertise, your passion for a chosen area will suddenly all fit together better than ever before, and that is largely because colleges are built on the development and pursuit of specialized interests. Not only will college allow you to pursue your area of interest, but it will also reward you like never before for being successful in that area. It is fair to comment that of all environments in which people study, train and work, college is probably the one place where the strengths of AS, such as the single-minded pursuit of a subject, are really recognized and valued. It is also one of the few workplaces where those with AS can play leading roles in research, and develop fulfilling careers. For all these reasons and more besides, assisting students with AS to manage their college experiences better is a service to the whole academic community.

Bullying of students with AS is quite common in elementary and high schools. College is often a refuge from this horrible activity. If you have been bullied at school, those experiences are less likely to be repeated in college. This does not mean that all social interaction stresses will disappear, but at least one of the nastiest forms of intimidation will be diminished.

The rest of the book now, please...

Now for the big question: *What have you let yourself in for?* Before dealing with it directly, which takes up the rest of the book incidentally, we state the motto that everyone with AS should adopt when confronting change: to be forewarned is to be forearmed. Repeat that phrase a few times before reading on. It means that you should try to get a good idea in advance of what is available in a set of circumstances and what obligations you will be under.

For example, suppose you need to use the library as a student. Of course you will need to use the library, so pay attention. If you sign on for a library tour and listen carefully, then when it comes to using the library you will be in a better position than not having taken the tour. Likewise if you are taking a laboratory based subject, then it is worthwhile arranging for a staff member (often called a *demonstrator*) to give you a tour of the lab. The demonstrator will explain the purpose of the lab within the learning context of your course and describe the functions of the various pieces of equipment. Actually it will be quite fascinating and you will enjoy it. All of this information will take some of the anxiety out of using the labs in the opening weeks of college term.

The Foreknowledge Principle

Having advance knowledge will help you enormously in dealing with change and unpredicted events. We will call the acquisition of this advance knowledge the Foreknowledge Principle. It is nothing fancy, but it serves as a commonsense rule for those with AS. We treat it as a fundamental rule guiding preparation by those with AS. The reason it is important is that people with AS, as you know yourself, often get distracted when it comes to getting organized. Planning ahead may not be your strongest virtue. In the examples above foreknowledge was obtained for library usage and laboratory practices. This foreknowledge will help when you have to immerse yourself in both environments. You will already have advance knowledge of your obligations, so you can now concentrate on getting the task done, rather than on any anxiety.

Life as a young adult in college requires a lot of organization, and frequently you are away from home and have to rely on self-organization skills. The fact that you are in college means that you are bright and a good problem solver. These are great strengths. Aligning these strengths in logical reasoning with proper preparation will enable you to manage many organizational demands. A good number of the recommendations in this book are designed to improve your organizational skills.

Academic commitments

For as long as historical records have been kept on college life, top of the agenda of complaints has been the allegedly boisterous and carefree nature of student life. It is not a secret but many of those stories about all-night parties, paddling in the college fountain and generally having a good time are in fact true; true, but tempered by more than a dash of the really hard work that accompanies student life. To be successful, you must work hard. Do not lose sight of the simple rule:

Intellectual Aptitude + Study = Exam Success

Neither aptitude alone nor study without some aptitude are sufficient to ensure success. As someone with AS you may be inclined to accept statements from people at face value, especially if these people present themselves as your friends. That is not something to worry about. It is a good trait, but you have to be careful that others do not take advantage of your good nature and openness. Do not allow your own sense of personal responsibility to be undermined lightly. Here is a concrete example that is worth remembering.

It is nearly impossible to avoid a certain type of student who will tell you that he or she is doing absolutely no study, but still managing to do well in exams. You may be inclined to believe these statements. In fact if you are impressed with the attention that this braggart showers on you, you may even consider following his or her supposed example. You should know from applying the Foreknowledge Principle that exam success is based on students (you) having the available material and students (you) meeting their (your) obligations to learn that material. Exams require preparation. They require material to be learnt, which means that time has to be set aside to learn it. When it comes to studying and exams, always act responsibly. Do not be misled by other students' claims about how easy the exams are.

Do not believe anyone who says they are passing exams without studying. You can be sure that they are probably spending as much time studying as anyone else. The lesson to be learned here is stated in the 'false friends' rule. If someone says something about their own activities and behaviour that is at variance with a process as you understand it, make a mental note of what they say and check it out. If what they say is untrue, consider avoiding their company. You do not have to challenge them over what they said. You know it is false. That's enough.

Your primary business in college is studying for your degree, diploma or whatever relevant qualification you've chosen to pursue. You have come to college to learn, and it is important periodically to remind yourself of that purpose. We are not suggesting that you spend all your spare time outside of classes in the library. Apart from its impracticality, you would lose touch with classmates and the social environment. Time spent studying has to be balanced against all else that is happening in the environment. Nonetheless, you do need to meet a minimum number of academic commitments pretty much constantly, and this requires a degree of planning. Applying the Foreknowledge Principle to each of your courses (and each new academic year) will make organization and planning more efficent.

Many students with AS find self-organization a very difficult task. Dealing with academic commitments requires a routine. Fortunately the college will provide the framework for the routine in terms of a timetable for classes and laboratories. Excepting illness and exceptional events, you should attend all scheduled classes and course activities. The stressful bits of these tasks entail finding where the various classes are being held and making sure to be there on time. Again work on gathering foreknowledge will be immensely helpful. If you completed the college planning project recommended in Chapter 1, you will already have covered most of what you need to know.

Academic staff and teaching

Throughout the book, when we mention 'academic staff' or 'faculty staff' we mean staff that teach and research. They may be temporary staff or permanent (tenured) staff. Academic staff teach by giving lectures (usually called classes in the USA). They give practical demonstrations of scientific principles in labs (experiments, in other words).

Every academic department will have a complement of teaching staff and perhaps several professors who are more senior in status than the lecturers (in the USA lecturers are also called either assistant or associate professors). One of the professors will also be known as the head of department. He or she is fairly much the boss in the department. Classes are given by all grades of staff and there really isn't any way of telling who is who until you get to know the staff names. Lecturers vary in style. Some like a large amount of interaction with a class; others simply deliver the material with little focus on direct question and answer sessions with students. If you are taking a subject that involves laboratory work, you will also meet laboratory demonstrators who supervise practical work.

The bulk of the material in your course will be delivered in lectures (classes).

Being asked a question in class in the first few weeks of college feels a bit like straying into the beam of an unwelcome giant searchlight. Many students, especially in their first year, dread being asked a question in class. Students with AS will have much in common with peers in this situation. However, there are certain types of classes known as tutorials, with smaller numbers of students, that rely on interaction as part of the teaching style. You simply cannot avoid the searchlight in a tutorial. A tutorial is intended to amplify points in the more formal classes and students are expected to participate in question and answer sessions.

In a tutorial the main issues for AS students are: *When do I start talking, when do I stop talking and how long do I talk for?* We have various recommendations for dealing with these tricky questions, but the key recommendation is to build your response around the question asked. Build any question you need to ask around something you can cite from your lecture notes or book on the course. Base all your interactions on what has been said or what you have read. If you think a question is unclear, ask for it to be repeated: *Could you repeat that question for me please?* If necessary ask for the question to be rephrased: *Could you rephrase that question for me please?* These types of requests are not unfamiliar to staff, so please use them when necessary. Restrain yourself from attempting to answer a question that you understand imperfectly.

You may find that staying relevant is a bit difficult. In fact at times you may be uncertain about the relevancy of your participation. It is difficult to gauge. Do not worry about this for the moment. A simple rule to follow is that once you have delivered your answer, ask the tutor or lecturer was it a sufficient answer. For instance, having delivered your answer you could then ask: *Was that answer satisfactory?*

Given its interactive nature, it is recommended that you prepare your material in advance for a tutorial. If you are well prepared, the interactions are more likely to be successful. The use of stock phrases, such as those above, may help you manage the tutorial with minimum anxiety. We emphasize that the main thing to concentrate on in any lecture or tutorial is what you are learning from it. Ignore any distractions by other students. Focus on getting the knowledge.

Managing your independence may require some form of support

College life has highs and lows. Some of these highs will be due to academic success in exams and projects, some will be due to fantastic parties and some will be due to just staying the course and coming out with that valuable scroll at the end of it all. There will be lows when things do not work out as planned, there are exam setbacks, or one's social life doesn't take off. As a student you are officially a young adult. You probably have the right to vote, the right to drink alcohol and the right to a driving licence. You will almost certainly have a bank account and may find yourself having to manage money for the first time in your life. By the way, managing money comes pretty high on the list of responsibilities. If you fail to manage your money responsibly, you may find yourself short of food, rent and clothes. We'll have a closer look at money management later.

You are quite independent in many ways. However, with all those rights (and they do stack up nicely) you are also likely to make mistakes (like every human being), to act irresponsibly, and generally you'll have the opportunities to do both. There will be occasions in college when you'll step outside the normal bounds of good manners and end up making a fool of yourself – to be blunt about it. With AS, you have encountered these types of situations before. Drawing the line between appropriate and inappropriate actions is extremely hard. The subtleties of a situation may be clear to your classmates, but you will miss them. These occasions are stressful and confusing, and you probably shrink inside every time you think of something particularly jarring in the past. However, they are also unavoidable. Everyone at some stage will experience confusion over something they did which seemed right to them but not to anyone else. The important thing is not to become fixated on the feeling of confusion to the point of paralysis, but to focus on the sequence that brought about the actions that produced the confusion. Understand the early steps in the sequence and work to avoid them in the future.

Tim liked having a couple of drinks with some of his classmates at the weekend. He had been diagnosed with AS in his teens and worked hard at self-monitoring. However, he found one of his classmates very irritating as he would talk about anything except the course. Tim and this classmate rowed a few times in the student bar. On these occasions Tim would leave the bar feeling very confused and very angry. Tim began to worry that he would lose contact with the rest of the group if the rows continued. When Tim discussed this problem with his counsellor, she suggested that he take a break when he felt himself getting angry and return to the bar after half an hour. Tim was requested to concentrate his attention on the many classmates that did not irritate him. He was also encouraged to pursue a more active listening policy and focus on points of agreement rather than disagreement. After several weeks, Tim returned to the counsellor to report that he was much happier and felt much more integrated into the class as a whole. No further rows were reported either.

In the case above, Tim believed he was stressing himself out too frequently, and sought appropriate assistance. Tim corrected behaviour that bordered on the irresponsible by acting responsibly. If he had failed to take responsibility for himself and change how he managed the build-up to stress, he would most certainly have lost the company of his classmates. Our point here is: everyone is capable of embarrassing behaviour, but only a responsible person will act to stop it and not repeat it. If you find yourself repeating the same behaviour and experiencing the same stress reactions, you may need assistance to analyse and manage the early parts of the sequence that brings out the behaviour.

The discussion above underscores that independence brings responsibilities and obligations. As someone with AS you probably have a healthy respect for rules and routines. These are great strengths in most circumstances and will help you keep out of trouble. In particular a healthy respect for the law and the consequences of breaking it should keep you away from illegal activities. The sudden deluge of freedom and responsibility that you've earned by getting into college can be daunting to manage. You now have many more choices to make and more importantly you will not have the same monitoring available as you were probably used to in high school.

Communication skills: your need for assistance

Distinguishing between acting responsibly and knowing when to get advice on how to act responsibly is a very useful skill to learn. The typical student will probably have these two activities fused together. AS students will find it more difficult to know when to exercise the second option and look for help. Sometimes you have to rely on self-help to see your way through a situation, but at other times (especially if there is a social dimension) you may need assistance.

> In class Alan tended to rock in his seat and talk to himself. Alan has AS and was unaware that other students found his behaviour distracting. Occasionally someone would shout at him or even nudge him. Alan would invariably say sorry but within a short space of time continue with his old routine behaviour. Eventually Alan was asked to discuss his behaviour with his therapist. His therapist pointed out that saying sorry is not enough, especially if the routine continues. A leaflet was given to his classmates on AS. Following that a system was devised whereby Alan would invite those nearest to him in class to monitor his behaviour. They were to ask him to stop if he slipped into his old routine. Alan found asking his class to help him monitor his behaviour very successful, and in fact by the end of the year he had largely given up his old routine.

Social groups and social demands

Apart from how you will perform academically, perhaps the biggest concern for most students with AS is how they will cope socially. There is no doubt that college life poses a unique set of social challenges, but they are manageable and that is the important message for now. The uniqueness of the challenges arises from the melting pot nature of student life. No other institution or workplace will bring together so many young people of similar ages but varied backgrounds, with everyone having 'studentship' as the common identity.

There are at least four groups to consider when assessing your communication skills strategies. The largest and by far the most significant group is your peer group, which will mainly be your classmates. You may have other companions from different disciplines who have also come up from your school, but by and large your social circle will be drawn from those sharing your courses. Your peer group will also include roommates (and housemates). It is very important to learn how to get along with your peers because these are often the frontline of support when it comes to getting lecture notes (if you have had to miss lectures due to illness) or additional information on academic activities. You need to exercise friendship skills quite carefully here. More to the point, a lot of social activities will flow from contact with your peer group. Your roommates are also very significant players in your student life. Sharing a house or set of rooms requires a capacity to negotiate and compromise. These are skills that require a degree of social sophistication. They will be present to a limited extent in those with AS so compensatory strategies are required. Your intellectual skills can be turned to your advantage when other classmates are looking for assistance. By making yourself available to help others, you will almost certainly make many friends.

Contact with academic staff and other people in authority can bring its own set of burdens. The most common problem is how to begin the conversation, and then how to cope with the reaction. Hopefully you met several of the course staff while planning your entry to college. It is unlikely that you met everyone involved however. In most cases we recommend deferring face-to-face discussions with staff until you have established email contact. This usually makes the transition to verbal conversation easier. Also a collection of emails creates a common framework for any discussion. It is important to remember that most academic staff are unlikely to be aware of AS, so you may need to brief them in advance, or preferably the support office will have already done this for you. The advantage of contact with staff is that the topics of conversation are usually based around the course you are taking. This helps keep a conversation on an appropriate track.

The final group to bear in mind, and in many ways the most delicate communication strategies are required here, is the opposite sex. One of the most enjoyable and interesting features of student life is easy mixing between the sexes. However, few students with AS find initial mixing with the opposite sex easy. A huge range of nonverbal behaviours is often deployed. These cover everything from glances and gestures through to body postures.

Michael was diagnosed with AS in his teens. While in college he would commonly report the following occurrence. He was talking to a girl for a good while and they seemed to be getting along. She seemed interested in him. Suddenly another boy would come along and hardly say anything to her, but she would end up going for coffee with the other boy. Michael could not 'read' what was passing for communication between the other boy and the girl. It is difficult to consistently interpret nonverbal communication. The feedback from your interactions may be misleading.

The scope for miscommunication and misunderstanding is large. No matter how well intentioned you might be in assisting an opposite-gender classmate, harassment is something to be particularly aware of as it can have very harmful consequences. The whole subject of understanding the rules of contact with the opposite sex is so complicated that we've devoted an entire chapter to it.

Getting along with others: understanding the benefits of compromise

Most people with AS find making choices in an unfamiliar environment stressful simply because they cannot predict the effects of their choices. Often there is an anxiety that something unexpected will occur and leave you completely unprepared. Over time, as the environment becomes more familiar, you will become more comfortable with your choices and, as you know yourself, the choices then become routines. In the right circumstances, routines can be excellent aids to managing your life, but they can also hinder attempts to get along with other students.

An important point to stick in your organizer is that behaviour has consequences. When we choose one course of action over another, then we must also accept that our choice has an effect on ourselves and usually others. Consider the following situation. You are watching your favourite science programme on television. One of your housemates wants to watch the football match. You agreed to this several weeks back but forgot that your favourite programme was on at the same time. He wants to watch the football, but you are putting up an argument that it's your favourite programme and science is more interesting than football anyway.

Question: How do you resolve this dispute without both of
            you wrestling on the floor for the remote control?

Answer: You stick to your promise and let him watch the
            football. That's it, pure and simple.

Rationale: The world will not end because you missed that
            programme. You will not die that night either
            because of football. Of course, you'll feel annoyed
            and angry, but you have got to set those feelings
            aside and focus on the next day. If your routine isn't
            flexible enough to accommodate the occasional
            football match then it is not healthy. Change it. A
            short-term sacrifice in routine can bring more sat-
            isfactory long-term rewards.

Comfortable routines

Part of what we want to look at in this book is how to get into comfortable routines. Routines can become unhealthy and block social development. We will define a comfortable routine as one that is as near stress free
as possible. However, we also want to look at avoiding becoming so comfortable with a routine that it becomes a millstone and prevents change
from occurring. Consequently, the comfortable routine must accommodate some flexibility. The TV viewing routine described above could be
characterized as unhealthy if it became inflexible.

You may have become attached to certain modes of dress or certain
types of meal or watching specific programmes. In fact, you may be so
attached to these items that you cannot picture doing without them. To
do without them would cause great anxiety and distress. In a tightly controlled environment, such rigidity in behaviour and choice can be accommodated. However, in college this behaviour can become a hurdle to
personal development. If we decide that routines are like plans, sequences
of actions taking you from an initial state to a specific goal, then you need
to develop plans that are in a sense opportunistic. They are capable of

being reformulated in changed circumstances. Interacting with other people requires some degree of opportunistic planning.

Interacting with the opposite sex: sex and sexuality

It is quite natural and healthy to experience an attraction to members of the opposite sex. You see someone and you like something about them. It could be their hair, their physique, their laugh or whatever. You would like this person to be your girlfriend or boyfriend. You will find the person sexually attractive and discover yourself on occasion becoming aroused around that person. These feelings and desires are very common, but they require monitoring. Feeling sexually aroused does not give you permission to tell someone that they are the cause of your arousal. Learning to distinguish between appropriate and inappropriate attitudes and behaviour is important. Self-control techniques are essential. These are not easy tasks for someone with AS. However, the last thing you want is for other students to complain that your behaviour is either abusive or at worst even dangerous.

There are many rules to be followed in this social area. They cover everything from how you look at someone, through to how you touch them. Undoubtedly there is a degree of mind reading required here which disadvantages those with AS. However, there are strategies which will help you cope and direct your attention appropriately.

Contraception can also be a source of anxiety for anyone with AS. Fortunately, obtaining contraception is not a problem. Contraception is usually available on campus for men in the form of condoms, though women will need a prescription from a medical doctor to obtain the most appropriate contraceptive. There is only one rule for contraception, whether you are male or female: use it! Above all else avoid unprotected sex. Couples should practise safe sex with condoms until each party is assured of the sexual health of the other. Vending machines are suitably anonymous sources of condoms, but acquiring condoms elsewhere can prove a challenge.

Paul was a final year student with AS. He had been dating a girl in his class for two months when they began discussing having sex. His girlfriend was not keen on chemical contraception. He agreed to use condoms. When Paul went to purchase condoms in the student shop he couldn't see any on the shelves. He was nervous about asking the shop assistant, a girl. Finally, he asked her if the shop 'sold combs'. Paul made three attempts to buy condoms that week. Eventually he spoke to one of the student support staff. She rehearsed with him what he had to say for 20 minutes and then brought him to the shop. She encouraged him to ask for condoms. When he did ask, he discovered that the condoms had been taken off the shelf due to theft. Much to his relief his request was granted. His support officer suggested that it might be easier if he bought several packets at a time, as this would lessen his need to make requests in the shop. He was pleased with this advice and able to conduct his future transactions with more confidence.

Managing anxiety and stress

Be reassured that many of the stresses and strains that you will experience in college will be shared by the typical student across the table from you, beside you in the queue, or behind you on the bus. Remember that your fellow students are there for a common purpose: to get through the exams. Consequently, while your experiences are unique to you, they are almost certainly not unique in themselves. Everyone will experience anxiety at times, rejection at times, be misunderstood at times and generally feel miserable. Likewise, everyone will feel good at times about life and what it has to offer, about friends, about achievements, and so forth. Obviously, there are specific anxieties related to AS, especially in the area of social interaction, but there is still much in common with other students.

How you choose to adapt to change and stress is the most significant behaviour to focus upon. Maladaptive reactions may only increase rather than decrease anxiety. Our capacity to deal with stress can be impaired for a range of different reasons. There is a piece of conventional wisdom which says that when one is feeling stressed out one should just 'get on with it'. It is an uninformed view and one you should quickly dismiss. If only life was so simple. For the AS student, getting on with it is rarely a

convenient or practical option. Learning to practise stress reduction techniques is highly recommended for anyone with AS. The main benefit of
these techniques is that they help to bring panic attacks under control in
most cases. In our experience, panic attacks are a common reaction to
stress among students with AS. Thankfully these episodes are manageable most of the time.

Rory was a science researcher who was diagnosed with AS in his
early twenties. He was a very successful researcher and highly
regarded by his colleagues. However, he admitted to his therapist
that he found social occasions increasingly stressful. He had
difficulties understanding jokes and small talk. If a group grew
beyond two people, he would experience a panic attack. At this
point he would become silent and wait for the group to dissolve.
Rory's case is not unusual. He was encouraged to control any
impending sense of panic by taking deep breaths (among other
recommendations). After a number of months using anxiety
management strategies, the panic attacks subsided and gradually he
began to relax a little more in company. He was much happier in
himself and consequently more willing to participate in
conversation as a result.

Certainly stress reduction techniques are very useful and advised, but
occasionally even these defences may be overwhelmed by an extremely
upsetting event. You cannot expect to live a stress-free life – that desire is
unrealistic. You will find learning to distinguish between justified stress
and unhealthy stress very useful. For example, if your flat or apartment is
burgled and your computer is stolen, that will be upsetting and justifiably
stressful. If, however, two months later you are still feeling stressed over
the burglary and the loss, you may need to seek assistance.

Prolonged episodes of stress are not healthy. If you find yourself
living with a long period of stress, then seek help from a therapist or the
student support services. Do not allow stress to go unattended. It can have
terrible consequences. Learning to manage stress and reduce its causes is
so important to those with AS that we are going to return to the topic a
number of times.

College societies and clubs: finding the right one

Every college will have a collection of sports clubs and societies that are worthwhile reviewing. Clubs are generally involved in some type of sport activity such as the soccer club, cricket club, rowing club, etc. However, the chess club is in there as well. All the rest are known as societies, such as the English literature society, astronomy society, and so on. Do not get hung up on whether 'club' and 'society' are really different. They are not. We will continue to use club and society interchangeably.

College societies provide excellent opportunities to meet with students outside your class. Usually the societies are specialized around one subject area such as astronomy, computer science, mathematics or drama, to give just a few examples. These societies are ideally suited to students with AS. First, they are based on promoting understanding of one subject. Second, they provide a venue for meeting like-minded people. Putting these two aspects together means that college societies should be high on your list of things to explore in the college social scene. Societies usually have regular meetings and almost certainly they will organize parties for their members. These are highly recommended activities for developing one's social life.

In your first year at college it is worthwhile becoming a member of a few societies rather than sticking to just one in your favourite subject area. This will give you a broad social calendar in terms of society meetings and outings. The first meeting of a society, when you meet the established members, is always a bit daunting. Try to persevere and commit yourself to attending the first three meetings before deciding whether you want to quit the society.

Of course you may be very lucky and discover that your college already has a support group for those with AS. If you do not discover one, ask the student support office if an informal group exists. You might even consider setting up your own college society. We offer recommendations on this course of action later in the book.

The virtues of AS

Having AS and being in college as well means that you are a special type of person. In particular you have an above-average IQ and good-to-excellent strengths in your chosen subject areas. Part of the survival strategy we recommend is turning those strengths to your advantage in the social realm. You should list your hobbies in order of the strength of your interests and make a mental note of other students that share your interests. Finding someone with similar interests will immensely improve your social life. However, there is a time and place to demonstrate your knowledge and expertise. Within classes and labs your expertise will be welcomed and acknowledged. In other settings the audience may be less enthusiastic, such as a disco in the student club. One of the greatest dilemmas facing anyone with AS is learning when to switch off talking about their topic of interest. Typical students will also talk at length about their interests, but they will also talk about other issues. Later on we describe various monitoring rules that students with AS should consider when in company. These rules are not easy to apply consistently and mistakes will be made, but remember no one is a perfect raconteur when it comes to speaking about something which passionately interests them. The secret of success for someone with AS is to play to their strengths but acknowledge their weaknesses.

Review and recommended reading

A number of people have written about their lives on the autistic spectrum. The books of Temple Grandin (1996; Grandin and Scariano 1986), Liane Holliday Willey (1999) and, more recently, Stephen Shore (2003) are particularly relevant as these writers are highly successful college graduates. Many of the challenges you face have also been faced by them.

In this chapter we have presented an overview of the areas of student life that students with AS will find challenging. We have also sketched a number of recommendations that will help you manage those challenges. We stress that we are not trying to 'normalize' a person with AS, but merely trying to assist him or her in managing their college life better and producing more effective interactions with other people.

We recommend strongly that students with AS spend time acquiring knowledge in advance of any decision: the Foreknowledge Principle. Practise using this principle. It will help with planning, organization and coping with the unexpected. Students with AS should take courage from the fact that many of the greatest thinkers and scientists in history have had very pronounced Asperger traits, (Ledgin 2002) . Arguably, western science would not have come about but for brilliant people with AS. Now then, that's one in the eye for the typicals.

3 The College Environment for the AS Student

Student life: the focus

As a student, your life and daily routines will revolve around activities in college. Most of your activities will be predetermined by your course timetables. Your daily routine may involve attending classes, tutorials and laboratory sessions. The number of hours per day you spend meeting your academic obligations will depend on your course. It is likely that you will have at least eight hours per week devoted to formal classes, and possibly as many as 20 hours. There are also labs to learn the principles of practical experimentation if you are taking a science or engineering course. Outside these times you will need to spend time in the library reading various books relevant to the course and preparing coursework. Whatever time you have left over will be divided between your social life and keeping yourself fed and rested.

Student responsibilities are defined by college, but occasionally a student can get so out of touch with academic responsibilities that his or her standards become inverted.

Andrew was a very diligent college student in his first two years. He had been coping with a diagnosis of AS since his early teens. He achieved reasonable grades in college and was a reliable student. However, he became increasingly isolated from his classmates and no longer joined them in company. He began spending a lot of time back in his room and would only venture into college in the late evening for a meal. He began exploring projects that were unconnected with his course 'just to keep himself interested'. His parents asked him to see his therapist. During the session he told his therapist that he was very busy and had never been so occupied. His therapist asked him what he did in his spare time. Andrew immediately replied, 'Study'. Almost at once, he understood how odd it sounded to say that his spare time was spent studying. He was astounded at how out of touch he was with college responsibilities. With the assistance of the college support office, Andrew was allowed to repeat that year with regular monitoring.

Andrew's story is not uncommon among students with AS. On the surface he is fully occupied pursuing interesting and stimulating projects. Unfortunately these projects are not relevant to his immediate course and his exam obligations. He is also not organizing his time effectively between the time he must give to course matters and the time he needs for a social life. In Andrew's case his formal student life had very much withered. Attention that he should have given to college tasks was instead diverted to tangential interests. Students with AS need to monitor carefully any tendency to develop such interests. Keep time spent on your interests in proportion to time spent with your courses. College obligations should be satisfied before other interests and hobbies are pursued.

When tangential interests overwhelm college work, there is a risk that a student may drop out of college. When typical students drop out it may be related to drug abuse, boredom with a course, or just a lack of intellectual ability. In the case of students with AS, dropping out is rarely for these reasons. Despite very good intellectual strengths, overenthusiastic pursuit of tangential interests can push students with AS out of college, leaving them disillusioned at the least. However, there are cases of people with AS dropping out of college to pursue their interests in a commercial setting. We can speculate with reasonable confidence that the computer technology industry has a number of successful people with Asperger traits. However, for every successful case, there are many unsuccessful ones. In the longer term it is preferable that you complete your college education and then seek employment.

The purpose in being there

There is only one sensible reason for coming to college and that is to learn. In turn this means studying for a qualification that will establish you on a career path. You may change your ideas about a career path while doing your degree, but your focus on getting the degree should remain relatively fixed. If you are not clear about your purpose in college then you might consider discussing your interests with the college support office. Every student will experience an ebb and flow in their enthusiasm for a course. Some courses may be very difficult or presented in an unappealing manner. Others may be tremendously stimulating and you find yourself looking forward to the next class. College is not like theatre and classes are not given to entertain an audience. Students are expected to pay attention to what the lecturer is presenting.

The major difference between college and high school is that you are expected to do more for yourself. College will not be able to offer the same level of support and structure that you probably found in high school. Comparing the two, you can see that when you missed classes in high school it was immediately noticed, but in college your absence may go unnoticed for longer.

The difference in reaction is partly due to the difference in your legal status. In high school you were a minor. Legally your family had charge over you and in law they could decide on the school you attended, and quite a lot else. In college, assuming you are over 18, you are legally an adult (in most developed nations anyway) and therefore responsible for your own destiny. If you decide not to attend classes, the college cannot write to your parents to apply pressure on you, but will write to you instead. Apart from preventing you from sitting exams, there is really very little colleges can do to persuade a student to attend classes and meet course obligations.

If you find yourself drifting away from academic routines and skipping classes and laboratory sessions, you need to understand why your behaviour patterns have changed. It is always a concern when the performance profile of a student with AS changes. Usually the student has been diligent and competent. If this happens to you, we recommend that you involve the support office in reaching for a solution. Part of that solution may entail a re-examination of your purpose in college and seeing if it can be recovered.

If you have genuinely lost your original sense of purpose then you need to consider a different course. Only in very extreme circumstances should you leave college behind altogether. More often than not when a student with AS becomes disillusioned and depressed, there are social interaction factors to consider rather than academic factors.

The reasons we emphasize focus and purpose in this section are because these can act as anchors around which to steady the organization of your student life. They help motivate your participation in college life and help you decide on priorities. Given the intellectual abilities of students with AS, there is no reason why they should lose a sense of purpose, provided tangential interests and social demands are appropriately managed.

Get the right accommodation

Humans, even students, need between seven and nine hours sleep every night (except for party nights, naturally). They also need to eat, and usually that means being able to cook for themselves occasionally. Keeping themselves clean is also very high on the agenda. As a student you will also want somewhere to study, and somewhere that you can treat as your personal space. These are the least set of features that any accommodation you have, or are considering, should offer.

College accommodation comes in many flavours, from on-campus accommodation in shared dormitories to single-occupant rooms. Many colleges also offer conventional apartments which can be shared by two or more students. Usually college accommodation is better value than off-campus accommodation (unless you are living at home) and is much more convenient. Many students like the sense of community that can be built in the college dorms or halls of residence. In assessing student accommodation on college grounds, we recommend that you only consider accommodation that offers each student a single bedroom. With AS you will need time out on your own, and without your own bedroom you will not have any private space. You can cope with sharing a living room and kitchen, but you must have a private bedroom for your own space. It is unlikely that you will get a completely private apartment. Sharing with other students is probably inevitable. In many ways this is a very exciting prospect and you can make lifelong friends out of your roommates.

If this is your first time in college apartments, make sure to read and understand the rules governing your use of the accommodation. Again bring the Foreknowledge Principle into play. Get the relevant information and process it in advance of selecting the accommodation. Along with checking out your bed for comfort and the various storage cupboards, make sure you have a study desk. Also check that there are sufficient electrical outlets for a computer and any audio equipment you have. In any case bring an electrical socket board with you for additional appliances such as a reading lamp.

If you are staying off campus, excluding your home, we advise that you carry out the same checks. Again, we recommend that where financially possible you only take accommodation that offers you a private bedroom. If you have to room in a house or apartment, it is probably best if everyone else there is also a student. Having a common interest around college life will help you maintain focus on your own course. Convenience to college is also a factor to consider. There is no point in taking a room several hours commuting distance from the college.

Irrespective of the type of accommodation, spend time examining the kitchen and bathrooms. If you are used to high standards of order in your home, then a disorderly kitchen or bathroom will be a continual source of annoyance. Avoid sharing with people who seem slovenly or disorderly. You are setting yourself up for an unhappy time otherwise. It may cost you extra in time and money, but if possible we advise students with AS to look for accommodation in advance of the general student population. The college support office will also advise you on suitable accommodation, but they may not be in a position physically to book the accommodation. The support office will help you begin the negotiations, but you will need to complete the transaction. Additionally, there may be a branch of a national AS organization nearby that can give you some assistance.

The role of the family

Most students get tremendous support from their families while they are in college. This support can be a mixture of financial, emotional and practical advice. Financial support can be direct, where your family subsidizes your studies in college, or your family may have helped you raise a student loan by acting as guarantor. If you have an extended family you will probably receive the occasional money order from a relative. Should you become short of money or lose money, you should discuss your options with your family.

Hopefully, your family will have a very good understanding of you as a person with AS. They will probably have been there when you were diagnosed and will have listened to the various reports from the experts. They will be able to offer you emotional support and comfort and, assuming you have a good nurturing family, they will be there in moments of crisis. If you are having problems in college, whether it is your studies, relationships or money, tell someone in your family. Do not keep problems inside. Going to college does not entail leaving your family behind. However, you may choose to tackle issues without reference to your family. Part of the process of maturing involves making this judgement. We advise you to factor at least one member into your deliberations if you feel a need to talk to someone. It is likely that your family will have made contact with the support services when you came to college. If you feel unhappy or depressed we strongly recommend that you tell someone in your family and the support services. There are many practical ways that your family can help out as well, from simply offering you travel to redirecting your mail. Parents may offer to organize your clothes and footwear, for instance. These offers, no matter how trivial, may take additional pressure off you.

Students with AS should consider what role their family will play in helping them through college. Monthly or weekly visits could be very useful in the first year away from home. A partnership approach is probably worth considering here. You need to tell your family that you appreciate their support and want to work out a schedule of visits. In return they may want to work out a schedule for receiving your phone calls or emails. Working out details of vacation breaks and what to do during them could also involve your family.

College is a major transition in your life and signals a change in your relationship with your family. It is often very difficult to know where to place boundaries between parts of your life that are yours and parts that you may want your family to know about. In between these two divisions is an area of uncertainty about your family's right to know. Everyone has this debate when they first embrace the independence of early adulthood. However, young people with AS may experience more confusion than most. Most students work towards a compromise, which is why partnership agreements are important. Your family should not insist on having access to you entirely on their terms and conditions, and you cannot have access to your family on your terms and conditions. We advise you to discuss making these arrangements explicit with your family. It will build predictability into contact arrangements. However, remember to promote flexibility. The unexpected sometimes happens and you may need to contact your family outside of your schedule (and your family may need to contact you in an emergency).

Operations of a typical college

Colleges do not vary much in their operations throughout the world. They may differ in courses, departments and facilities, but the essential structures are the same. Basically a college divides into two parts defined by their purposes. One part deals with administration and finance and the other deals with teaching and research. As a student your interaction with administration will be largely confined to registration details. When you register for a new year in college or a set of exams, pay fees, or need to get library access, you are dealing with various arms of college administration. Attending classes and laboratories on the other hand involves you with the teaching and research arms of the college. The bulk of your college interactions will be with these academic parts of college. Note the contact details of important services in your computer or organizer.

Staff

College staff also divide roughly into two camps. You will interact with both administration and academic staff. Administrative staff, including security and catering staff, registration and exam staff and library staff are concerned with the running of services in the college. When interacting with these grades of staff, it is important to be polite and at the same time to the point. For instance, the type of conversation you will have with a security guard should be of a different nature than that with one of your classmates or a tutor. It is unlikely that a security guard will share your interest in quantum mechanics, for instance. If you need to speak to a member of the administration staff, use the Foreknowledge Principle and base your question around your model of their job. You may have difficulty initially in formulating a relevant request, but practice will help. If you have time, it is helpful to write out your request in advance and bring it with you. Most of the time, your interaction can use stock phrases. For instance if ordering food in the canteen, a more than sufficient phrase is: *Can I have the burger and fries please?* When you bring books to the library checkout desk, a suitable phrase might be: *I would like to borrow these three books please.* Of course, when you speak to someone, you can be reasonably sure that they will reply to you. In Chapter 6 we look at strategies for managing conversation.

You will mainly interact with the academic staff. This group divides into different grades, with different responsibilities. Academic nomenclature varies from country to country (even academics themselves find it confusing). In the USA, most teaching staff are divided into professor grades. In the UK and Australia, professors are generally senior staff, and the rest of the teaching staff fall into the grade of lecturer. Moreover, the grade of tutor in most modern colleges is reserved for junior staff. The older universities, on the contrary, treat the grade of tutor as a very prestigious post. To avoid being distracted by these differences we will treat colleges as having professors, lecturers and tutors (or demonstrators) in order of descending seniority. Generally, your classes will be given by the lecturers and professors. Tutors will give tutorials designed to expand on details in lectures and check your coursework. If you are taking an experimental subject, you will attend laboratory sessions which are managed by demonstrators. The division of responsibility is not rigid, but the model presented here is fairly uniform, no matter what college you attend.

Usually each course year has at least one member of staff as the course coordinator. This person is responsible for overseeing the smooth operation of the course. If you are having general problems with your courses, this is the person to contact with your concerns. If you have problems with a specific course, then you contact the member of staff giving the classes on that course. This is a very important rule to note. A member of staff will feel disrespected if you complain about his/her course without bothering to contact him/her first with your complaints.

An academic advisor, known as a *mentor*, is commonly available to students. The role of the mentor is to provide support for your academic efforts and to offer advice if you feel under pressure. Mentors are usually academic staff themselves, so they will be familiar with the pressures of coursework. If a mentor judges that your issues go beyond simple academic difficulties, he/she will suggest involving the student support office. Mentors will have a schedule of appointments for you. It is important to attend these appointments as failure to do so may cause a letter to be sent out asking if you are still in college.

Your lecturers will make themselves available for consultation. Usually they will post a schedule of times that they are free to see students. If you need to speak to a lecturer outside of these times, you will need to make an appointment. In these cases it is best to email or ring the lecturer to make the appointment.

Services

College services include activities connected with security, building maintenance, catering, power, heating and water supply. These services make life possible in college. If you have on-campus accommodation, you will need to know how to contact building maintenance. If you see a crime being committed you will need to contact security. Catering obviously handles the student canteen requirements. The other services are largely in the background and, though you use them all the time, you are unlikely ever to need to call them directly.

Larger colleges will have their own medical centres. It is important to note the relevant contact details in case of a medical emergency. If your college provides 24-hour medical coverage, that is fantastic. If it does not, then note down the numbers of the nearest 24-hour medical centre. This might be a local doctor service, but it is more likely to be a local hospital.

Student services are provided by your local students' union (or whatever the student representative body is called) and the college.

Usually both the student union and college produce guides about basic services for students. Keep these for reference. Student managed services vary considerably but they will usually include a welfare advice service, an accommodation service, a shop for student needs and possibly a crèche. As a rule the larger and wealthier the college, the more student-managed services available.

A most important service, which is also part of college administration, is the student support service office. We have mentioned the support office a number of times so far. This service should not be confused with any student service offered by the local students' union however. The student support office with its complement of disability officers and counsellors offers a variety of psychological services. Anyone with AS is advised to make themselves known to the support office staff. Remarkably successful partnership arrangements can be reached with support staff that will help you through college. We will discuss building a relationship with the student support office in Chapter 5.

Academic responsibilities

You are in college to learn and that means attending to a variety of academic commitments. Most of your commitments are straightforward and require a routine of class attendance followed by coursework completion. Small groups and group projects can pose problems for students with AS. We suggest a number of useful coping strategies in Chapter 6. If you have applied the Foreknowledge Principle you should have an electronic diary with your course timetables entered into it. This diary should be used as a checklist to measure your performance and commitment.

Attendance

In high school your attendance will have been closely monitored. Possibly you had the benefit of an individualized education plan (IEP) that imposed a structure on your routine which suited your needs. In college you are responsible for your attendance at classes. It is highly unlikely that anything remotely similar to a previous IEP will be put in place. Non-attendance at classes is an illogical choice when you think about it. If you are not in class to hear the lecturer you may miss important exam tips. Students who fail to attend lectures often misunderstand the emphasis in a course, and this can hinder exam preparation.

If you find your attendance slipping on a course, it may be that the lecture hall environment is too stressful. Your reaction may well be due to difficulties with note taking or reading what is on the whiteboard or projected onto a screen. Follow up on our suggestion in Chapter 1 and use a good-quality digital voice recorder to supplement your note taking. Move up to the front of the class and sit beside students who are concentrating on the class. You can transfer the recordings onto a computer in the evening and listen to the lectures again while reading the day's notes. This activity requires organization and commitment – and headphones so as not to disturb anyone else. If this arrangement is not working for you, then you will need to speak with the course mentor or the student support officer to discuss other remedies, such as the provision of more detailed notes and possibly special assistance from someone else on your course. Above all else, remember that lectures keep you in touch with the course and your fellow classmates. Pulling out of lectures inevitably will collapse your academic ambitions and social network.

Unsurprisingly, poor lecture attendance correlates strongly with weak exam performance. The inference is obvious: lecture attendance improves your chances of doing well in exams. If you begin missing classes, and this will be obvious when you look at your diary, then you might want to discuss what is happening in your life with someone from the support office. The primary reason for diligent students with AS not meeting their attendance commitments is depression. Depression can arise for a number of reasons, but social interaction stresses must be considered. We will have more to say on this condition in Chapter 9.

Coursework

Your coursework is parcelled out in a series of assignments. In school this was called homework. There are three sensible reasons for completing your coursework. In the first place, coursework keeps you in touch with the course. Therefore it reminds you of your purpose in college. Second, many courses operate a system of marking called continuous assessment. Your coursework counts as a percentage of your end-of-semester exam marks. A poor coursework mark will pull down your exam marks. The third reason for pursuing coursework, especially given the intellectual ability of those with AS, is that it is a direct measure of your motivation to complete the course. High quality coursework is a sign of a highly motivated student. Again, refer to your diary here, but if you find your coursework marks declining or if you keep missing coursework deadlines, you might want to discuss the situation with your mentor or a member of the support staff.

There is one rule covering coursework and that is to have it done on time. If you cannot meet a deadline, you can ask for an extension or else ask whether any special tuition can be provided for you. If you keep missing deadlines, we suggest you follow the advice above. You may find raising these issues difficult, and we suggest that you email your requests. If necessary discuss your options with the support staff and consider their recommendations. You may want one of them to ask the course lecturer to have your deadline extended.

Tutorials

Tutorials are designed to elaborate on details in lectures and to check students' coursework. The first thing that a student with AS will notice is that the numbers attending a tutorial are a lot less than at a lecture. Smaller numbers means less anonymity. Students will introduce themselves to each other when a new tutorial season begins. You need to be prepared for this event. It is useful to have set responses such as: *Hi, I'm Tom and I'm from Brighton.*

Interaction with a tutor is inevitable in a tutorial and this can be a source of major anxiety for AS students. The interaction is based on the tutor asking questions of the group and then requesting answers. The activities that require foreknowledge and planning are: when do I start talking, when do I stop talking and how long do I talk for? If you are asked a question then the main strategy is to build your response around the question asked. For instance, in a computer programming tutorial you could be asked by the tutor: *Describe an algorithm for searching the contents of an array for a particular element.* Your reply should begin by including the question: *An algorithm for searching the contents of an array for a particular element would …*

Likewise, build any questions you need to ask around something you can cite from your lecture notes or book on the course, rather than say to the tutor: *I do not understand this.* You need to be specific. Avoid vagueness. Suppose you are taking a mathematics course in number theory. You have a problem understanding the proof of theorem X (substitute the problem theorem's name for X). Be very explicit asking for help: *I do not understand how line 6 in the proof follows from line 5. Can you explain this to me please?* Base all your interactions on what has been said or what you have read. If you think a question is unclear, ask for it to be repeated: *Could you repeat that question for me please?* If necessary ask for the question to be rephrased: *Could you rephrase that question for me please?* These types of requests are not unfamiliar to staff, so please use them when necessary. Restrain yourself from attempting to answer a question that you understand imperfectly.

Group work

As you progress through college you will be given project work to complete. Projects usually take a few weeks and can be seen as long pieces of coursework. A number of your projects will be group based. This means that you have to work on a section of the project as part of a team. It also means that you cannot schedule the project around your own routines but will have to negotiate responsibilities and meeting times with the others in your group. One option is that you use your analytical abilities to identify a component of the project that is suited to your talents and state of knowledge of the course at that point in time. However, we recommend that you identify two areas that match your skills, and present these to the group in order of preference. You should certainly look for a position of responsibility in the group and not accept someone else handing you a section to complete. Students with AS may find group work stressful due to the social interaction requirements. It can help to explain what having AS means to members of the group. The support office may have a student-friendly leaflet that you can distribute (preferably to the course lecturer). When your group has its initial meeting to assess the project and divide up work, that is the time to volunteer your expertise for a specific section. If you cannot reach some type of partnership arrangement with your group, then you need an external arbiter. The ideal person is the course lecturer. Suggest to the group that he or she act as referee in any dispute over the division of responsibilities. Above all else, try not to alienate the others in the group by insisting on your own schedule. It is OK to ask other members of the group if you are being unreasonable. Inviting them to monitor your interactions can help you greatly in the longer term. Maintaining good relations with your group can bring dividends when you need help.

Domestic responsibilities

When you live at home many seemingly trivial tasks are done for you. Soap and toothpaste are available. Toiletries are in stock and food is in the kitchen. Your clothes are washed and ironed (probably) and someone reminds you constantly about your hair, your appearance, bringing an umbrella out in the rain, and so on. Replacement lightbulbs are stored in a particular place. Cutlery, plates, cups, pots and pans are in abundance. A home is a very organized environment when you think about it. Once you move away from home you have got to manage your domestic responsibilities largely on your own. Use your computer to record your domestic needs and expenditure. Generate weekly shopping lists.

Hygiene

A schedule of personal hygiene means simply washing yourself frequently and changing your clothes regularly. Many young men and women are unaware of the impact of bad hygiene on their social life, especially with the opposite sex. Having a shower once a day and a daily change of underwear and socks are basic requirements in the hygiene schedule. Regular dental hygiene helps suppress bad breath and is also recommended. We recommend that you create a checklist of toiletries you use. As they begin running out, use this list to create a shopping list. When shopping for toiletries it is convenient to buy three or four of each (four bars of soap, four bottles of shampoo, four tubes of toothpaste, etc.) at one time. Do not wait for them to run out before buying more, but decide that as soon as you open the second-to-last item in any category that it is entered into a new shopping list. Forward planning cuts down on stress. Maintain an adequate supply of toilet paper. Women should ensure that they have spare sanitary towels or tampons in their toilet bag.

It is rare for other people to comment directly to your face about your personal hygiene. Consequently you need to monitor your own hygiene practices. If you find yourself departing from your hygiene schedule over a period of time, you may want to discuss this change in behaviour with a support counsellor or your therapist. Falling hygiene standards can indicate the early stages of depression.

Food

Food is a topic close to every student's heart, mainly because they either think they are not getting enough of it or do not appreciate the quality of college food. You will find yourself eating in college and cooking for yourself, to varying degrees, during your college years. A varied diet is a healthy diet. Try to avoid becoming rigid in your choice of foods. Experiment with new foods in small amounts. A balanced diet is better for your all-round academic performance and will also keep your body in better shape.

Shopping for food takes a bit of practice and it is likely that on the first few occasions you will buy too much of one item and too little of another. One way to minimize the stress is to develop your foreknowledge of what is involved in shopping. Calculate how much food you will need to have on hand in your apartment or room. Until you become comfortable with cooking for yourself, focus on having healthy convenience foods. Carbohydrates in the form of bread, pasta and rice are always convenient. Protein is cheaply got from cheese, tinned fish and beans (tinned or uncooked). Red meat is an important source of iron. Vegetables are necessary for fibre, vitamins and trace elements. Fruit is nice and healthy. If you like milk, it is a good source of calcium and vitamins. Stimulants such as tea and coffee are refreshing.

You do not have to buy a lot to feed yourself well, but you do need to watch what you buy. It makes sense to keep your intake of sugar and animal fats low, but you do not have to exclude them from your diet. To avoid an overly rigid shopping routine, allow yourself one small luxury every time you shop – a bar of high quality chocolate perhaps. Change your choice of luxury item regularly. Also vary your choice of brands every few weeks. This will make you more receptive to accepting change in your diet and be much more fulfilling over time.

Shopping requires interacting with shop assistants. We recommend that you create a shopping list before going to the supermarket as it will give you some idea of how much you will need to spend (and whether you can afford it). The shopping list will take a lot of the stress out of shopping.

Clothes

Wearing clean clothes and looking clean will help in making and maintaining social contacts. To put it another way, if you look dirty and dress dirty, people will avoid you. In hot weather you may need to wear a fresh shirt every day. In a cool climate you should aim to have at least three but preferably four fresh shirts available per week. Jumpers, skirts and trousers may remain wearable for four or five days, but after that they should be washed. Some students with AS develop a very rigid style of dress, which eventually becomes a uniform. Their clothes may be perfectly clean but their routine needs to allow for some experimentation with clothes and colours. If you have a sensory reaction to certain materials, avoid them (cut the tags off clothing if they irritate you).

You do not need the latest fashions to look good in clothes. Better that your clothes are clean and well maintained than fashionable and grubby. If you are strongly attracted to just one style of dress, then you may need to consider having a few sets around. For instance, parents can help here by providing two or three similar outfits to wear while the others are being washed. We recommend that if you are strongly attracted to one style of clothing, you wear it but establish a rotation with different types of clothes being introduced gradually. Having some variety in dress will suggest to others that you are flexible. Sticking to the one style of clothing indicates rigidity, which does not help develop a social life.

Money management

The universal rule of money management is not to spend more than you can afford. Students are generally on tight budgets and have to be careful with their money. The easiest principle to adopt is to determine what you need to spend in an average week on food, rent and standard bills, and do not exceed that amount. If you find yourself constantly running out of money then you may need to discuss refinancing options with your parents, your bank or your college support office.

Expenditure has to be prioritized if it is to be managed effectively. In order to remain alive you need money for food, and to remain in college you need money for accommodation. Therefore food and accommodation are top priorities. In addition you will need money for books (and possibly travel), not to mention clothes and the occasional night out.

Many students take up part-time work to have a little extra money. This is a useful option to explore, but you should check that the work does not interfere with your academic commitments. Any work that prevents you from attending lectures should be turned down. If you do take up part-time work, make sure you quit it in time to prepare for exams. Working outside college can bring its own set of burdens. Between work and college responsibilities you may not be able to give yourself sufficient private time to relax and unwind. This combination would not be good for your stress reduction. Part-time work will also take time off your college social life and may prevent it from taking off. The bottom line is that if the part-time work diminishes your academic commitments then think long and hard before taking it up. Ultimately you may want to discuss the implications with a student support counsellor.

Now that you have access to money, and you need to have some with you every day, you also have to work out how much to have with you in cash. It is not a good idea to carry a lot of cash about, but you do not want to leave yourself short either. A reasonable strategy is to work out what you need to spend per weekday and carry that amount plus 20 per cent in case of emergency. We call this the '120 per cent rule'. At the weekend your spending pattern will be different, but try the 120 per cent rule for at least three weekends before modifying it. Keeping an account of your weekly, but preferably daily, expenditure will help you create practical budgets.

Social life

College social life is really all about being in the company of other students. Whether you are skiing in Aspen, hiking in the Scottish Highlands, or drinking beer within the shadow of the Sydney Opera House, you could be with a group of students from college. Friendships made in college can last a lifetime and it is worthwhile making a special effort to cultivate friends. Making friends is not easy and it will often be difficult to distinguish between acquaintances and genuine friends. Social interaction among students is different from social interaction in school. For a start the interactions may involve a group of equally talented academic achievers with interests in the same specialist areas. This is a change from school. Social life will also introduce you to a more definite adult way of doing things. Drinking in bars and clubs will become more familiar. It is inevitable that you will encounter illegal drugs at some stage (if you did not already in school). Clearly this is an exciting period of your life, but it also requires self-control and stress management skills.

You're on your own now

Being independent gives you opportunities to develop self-focused talents. These talents should be developed to help you enhance your independence. Self-assertion means identifying situations where you need to assert your point of view and then doing so in a calm manner. You will need to justify your point of view and tell your fellow students that you respect their points of view. Group work typifies situations where self-assertion skills might be needed. At all times be calm, be logical and listen to alternative opinions. Know what outcomes you want and be prepared to compromise. Treat the operation as an exercise in logical argument and persuasion.

You will also need to develop study skills to work independently. The level of supervision available in high school is no longer available. Being able to manage your own coursework load requires organizational, planning and motivational skills. Starting your coursework promptly rather than shelving it for a few days or weeks is a useful habit to develop. Once you begin your coursework, do not shift focus randomly. Try to finish it as quickly as is compatible with the desired quality of finished work. When the coursework is completed, check it over for mistakes or omissions before delivering it to the member of staff responsible.

You will also be responsible for looking after your health. If you feel unwell, you may need medical assistance. If you feel depressed or disillusioned, you may need to have a discussion with a counsellor (or your therapist). Taking responsibility for yourself is a big responsibility, but you will manage it successfully.

Acquaintanceship is not friendship

You will meet many people in college, but only a few will become friends. One of the features of AS is a tendency to accept people at face value. This is a noble attitude if everyone around you was scrupulously honest and trustworthy. However, the world has a mix of people. Distinguishing between different types of people begins by learning to distinguish between acquaintances and friends. An acquaintance is best defined as someone you know only a short time. For instance, when you first arrive in college you will be making acquaintances. As you spend more time with your fellow students, you will find that your circle of acquaintances has shrunk to a group of 'regulars'. Before deciding that anyone in this group is a friend, ask yourself: *How long have I known this person? How often do I see him/her? What interests have we in common?* You will need to ask yourself: *Is this person asking me to give him/her something of mine before I have known them for a suitable length of time? Have I evidence of interests in common? Would he/she help me?* As an extra safeguard, ask yourself whether this person has ever insulted you. Have they borrowed anything from you but not returned it? If you are satisfied with your answers to these questions then you could consider this person a friend. However, be cautious about revealing information about yourself, especially about your finances. Remember, proceed slowly and try to control impulsive tendencies.

Take your time assessing potential friends. Think about what you want from a friend and what you have to offer. No matter how friendly a fellow student is to you, if he or she is involved in any illegal activity or risky behaviour, avoid that person. False friends are often difficult to identify. They can take advantage of your good nature.

> Paul was a student with AS who met another student at a college society. Paul mentioned in passing to his student support counsellor that he now had a friend in college. He was very pleased. When the counsellor enquired into the nature of the friendship it turned out that Paul had known his friend for four weeks. They met at weekly student society meetings. At each of these meetings Paul's friend had borrowed money from him. He promised to pay Paul back each time. The counsellor advised Paul not to lend any more money and to ask for the money he had lent to be returned. Paul explained that he was willing to lend this person money since he was a fellow student in the same institution.

The friend was not a true friend but someone who abused Paul's trusting nature. Paul's reasoning was flawless. We are students. We are pursuing a common purpose. Therefore, we share common values and respect one another. Paul rushed into friendship before answering the questions outlined above.

Managing the challenges

Coping with change is one of the biggest challenges facing anyone with AS. Hopefully, you will apply the Foreknowledge Principle as part of your planning strategy. It is often useful to make a brief list of what has changed between one situation and another. For instance, if you change accommodation, make a short list of what has changed between the old arrangement and the new one. When you are moving from one college year to another, get the foreknowledge on what the next year will offer you. It is onerous, but if you put in a bit of extra planning time during the holiday, your life back in college will be less stressful. If you are uncertain about the implications of change, then consider discussing your concerns with someone whose judgement you trust. This person might be a member of your family, a therapist, a student support counsellor, or a member of the academic staff. Discuss your concerns in terms of the feelings you are experiencing about change. Above all, if you are becoming depressed or disillusioned when confronting change, then seek assistance from the student support office.

You will experience conflict with others from time to time in college. Conflict often arises when people cannot agree to tolerate each other's point of view. It can also arise when a person's behaviour towards another is inappropriate and abusive. When a clash of opinions is at the heart of a dispute, you have the choice of examining whether your position is fair and correct, or else seeking a referee to resolve the dispute. There are no easy solutions to disputes. Most solutions involve some element of compromise by both parties. Remain calm and reasonable at all times however, and this will help diffuse any tension. If the conflict seems likely to turn into violence, then remove yourself from the situation and seek assistance from someone in authority.

We recommend that you keep a daily diary, recording your schedule for each day and any departures from it. In Chapter 8 we detail the type of feelings and signs that you should look for. Use the diary to record your feelings. If you find yourself recording only negative sentiments, then consider having a discussion with a student support counsellor or a therapist.

Drink

Having a few beers with classmates is quite common. Moderate drinking of alcohol is tolerable while you are in college, but be careful to schedule your drinking so that it will not interfere with your studies. Avoid drinking while you are taking exams. If you find yourself in the company of students who spend a lot of their time drinking, then you need to find new company fast.

Oscar Wilde once quipped that he had discovered that alcohol taken in sufficient quantities caused inebriation. If you drink alcohol, then inevitably you will get drunk on occasions. These can be quite pleasant, good humoured experiences, but alcohol disinhibits our behaviour. When we are drunk, we may behave out of character and inappropriately. Regular bouts of drunkenness are unhealthy and may be symptomatic of underlying psychological distress. Drunkenness can also lead to law breaking and delinquency, so be careful.

If you are drinking, then be moderate in your consumption. A few drinks can be good fun; too many can cause problems. Also alcohol costs money and you need to manage money carefully while in college. No one can prescribe what the right balance is for you, but over time hopefully you will develop your own mature judgement on this matter. If you find when reading back over your diary that you are drinking too frequently or missing deadlines due to drink, then we suggest you look for assistance from a student support counsellor or a therapist.

Drugs

Illegal drug consumption is taking place on a massive scale. It is impossible to avoid being in situations where drugs are used and probably sold. Cannabis is the most commonly available illegal recreational drug, followed by ecstasy. Both these drugs are regularly used at parties, so do not be surprised to see people smoking dope or handing out pills to one another. What they do is their business. Your concern is what are you going to do when people around you are taking these drugs.

The first thing to remember is that these activities are illegal. If you are caught with illegal drugs, you may end up with a criminal record. Many employers are reluctant to employ people with drug convictions, despite their qualifications and talents. A conviction for drug possession could seriously interfere with your career development after college.

The second thing to look out for is false friendship. There have been cases where young people with AS became attracted to the drug culture because they were accepted into that group. Regular drug users are a loose collection of people with a high tolerance of different moral and behavioural standards. Anyone can join the group as long as he or she participates in drug taking. All that matters is getting high and taking more and more exotic drugs. Some people with AS experience a sense of belonging in these subcultures because they are accepted for who they are. This is a misleading impression and untrue. In these few cases the individuals have confused the indifference of the group with a feeling of being accepted. You can avoid making the same mistake by asking yourself the set of 'friendship' questions about drug users you may encounter.

Keep well away from the company of anyone involved with illegal drugs, especially addictive drugs such as heroin. At the end of the day, you want to manage your life so that you are a success. If others want to take a different path, that is their choice. You make the right choices for you.

Recommendations

In this chapter we gave a broad overview of the practical demands, academic commitments and social rules that will influence the college experiences of a student with AS. Along the way, we emphasized the importance of foreknowledge as a lever to managing change and your reactions to change. Being responsible for oneself is an incredibly important job and you will need to work hard at it to be successful and content. Use your computer or organizer as a reliable witness to your daily life. Creating schedules as checklists is useful in helping you monitor your own behaviour. Try to include other people in the monitoring process as well. Sharing the responsibility for monitoring your behaviour will take away some of the stress and help others genuinely to relate to you and understand your needs. You will make friends, but take your time. Protect yourself. You will have a great time in college, and you have the ability to achieve very highly. In the next chapter we will have a look at the specifics of the academic commitments.

4 Attending to Academic Demands with AS

College life is overwhelming at times. Keeping a steady focus on your studies and academic commitments can be hard. Adapting to new routines and adjusting to changes in existing ones may produce anxiety and confusion. Everyone around you will find change unsettling to greater or lesser degrees. Change and the challenges it brings are inevitable no matter what career one follows. College has certain advantages over other places of work in that change within courses is generally predictable, so with some foreknowledge you can prepare for these changes. Timetables provide scaffolding for your daily and weekly routines. You will have much in common with typical students. Never forget that you have more in common than not in common with them. Use this commonality as a foundation for social interaction. You are more like other students than different from them.

Is life that different for the AS student?

Despite the overlap in interests and abilities between typical students and those with AS, there are differences in social emphasis and behaviour that should be acknowledged. In terms of raw intellectual ability, AS students have the potential to be very successful academically. However, academic progress and success do not occur in a social vacuum. Interaction with others is desirable and inevitable.

What are the main sources of anxieties you may experience? Briefly, these are meeting new people, making friends and generally fitting in. Be reassured that everyone has some difficulties with these areas when they first come to college. What typical students may take for granted in a social interaction, you may have to logically deduce. Let us take a look at a joke interpretation as an example of what is required (see box).

> A man arrives in a bar one night and has three drinks in rapid succession, and then leaves the bar. He continues this routine for several weeks. Eventually the barman asks him why he has three drinks in rapid succession. The man replies that he has one drink for his older brother, one drink for his younger brother and one for himself. The man continues the routine for several more weeks. However, one night he comes in and only orders two drinks. Amazed by the change in routine, the barman asks him whether one of his brothers has died. The man replies: Oh no. They are both very well. It's just that I'm off the drink myself.

Jokes work because they confound the audience's expectations. When someone tells you a joke you may not get the punchline immediately. That is OK. A joke is unfolded in a sequence. Take any component out of the sequence and the joke will fall flat. Understanding the humourous implication of a joke means understanding the whole of the sequence, not just one or two parts. If you treat understanding jokes as an exercise in code breaking, this may help you enjoy them more. Spend some time studying humour. Obtain a few joke books and look through them for patterns of humour. Jokes are amusing to read, but the real hitting power of a joke comes from its being spoken. Professional comedians are very skilled in pacing the verbal delivery of their jokes. They do not read them to their audiences, but animate each joke. Finding the humour in the jokes is not always easy, but all you can do is listen, analyse and hopefully get the punchlines.

Another reason for focusing on jokes is to get you to think about communication. Jokes may be good to read, as we have said, but they are much better when communicated well. The comedian is a good communicator if his audience laughs. Communication skills are important when you need to get your message across clearly to others. In the comedian's case, if he doesn't get his message across successfully he's out of a job. Definitely you want to be understood clearly. Likewise, when other people speak to you, they want you to understand them. Since they will not have a clue about AS, this gap in their knowledge can sometimes cause you considerable anxiety. Their expectations of your listening and communication skills are similar to their expectations of anyone else's. That is the tricky part. They do not know what it is like to have AS, so the scope for miscommunication between you and them, and them and you, can get quite big at times. We will have much more to say on this in Chapter 6.

If you look again at the three sources of anxiety – meeting new people, making friends and generally fitting in – you will notice that each of them is related to using communication skills. Most of the time these skills are really no more than knowing how to start, stop, continue and interrupt a conversation. There is a well-kept secret among typical students that is rarely revealed, but if you swear to keep the secret, we'll let you in on it: few typical students are complete masters of these communication skills. What we experience in everyday life is an uneven distribution of these skills in the population. Some people have really mastered communication skills, and some have not. In between there is a whole mix of people with degrees of communication skills.

Whether your life in college is different from that of other students and whether it is more or less stressful, are in fact irrelevant questions. The relevant question is whether you can manage your life in college sufficiently to achieve a reasonable degree of contentment. Part of that management will involve a willingness to examine your social communication skills. Closing the social skills gap between others and yourself requires time and preparation. It will never close fully, but at least you'll be more content. Your differences can also be your strengths. Dedicated commitment to topic, fastidiousness about work and reliability are the necessary characteristics for success. Self-confidence is based on the development of your strengths. You can address any experience of difference by first being secure in your strengths.

Social naivety and exploitation

Most people with AS are trusting of other people and accept them at face value. This is a praiseworthy trait. If the truth be told it is a noble trait. Most people you interact with will merit your trust. They are not out to harm, cheat or abuse you. However, a minority (a tiny minority) will injure, cheat and abuse almost anyone, if given the opportunity. We mentioned in the last chapter that distinguishing between friends and acquaintances can be tricky. We suggested a few questions that you can ask yourself in reaching a decision.

Despite these safeguards, a false friend can sometimes arise and gain your trust. False friends are insincere and manipulative. They pretend to like you. They get you to like them and then they take advantage of you. Their main interest is in extracting money, support or information from you. They may even attempt to involve you in crime. The false friend may borrow money from you on some pretext (and they are really good at telling lies), but 'forget' to return it. The false friend may seek to borrow books but 'forget' to return them. The false friend may ask to use your apartment while looking for another one, but 'forget' to pay their rent or buy food. Recognizing your superior intellectual skills, the false friend may ask you to help him or her (who said false friends are exclusively male?) with coursework or exam preparation. In this latter case, he or she will take a sudden unexpected interest in you near exam time, but just as suddenly avoid you once the exams are over. Protecting yourself against false friends is not easy. Everyone, and we mean everyone, has been duped by a false friend at some time.

Brendan was an engineering student with an open disposition towards other people. He had been diagnosed with AS in his primary school. Brendan was glad to get to college as it took him away from much of the bullying he experienced in school. He was keen to make friends and frequently rushed into friendship without exercising good judgement. Brendan met another student who persuaded him to drink in the city centre and go clubbing. Brendan enjoyed the company, but often found himself going home alone when his friend met a girl in town. In fact, as he later told his therapist, his friend would often abandon him in a club if another group of students came along. Brendan had a car and was happy to drive his friend from club to club. However, his friend always dictated the nightly schedule. Eventually, the friend dropped Brendan.

Why do you think the friend wanted to hang around with Brendan? The friend, of course, was a false friend. He wanted to go clubbing in the city centre and Brendan could be persuaded to act as his chauffeur. Why do you think Brendan wanted to hang around with this friend? You might say that Brendan's need to have a friend meant that he was not very selective. However, equally you could answer that Brendan was a decent guy whose good nature was exploited. The second answer says: it was not Brendan's fault that he was exploited. If you ever find yourself exploited by a false friend, then remember it is not your fault that this person exploited you. The false friend is the villain, not you.

The *friend or acquaintance questions* will help you distinguish false friends (who are a particularly nasty type of acquaintance) from real friends. The rule is not to rush into friendship. Take time to assess people. Do we have interests in common? Do I feel threatened by this person? How long have I known this person? Is this person treating me in a way that makes me afraid, uncomfortable or confuses me? Pose these questions to yourself in an effort to prevent exploitation. If you have been exploited by someone, then think about talking it through with either a student support counsellor or a therapist. Do not repress feelings that make you feel bad about yourself.

The hidden curriculum in college

You have more than likely heard of the importance of the 'hidden curriculum' in guiding participation in and interpretation of social conventions. In practice the 'hidden curriculum' is just another way of referring to the social conventions that make possible effective communication. In school, for instance, you have conventions about interacting with teachers and other pupils. As you move up through schools, especially high school, the conventions are less easy to state in words. Indirect uses of language occur more frequently. Body language and gestures reveal more than before. Eye glances and even the tilt of someone's head may carry significant meaning. At times you may have thought to yourself that if only everyone wrote emails to one another communication would be much clearer. In reality of course, we rely on spoken language for most of our communications and reserve text for special purposes.

In college, people still use social conventions that you may miss on occasion or even find mysterious. However, as students mature they may be more willing to bring clarity to interactions if you ask them. If you are not sure what someone is trying to convey to you then simply say: *Could you explain what you mean? I didn't follow what you said.* If someone reacts in an unexpected way to you in conversation ask for clarification: *I sometimes say things that can seem a bit odd. What did you think I meant?*

In a group setting this is more difficult to practise. People use a large amount of non-verbal communication in groups. But you are in college, in a learning environment which is supportive of questions. In these circumstances, it is acceptable to ask a classmate to explain what is happening. At one level you might ask someone to explain the meaning of a gesture. At another level you might ask someone to explain a sequence of interactions. The issue to ponder is not *Why is X making that gesture?* but *What does that gesture mean?*

Perhaps you have attended social skills programmes and found them useful. That is tremendous. Nevertheless, we advise people with AS to approach learning the language of social convention, gesture and nonverbal expression as if they were learning a second language. We will have more to say about this idea in Chapter 6, but for the moment just try to picture yourself amidst a strange tribe of people. You do not know their language, but in order to get food and shelter you will need to make yourself understood pretty quickly. What will you do? You will observe and logically analyse all the interactions until you have built a model that explains the interactions. You will test your model by interacting with the tribe yourself. Your model might be wrong in places. It might be incomplete, but you will keep refining it until you have a fairly consistent interpretation of all that is happening in the interactions.

What we are asking for here is that you apply your intellectual skills to analysing and comprehending the hidden curriculum. Your model might be deficient, but keep refining it until you are satisfied with its consistency.

CARRY-OVER FROM HIGH SCHOOL

What you learnt about social conventions in school is still relevant in college. If you have notes from social skills programmes you attended while at school then reread them occasionally. Staff have to be treated with the same level of politeness. Clothes and hygiene are still incredibly important to get right, and determining the expectations of others is still extremely important. Knowing what to say, how to say it and when to say it and understanding the responses of others will occasionally cause misunderstandings and confusion.

In school you may have had an individualized education plan and a resource teacher. In contrast, in college you will need to rely more on other students for help. This may be a novel experience for you but it will be a rewarding one after a good deal of practice and some trial and error.

If you were bullied and mocked in school, you are much less likely to experience this unpleasantness again in college. It is a point we made above, but it is so important that it needs to be emphasized again. In school you may have pulled back on occasion for fear of an aggressive or abusive reaction from a pupil. These nasty reactions are much less likely to occur in college. Colleges are designed to support questioning. Asking another student for help or clarification is completely compatible with the ethos of a college education. If one student is unhelpful, make a note and ask another student. Again it is best if you apply the friendship questions when asking for help from other students.

Interview with a psychiatrist

Michael Fitzgerald is Professor of Child and Adolescent Psychiatry at Trinity College, Dublin. He has been involved with autism and AS research for over three decades. During that time he has seen several hundred patients with AS. Interviewer is John Harpur (JH).

JH: Michael, let us consider a person with AS making the transition from school to college. What are the important issues confronting them?

MF: There are a number of points to consider depending on how content you were with your school experience. If you found school a reasonably pleasant experience, then college will be less anxiety provoking. But if school was not a nice place, then your trust in other peers might be greatly diminished. When you arrive in college, you may not expect people to treat you any better than they did in school. In these cases, history tends to repeat itself and some students become very anxious about any social interaction. Their anxiety makes settling into a routine difficult. And regrettably some people will leave college prematurely. I would always recommend that a student join several college societies in the first year, just to create a social calendar. The principle is that if you want to make friends, then you have to meet people. That means putting yourself out some of the time – may be a lot of the time.

JH: What advice can you offer someone moving from school to college?

MF: My main recommendation is to treat college as a different type of environment. Seeing college as just an extension of school often prevents students with AS from escaping their school-derived anxieties. But I would like to repeat the earlier point: get involved socially as early as possible. Get a social calendar together that will force interaction with others, and give yourself at least three months with this schedule of meetings, debates, outings and whatever else. Admittedly, this is a very difficult part of college life, and regular contact with counsellors or therapists can really help someone manage the first couple of years in college. If students around you know that you have AS, that can also help them to help you. Making the decision to tell others is not easy. It is probably best to consult with your counsellor or therapist on the timing.

JH: Is there a 'rule for attending counsellors' that you would suggest?

MF: That depends on whether the person is diagnosed before coming to college or while in college. If you have been diagnosed before coming to college, you've probably been doing a lot of background reading. Also you will have had time to adjust to the diagnosis. I would recommend registering however with the student support service and arranging a schedule of appointments for at least the first term in college. Continue seeing your therapist as well. If you are diagnosed in college you may need very regular contact with the support office, and with your therapist (assuming you have an external therapist). A person-by-person approach is the probably the wisest when deciding on the specifics of an appointment schedule.

JH: Finally, Michael, what is the general outlook for a student with AS in college?

MF: Communicating socially with other students will be unavoidably stressful at times, and confusing. Communicating about course topics and laboratory protocols will be relatively easy to manage, by contrast. The intellectual abilities of students with AS will help them analyse interactions and prepare responses, better than in school. The reason I say 'better than in school' is to underline that college is more respectful of people usually. If the student gathers sufficient foreknowledge about events and courses and tries to engage socially – some trial and error is inevitable – the outlook is very favourable. The neurologist Oliver Sacks has a book entitled *An Anthropologist on Mars*. In it Temple Grandin, who suggested the title, describes dealing with others as similar to understanding an alien civilization. Students with AS similarly might regard themselves as scientists trying to understand the outer world of social conventions. The history of science is full of successful thinkers with strong AS characteristics.

Interacting with academic staff

Students with AS should consider developing two interactive modes with staff – text and speech. The latter will initially be more difficult until familiarity with the staff is established. But you will sort it out over time. Remember that all students find interaction with academic staff awkward to some extent. One thing to be aware of is that staff like their personal space to be respected. There are simple rules to observe. For example, enquiring about staff members' mobile phone numbers is generally discouraged. There are lots of privacy issues here, and unless a staff member volunteers their mobile phone number to you for a specific purpose, do not ask for it. Do not pick up papers or books in a lecturer's office unless you have permission. Defining the 'space' boundaries is tricky. Again, as a rule do not look over someone's shoulder to read their computer screen. That is considered impolite. Likewise always ask if you may sit down before doing so. If you have to show material to a lecturer for assessment, try to avoid standing too close, especially if they are sitting down. A good rule to follow is to keep at least the length of your forearm, but preferably the length of your arm, between you and a staff member. (You should try out this rule with most people you meet, unless you know them very well or they are family members.)

The use of text as a communication medium for those with AS opens up a variety of interaction and support possibilities. Text is good for clarity and lack of ambiguity. Email is an example of a fast text communication technology. Ask either the course mentor or a support office to encourage departments to introduce a policy allowing questions to be submitted via email rather than asked orally in a tutorial, laboratory or lecture. Of course, there are occasions when oral communication is absolutely right for the task, but if the answer is not urgent then email should suffice.

Students routinely email lecturers about a variety of matters, but what is being suggested here is that the AS students keep lists of specific questions arising from a laboratory session, tutorial or lecture for emailing afterwards. Text communication in this case has two advantages. First, it largely replaces oral interactions which may especially help the recent student arrivals get some confidence in the environment. Second, it will assist in developing oral interaction skills. A policy like this will help you, but it is never going to be perfect. Texts can be mislaid; emails can go undelivered and unread. So it is important for those with AS to become aware of these possible gaps in the questions-as-text policy.

A policy is only as good as its implementation. Allow for staff being overworked and very busy if your emails are not answered promptly. Just as it took you time to compose your email, it will take your correspondent time to read it and compose a helpful reply. Also consider that staff may not have time to deal with every written question that they receive. Ask yourself if the time frame within which you expect a response is reasonable to the sender.

Despite its many advantages, email communications may often drag out an issue much longer than one party feels is necessary. For typical correspondents, a five-minute verbal conversation may avoid several hours of clarification–focused emails. It all depends on the topic of discussion. If you find yourself batting the same topic (or series of questions) around in the email for more than five exchanges, and not making progress in your request or improving your understanding, then you should adopt a different approach. We would suggest you send an email to the staff member, and to the course mentor, which reads something like this:

> Dear <staff member name>
>
> We have had five exchanges of email on<topic name>. I thank you for your help. However, I am still not clear about <topic name> and I would like to meet with you. Could you send me an appointment please? I am copying this email to the course mentor as I may need extra tuition to understand <topic name>.
>
> Yours sincerely
>
> <Your name>

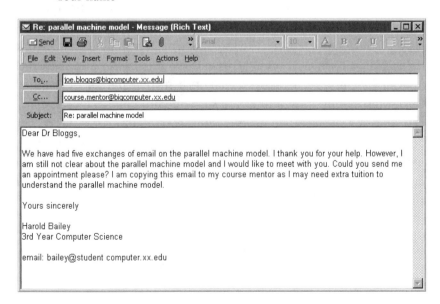

Figure 4.1 Example of email to staff member

What we have above is an interaction template. You fill in the blanks to generate the actual communication. An example of the template completed (with fake names) is given in Figure 4.1.

However, having recommended email as a communication medium, it is important for you to monitor the nature and frequency of your communications. If you ask too many questions and send too many emails, you may confuse yourself and lose the thread of the discussion. Never use abusive language or make emotionally charged accusations when emailing members of staff. Be neutral, objective and to the point. Email communication requires a little foreknowledge to make it most effective. A short email is easier to read than a long one. A question that quotes from a book or lecture notes (such as in tutorials) may be answered more quickly. If you need to ask four or five questions put them in one email, not in four or five separate emails. Allow at least three days for a response; longer, up to a week, for a series of questions to be answered. If you do not receive a response within those time frames, send an email enquiring if your original email was received. If for whatever reason email communication between yourself and a member of staff breaks down, contact the course mentor and your student support counsellor immediately.

Many staff members receive too many emails already, so additional emails need to be focused. Ordinarily a staff member would discuss email etiquette with a class and suggest a format, about what is and is not appropriate in content and length. Ask for a copy of the rules to be emailed to you. Explain (in email or orally) why you would initially prefer to communicate by email. If this poses a challenge, involve the student support office. Most importantly inform the staff on your courses that you may need some assistance in monitoring your interactions. For instance, you could inform staff to tell you when to cut down on the volume, content or length of emails. It is best to deal with these requests in private. Ask the course mentor for an appointment, or email each lecturer individually. An example of a simply phrased request would be:

> I need to inform you that I would welcome help in monitoring my interactions with other people. If my emails are too long, or have too much content or are too frequent, please tell me what I need to reduce. Please continue to help me monitor my interactions after that point.

Staff will value your honesty and openness. You will get their assistance. If staff members are not informed of your requirements, they may become hostile to the emails.

Departmental staff: etiquette and expectation

Speaking to staff members follows the same rules you learnt in school. If you need to raise an issue with a staff member about course work or course content, try to avoid challenging your teacher. Most people in authority, not just academics, do not like to be challenged. If you are raising issues, avoid using judgemental or emotive language. Stick to facts. It is difficult to distinguish at times between being assertive and being rude. If a staff member tells you that you have crossed the line between the two behaviours, then always apologise. You should say something like: *I'm sorry if I offended you, but sometimes I become too impassioned. Please stop me if it happens again. Can we return to my original point? Perhaps you could help me rephrase it?* You might say to yourself that this is a bit long winded, but this reply performs three tasks. First, it says that you can apologise when necessary. Second, it says that you are serious and want to stay 'on topic'. Finally, it asks the hearer to help you to monitor your behaviour and assist you to achieve your goal of getting a response. Your sincerity will impress any audience.

If you become very frustrated, there are a few rules to follow: Not shouting or using bad language are the two most obvious ones. These rules are part of the basic interaction etiquette that staff members expect from students. Of course, students expect the same courtesy from staff. If a staff member shouts at you or is abusive to you, you need to tell that person that (1) you do not like their behaviour; (2) you do not like their attitude; (3) you will have to report them to the head of department.

Respecting another person's space is immensely important during interactions. We mentioned above using the 'arm's length' guide as a way of separating your space from someone else's personal space. This is simply a guide. You will need to compromise with it occasionally. It is not practical to operate the rule in a crowded lift or car, for instance. In these cases, you might try to keep a forearm away from someone else. If that is not practical then you may have to accept a discomforting sensation for at least the duration of the journey. The thing you are not allowed to do is fight with other people over this inconvenience.

If you are working in a laboratory it is likely that other students will bump into you accidentally – you will also bump into people. As the need arises to check your work, the staff that manage laboratories (the lab demonstrators), will lean over you, look over your shoulder, and possibly even grip your hands to show you how to hold equipment to keep yourself safe. All this behaviour is quite normal. If a demonstrator asks you how an experiment with a pendulum is progressing, do not think that he has singled you out for attention. He checks on everyone. Again in these circumstances, foreknowledge can play a vital role in managing anxiety. Find out what a lab entails from the course mentor or lecturer. Ask the support office if it has any material describing the environment of a lab. Visit the lab in advance and get a sense of its space and layout. If necessary photograph the lab for later study. As a general rule, all sources of advance knowledge should be used in an attempt to infer etiquette and expectations.

What happens if you are the disruptive force in class? Academic staff have a low tolerance of class disruption. Laughing aloud, rude interruptions, talking or distracting others by your behaviour are not allowed. If you engage in any of these activities, it is likely that you will be reprimanded. When disruptive behaviour continues, a student can be suspended from a course. It is an extreme consequence and you do not want to find yourself appealing against a suspension. One way to avoid this consequence is by involving the student counsellor early in any disciplinary dispute between a staff member and yourself. The counsellor will try to broker a compromise between you and the staff member (or members). This may involve you agreeing to have someone from the support office observe you in class and discussing your behaviour afterwards. Also you will be expected to produce a behaviour management plan for the affected academic staff. This plan will be put together by you and your student counsellor (and external therapist). Partnership relations are coming to your aid again. The academic staff and the counsellor will monitor your compliance with your new behaviour management plan. In the short term regular supervision of your behaviour may be irritating. In the longer term it can only be of benefit to you.

The importance of working to a plan

Every time you step into a house, take a ride in a car, use a domestic appliance, you are benefiting from the realization of several plans. In fact all man-made objects surrounding you started out as plans on paper. If you think about a simple sponge cake, it can only come about by following a recipe. At its simplest a plan is a recipe, a set of directions for achieving a specific outcome. For a sponge cake, we mix the ingredients together following a sequence of instructions. Then we put the mixture into the oven. The cooking takes so many minutes at a set temperature. Finally, we get a nice cake to eat. Once we begin with the right ingredients in the right proportions, and follow the instructions, we are pretty much guaranteed to get the outcome we desire.

However, not only do we devise plans to help us manufacture items, but also we develop plans that help us manage our behaviour in order to achieve social goals. For instance, you might have it in mind to meet a friend across town tonight (the social goal). You need to check what transport is available. If you are using public transport, you go to the relevant departure point, get on a bus, pay your fare, sit down, get off the bus at the stop nearest your friend's house, walk to the house and ring the doorbell. What results from all of these behaviours (actions)? Your friend opens door and welcomes you in (the goal).

Breaking down your behaviour into such small detailed steps might at first seem odd, almost a foreign way of thinking, but a fundamental characteristic of effective minimum stress organization is just such planning. Admittedly some of the planning may be so routine that you no longer need to think about the intermediate steps, until something goes wrong. Nevertheless, when doing anything that could lead to anxiety and stress, think first about putting together a plan.

The famous English eighteenth-century wit and lexicographer, Dr Samuel Johnson, once commented that the path to hell is paved with good intentions. A plan is only as useful and effective as your willingness to see it through. There is very little point in putting together plans that you are not keen on pursuing. Even when your motivation to complete a plan is high, you may still have to consider whether your proposed plan is realizable. Leaving aside social communication issues for the moment, this type of critical thinking is particularly important when preparing for exams.

Identifying goals

Goals are really another way of talking about achievements that you would like to bring about in various areas of your life. You might have career goals, academic goals, personal development goals, sport goals, social goals and so on. What matters in selecting any goal is whether or not it is realistic. Suppose you want to ask a girl in your class to the cinema. This is your goal. Is it a realistic goal, you need to ask yourself. Do I know this girl? Have we had conversations? Has she given any indication that she enjoys my company? If you have never spoken to the girl, it is probably unrealistic to expect her to accompany you to the cinema. Chapter 7 has more on this topic. For convenience, we will describe all planning that culminates in interactions with other people as essentially directed towards social goals.

> Alan had been diagnosed with AS before coming to college. He was a mature student. The age difference between Alan and his classmates was about 15 years. Alan seemed to fit in well with his group and, while quiet, coped well with college. During his second year he developed very strong feelings of attraction towards one girl in his class. She however was involved with another classmate in a stormy relationship. Alan's openness made him the ideal listener for her complaints. He became attracted to this girl and eventually invited her to go away for a weekend. She was quite shocked and rejected his suggestion. Alan was confused by her rejection. He became very depressed. His therapist persuaded him to remain in college and negotiated a break of three weeks to help him calm down and comprehend that a romantic relationship needed to progress more slowly (going to a movie rather than going away for a weekend). Alan eventually returned to college.

There is more uncertainty associated with social goals then any other type, since by and large people are not completely predictable. Other people may have a variety of desires and understandings of other people and events that you will find difficult to grasp at times. Alan's behaviour was not unreasonable. It is very difficult to get a clear understanding of the dynamics of other people's relationships. Alan's case shows that sometimes goals that seem reasonable and attainable are frustrated by other factors. Perhaps deep psychological factors are at play. Even the best 'mind readers' among typical students can be misled in these circumstances. The only general lesson is that if you are interested in a relationship with someone else, try to ensure that they are not encumbered by a 'not yet dead' previous relationship. The other lesson to draw, and you may be familiar with this one, is that logical analysis and planning can be undermined by the emotions. You may consider your goal perfectly realistic. Your planning is thorough, you have completed your background checks, but when you are ready to act the other person says 'no'. Everyone finds this outcome frustrating. Experience tells all of us that the past behaviour of other people is not an infallible guide to their future behaviour. Events unknown to the outsider can upset expectations. For example, if another student had a recent bereavement in their family, it would not be appropriate that he or she accompany you to a party, even if you have partied with this person before.

Goals that are associated with academic activities are academic goals. In comparison to social goals, academic goals are much more straightforward to grasp and plan. To progress through college you have to meet these goals. Fortunately the goals are transparent and defined by your course structure. For convenience, we can divide academic goals into short and long term. The only difference between them is that the achievement of long-term goals is dependent on achieving short-term goals. Typical short-term goals are class attendance, laboratory attendance, completion of coursework and success in college exams. Longer-term goals are: achieving your degree (or whatever the relevant qualification), possibly aiming for a particular grade; securing a scholarship in another college; focusing on a career path in a particular college or company. These longer-term academic goals are dependent on your performance, but interpersonal skills cannot be ignored. In many cases, you will need character references from your course teachers. These references may refer to your capacity to work in a team, to take part in group activities, and so forth. If you require a character reference then please discuss the reference, and why you want the particular position, with the referee (the person giving the reference). Your goal is a good but fair character reference, so plan your approach to the referee carefully.

An interesting and exciting property of academic goals for those with AS is that they are usually competitive. This quality provides opportunities for your intellectual abilities to shine, and to enhance your standing among your peers. Again notice how success in one area can help you enhance your social status. We will return to social goals and plans in Chapter 6, but in what follows the focus will be on academic planning tasks.

Organization of resources

Let us assume for one moment that you have been charged with building a house. It is a conventional house made with bricks and a slate roof. A daunting task? Yes indeed, but you will work to a plan to complete the task. Just look around your home at the moment. Notice the different materials, services, furniture, floor coverings, structural elements and so forth that define the physical presence of your home. Even with little knowledge of building terminology you could compile a huge list of what is required to put a home like yours together. In practice builders find this task so daunting that for all but the smallest of projects they employ quantity surveyors to work out all the materials they need. For a builder this is the first step in the organization of resources. Without estimating the resources he needs for a project, the builder may be unable to complete it.

In the case of the plans we have mentioned, the same rules apply. For a plan to have any chance of success, an estimation of resources is required. For instance, if you are inviting someone around for a meal, you need to make sure that you have cutlery, plates, glasses, cups, and the food. These are basic resources for the 'having someone around for a meal' plan to work. Of course, at times we may have to improvise if one of the desired resources is absent. A cup can be used instead of a glass, for example. It is worthwhile making out a list of what's required if you are inviting people around. However, knowing the requirements necessary and committing oneself to meeting the requirements can be difficult.

Tony invited two classmates around to his new flat for dinner. He spent the afternoon planning the meal. Tony had been diagnosed with AS in his late teens. He was remarkably capable intellectually if not distracted from his tasks. On this occasion Tony noticed that the front of the dishwasher was about 10mm proud of the rest of the units. He had been in the flat for one week and was surprised that this blemish had escaped his attention. Tony spent the rest of the afternoon and evening trying to reseat the dishwasher. This required that he remove the unit and disconnect the water and electrical supply to the dishwasher. During the latter stages, Tony's classmates arrived to find the kitchen in disarray. No food was prepared and Tony was working on the dishwasher unit. His classmates assisted him with the dishwasher and eventually they persuaded Tony go to a restaurant with them.

Tony's difficulty was not in identifying requirements, but in remaining focused on meeting the requirements. Tony had plenty of foreknowledge but he needed to commit to the foreknowledge. Possibly the dishwasher needed his attention, but not when two classmates were coming over for a meal. The priority task was meeting his obligations to his classmates. When Tony raised this event with his therapist, he explained his behaviour in terms of needing to deal immediately with any problems in his environment. Tony's attitude towards problems was reactive and impulsive. This meant that while he could identify the basic requirements necessary for a plan, occasionally he would set these aside to deal with other less relevant issues. A solution strategy was suggested to Tony. In future he would list any problems (distractions) in his diary and mark the urgency of the problem in days. Urgency was defined in terms of threat to his and others' health and safety. The more days assigned to resolving the problem, the less immediate did it become. This problem classification scheme was monitored over a period of months, during which Tony's requirements planning improved greatly.

Tony's experience is not at all unusual among those with AS: good intellectual analysis of what is required, accompanied by weak follow-through on actions. In the case of exam goals, students with AS are capable of identifying what needs to be done, but often find themselves partially or wholly deflected from committing to doing the work. It is not uncommon for these students to identify all that is required of them to be successful in a course, but yet fail to actualize the requirements through study.

Once you have clearly identified requirements, then the next stage is to act on those requirements and execute your plan. Use your diary to record your progress with academic goals. If you find yourself underperforming, then talk to people such as the student counsellor or your mentor about your situation. They will offer you advice on study preparation and monitor your ability to stick with a plan. The important lesson is that knowing what resources you need is the first part of the solution; using them effectively is the other part.

PRE- AND POST-CONDITIONS

When we discussed organizing resources, above, we were focusing on resources playing a particular role in a plan. Not every resource is relevant to a plan. Having four pairs of shoes, for example, doesn't count as a resource for inviting classmates for a meal. Only certain resources serve as a foundation for a plan. These resources become the pre-conditions that must be in place for a plan to succeed. Intrinsic to learning to plan and organize for events and people is learning to identify essential resources (necessary for success) from inessential ones. Sometimes you may want some help to do this. Ideally this help should come from friends, but you may instead consult with family members, student counsellors or therapists.

When we talk about pre- and post-conditions we are talking about resources and outcomes. What is a condition? Technically we might think of a condition as something that is true or false, available or unavailable, achievable or unachievable. A builder cannot begin a house unless the materials are available. A scientist cannot plan an experiment unless basic apparatus is in place. Without water, you cannot make a cup of tea. In everyday life it is convenient to think of conditions as requirements that must be met. For instance, to have lunch in the student canteen – your goal – you must meet the condition of having lunch money. Having money is a precondition for buying your lunch. If you need to borrow books from the library, you must have a valid student ticket and not have exceeded your borrowing quota. These are pre-conditions. In addition the resources – books – must be available to you. When you need to revise for exams, pre-conditions include having the relevant course notes and books, finding a suitable place to study, and making sure you have pens and paper.

Social communication also involves pre-conditions. For instance, if someone asks you for a loan, a pre-condition is that you know this person as a friend. If you want to enter into a conversation, pre-conditions such as willingness to listen to others, keeping appropriate distance, and monitoring of any tendency to interrupt all have to be met.

Post-conditions are similar to outcomes. In other words a post-condition is how we expect the world to be once we have completed our plans. Recognizing post-conditions is an important step in under-standing the completion state of your plan (achieving your goal). Taking an expanded lunch example again, if the pre-conditions of having the canteen open, having food on offer and having money for food are met, you can reasonably expect the post-condition of eating your lunch to happen. In the case of exam preparation, if you have met the pre-conditions for studying, then the post-conditions – the outcomes – should include exam success. If your goal of exam success is not reached and you can look back in your diary and see no gaps in your alignment of resources and planning, then talk to the academic staff about your concerns. It is always important to use both our successes and our failures to guide our choices and behaviours.

Applying post-condition reasoning to social circumstances is usually a lot trickier however. As we said earlier, predicting other people's behav-iour is an uncertain exercise on occasion. For example, if you invite someone around for dinner with the goal of forming an intimate relation-ship, then among the post-conditions, you would expect some degree of intimate behaviour such as hand holding, caressing or kissing. If none of these post-conditions are met, you may find yourself confused and won-dering about what had been achieved. This can happen in the most mundane of circumstances. You may plan to join a group of students in conversation. After a while they head off to the bar. No one has explicitly said: *Join us in the bar.* On the other hand, no one has said: *Do not join us in the bar.* Understandably people with AS often cannot determine if they have successfully participated in conversation. Our advice is that unless a negative post-condition is encountered (*Do not join us in the bar*), ask if you may proceed: *Are you guys going to the bar? Can I join you?* If you have difficulty recognizing that you have achieved your goal, you have no option but to ask. You may not always like the answer, but not asking will just increase any sense of outcome uncertainty. There is the possibility that you will be misled or misinterpret events. Someone in the group might reply: *Sure, join us in the bar.* Unbeknownst to you the group has decided to go to a different bar. These occurrences are unfortunate but they happen to everyone from time to time. The important decision is not to let these events get you down. Spend time analysing the situation in an effort to pre-empt it happening again. If you are caught out again, keep away from that group.

Actions to complete

In between getting organized, identifying what you need to realize your goal, and achieving it, you need to complete a sequence of steps. A plan is only as useful as its execution. If you are planning your coursework, then becoming anxious because you are, say, short of one coloured marker will not be helpful. On the other hand if you begin your homework without any markers at all, then there is just cause for some anxiety. One of the biggest challenges facing students with AS is staying focused, 'staying on task'. Consider what seems like a mundane case below.

> Bill worked as a kitchen maker in a family business after his apprenticeship. He was competent at designing kitchens. He was also competent at calculating materials and cutting lists. His main weakness was a tendency not to complete jobs. For instance, he would make the carcass (frame) but would 'put off' making the doors and fitting the trim. There was always a tangential job that required his almost total attention. Normally his brother would complete Bill's projects. However, after a car crash Bill's brother was unable to work for several months. The business began to suffer as other employees were less understanding of Bill's work patterns. Bill was unable to cope with the stress and daily friction with the other staff. Eventually Bill suffered a nervous breakdown. During counselling, Bill was diagnosed as having AS. He was 23 years old.

Bill's case is not unusual. He could clearly identify the beginning and end of his projects, but had great difficulty completing them. Bill had the classic difficulty of grasping the *whole*. Another case relates to a student.

Mary had been an excellent student in her school and had won several awards. She had been diagnosed with AS at the age of 14. She chose a science track in college and, based on her school work, parents and teachers assumed she would be very successful. Mary's attendance records in college were exemplary. However, she struggled through her first and second years. In the third year, she failed her exams and resolved to leave college. An examination of her performance (conducted by her parents and therapist) showed that Mary paid great attention to her notes. After classes she dutifully rewrote her notes and used different coloured highlighters to indicate the significance of points. She had an elaborate colour coding system of her own. Mary's continuous assessment was a weak passing grade. An examination of her study practices revealed that she was too selective in rewriting her notes and recoding them again (several times for certain courses). She was too selective in her treatment of topics. When revising, she focused on notes that she considered particularly elegantly reworked. Unfortunately this strategy meant that important topics were ignored.

Mary did not go off on a tangent outside her courses but within them. By successively narrowing her study focus actions, she ruled out attending to the whole of the course. No matter how competent one is in charting the initial requirements and identifying the goal to be achieved, unless the action sequence between the initial and final state is defined and monitored, there is a danger that the plan will fail. The key issue to define is what needs to happen to go from one state to another, and then to carefully monitor one's progress. In the case of academic courses, it is essential to have a study action plan that includes the whole of the course. This is why carefully designed study schedules are so important. If you have weaknesses in this area – and you could have in the initial years in college – then discuss your requirements with the student counsellor and the course mentor.

Flexibility: it's not a straitjacket

It is important to build flexibility into a plan. Often, despite all your planning and preparation, something unexpected will happen to frustrate your plan. This can be confusing and stressing. What do you do when your plan, which embodies your expectations, is deflected or fails? Suddenness in other people can be upsetting. Their thoughts and intentions are unclear. A lecturer walks into a lab and tells the class that the planned experiment is postponed due to a shortage of resources. Instead, the class will perform a different exercise. No one likes that, but these events are common. They are very minor upheavals compared to an airliner crashing, or an earthquake. So when your schedule is upset, try to keep a sense of proportion.

Assume you have made an arrangement to see another student for a night out. For whatever reason, the other person does not turn up. What do you do? How do you feel? If you were hoping to meet a member of the opposite sex, then you will be disappointed. Anyone would be. If you had planned on meeting a friend and heading off to a concert, for instance, you can still go on your own. OK, it's not as much fun, but it is better than feeling let down and upset. Often it is easier to give in to your feelings of being 'let down' rather than explore alternatives. In making a plan, you implicitly classified the event as a having a certain personal significance to you. When the realization of your plan is frustrated, you need to look at reclassifying the event so that it is still of positive benefit to you. Reclassification is another way of saying redesignate the significance of the event. Suppose an important lecture with a visiting academic is cancelled. You have been looking forward to the lecture and meeting the speaker. His area of research is very similar to your interests. When he has to pull out of the lecture, you are entitled to feel disappointed, but use the time to read something extra about his work, or even to catch up with some social contacts in your class. Try to develop some flexibility in your reactions to disappointments.

People with AS usually attach great significance to arrangements with others. Sometimes the arrangements are violated by the other person, who is probably unaware of their significance. Other people will often not understand what an arrangement means for you. That is one of the facts of life. If these events provoke great anxiety, perhaps a visit to the student counsellor is in order.

Plans will go awry. When formulating any plan, try to formulate at least one alternative if your main plan doesn't work out. It is not uncommon when making dates with the opposite sex for a certain percentage of 'no shows' to occur. Remember that dating involves two people coming together who do not know each other well. Often a potential date is just an acquaintance whom you find attractive. Dating is very important and when someone does not turn up it can be very upsetting and confusing. When making a date, bear in the back of your mind that circumstances may prevent a person from turning up. If he or she rings you in advance telling you that the date is off, at least you know not to turn up. On the other hand, if you turn up and they do not, what can you do? Of course you may rage a little, that's understandable, but after that use your time to visit an art gallery or have something to eat in an unfamiliar restaurant. These actions will help you reclassify the significance of the 'no show'. In simple terms it is a strategy for turning a negative experience into a small positive one.

Working with a schedule

What is a schedule? Well, a schedule is a way of laying out plans that involve doing tasks within certain time limits. People often talk about their appointments schedule, meaning a description of the people they have to meet at certain times and dates. Your courses in college are based on schedules of classes and practical work. Each activity is given a time, location and date in the college calendar. A railway schedule is a timetable describing the origin and destination of trains, and the times they will arrive at various stations. Essentially schedules are timetables for events. They are useful because they help us organize our lives. They help us plan effectively.

Basic schedule properties

You should treat a schedule as a plan that lists all the tasks (jobs, work, study, etc.) that you must attend to, and when you should attend to them. Schedules are a way of listing what events should happen at certain times.

In college the fundamental schedule is the course timetable. It organizes your life in college, during the day at any rate. The course schedule – timetable – describes where you have to be at certain times. It also gives you vital foreknowledge about your courses and informs your expectations. Without such a schedule, life in college would be random and very confused.

It is worthwhile putting together a nonacademic schedule to deal with domestic and social responsibilities. For instance, a domestic schedule is very helpful in planning money withdrawals and expenditure. It will also help you organize your washing, and so on. We've covered the advantages of planning your domestic life earlier, so we do not need to go over all the details again. A social schedule, involving college societies, can also be immensely helpful in filling your social life. A weekend schedule can help plan visits to friends and family as well as outings to sites of interest (museums, planetariums, etc.).

Advantages for AS in schedules

Schedules help organize your life, but remember a schedule has to be followed. A schedule has to be implemented. While schedules are essential for some areas (study), they can be hindrances if applied rigidly to your social life. A social schedule should allow for alternatives if arrangements do not work out. A social schedule should be qualified. For instance, you might plan to visit John in Vermont every second weekend. Great idea, but what about the snow? Have you factored that into your schedule? We are back to the issue of being realistic again. A flexible social schedule is essential if disappointment and anxiety are to be minimized and managed appropriately (and we do not underestimate the difficulty).

It is hard to overstate the negative impact that poor personal hygiene and unclean clothes can have on peers and people in authority. Often an unkempt, dishevelled appearance serves to reinforce prejudices among these groups. Certainly social intimacy is nearly impossible to achieve unless basic hygiene and cleanliness are respected. A domestic schedule can be hugely beneficial to someone with AS. It can save them from distractions and shield them from mistakes.

Attendance and work completion

Schedules also help manage course attendance and coursework completion. They help you monitor your own performance. But you need to review your actual performance against your schedules on a regular basis. At least once a week look over both, and if there is any deviation in attendance or performance, explain why to yourself. If the deviations persist, you may want to discuss your commitments with the student counsellor or course mentor.

One of the most important schedules you will need to develop is a study schedule. You use a study schedule to keep you in touch with the courses and coursework. As you get nearer to exam time, you will need to revise your schedule and allow more revision time. A study schedule should be balanced between time given to revision and time given to relaxation. Overdoing either one or the other activity can pose mental health hazards. Try two-hour sessions initially, followed by 15-minute breaks. When you are approaching exams you might be studying ten or more hours per day. Give yourself a ten-minute break every two hours, with a 45-minute break every three hours. Remember to eat regularly, and even though you are pressurized at these times do not overlook personal hygiene.

What are the main components of a study schedule? The main components are simply time slots set aside for studying aspects of your courses. Students differ in ability and take very varied courses. Consequently, it is not possible to produce a set of specific schedules here. In general you will need to identify the modules in your courses and assign time to each module commensurate with your ability. This implies that you assign more time to studying modules in which you consider yourself weak, but do not overestimate your 'strong' modules. No matter how you divide up your time, each study session should be task focused. This simply means that every time you sit down to study, you set yourself a goal for that session. Studying is not reading and it is not stream -of-consciousness thinking. For studying to be effective it needs to be a wrapper around a particular task. Rather than saying to yourself *I'm going to read 100 pages of book X*, instead focus on a topic (or topics). You might say to yourself: *I am going to study the first two chapters in book X as these cover the introduction to and development of topic Y*. Again bring in your knowledge of planning and organization in tackling this task. One other reason for doing task-focused studying is to minimize distractions. Sometimes people with AS will start out happily studying one topic, but before completion switch to another that has caught their attention. If you find this happening, measure your actual performance against your study schedule. Is there a deviation? Is there a large deviation? Can you give a logical explanation for the deviation?

Getting ready for exams

Everyone finds exam time stressful. One way to minimize stress is through organization. Have your study schedule planned and be satisfied that it is realistic for you. Unexpected events can be very anxiety provoking and confusing at these times. A sensible planning approach is to have alternative strategies built into your daily schedule in case the unexpected happens (the library is closed due to power outage, the computer network has crashed, your friend cannot find the important book you want to read, etc.). These strategies should allow you to redesignate the significance of an event quickly. This strategy is important in helping students with AS break out of 'bad' thought patterns. If you get completely hung up on what has not happened, you will find it difficult to focus on what needs to happen.

Be ready for the unexpected

Jim was a student with AS. He had quite limited social contacts in college, but was very successful in his studies. Coming up to his final exams, he developed a study plan which involved him spending ten hours per day in the library. He always sat in the same seat near his subject area shelves. During exam time the library becomes very crowded. One morning he arrived late due to a delay in his bus arriving to campus. When he reached the library, 'his' seat was occupied by a female student. Jim asked her to get out of 'his' seat. She refused whereupon he pulled the seat from under her. He also hit her on her back with his fist. This was a serious situation. He was escorted from the library by security staff and arraigned before the Dean of Discipline. Fortunately Jim's AS was well documented in the college. He was not suspended on the understanding that he apologize in person to the other student. He was fortunate that the other student accepted his apology and did not press for further disciplinary action.

Well what happened to Jim then? Jim had a great study plan. He was diligent about monitoring his progress and he was a high-ability student. He explained to his therapist afterwards that when he saw the other student in 'his' seat he experienced an intense feeling of panic. So intense was this emotion that it overpowered any normal common-sense reaction. His carefully assembled foreknowledge had been violated, and all he could focus on was removing the source of difficulty. The significance of his study plan was so immense in Jim's mind that any violation was likely to undermine his self-control. If we step back from Jim's situation for a minute, it is obvious that every student finds exam time stressful. Your nerves are on edge coming up to exams. You are intensely focused on your subjects. Any interruption of the study process can seem catastrophic. But it is how you deal with these upsets that is important. Think *How can I redesignate this situation?* rather than *Oh my goodness, he didn't turn up. He hasn't brought the chemistry text. This is terrible. What can I do? Oh my goodness, he didn't turn up.*

Inevitability of stress for AS students

Try not to panic if you feel stressed. Panic will only overpower your capacity to think logically and will make a crisis out of a difficulty. The exercises in Chapter 8 will help you manage anxiety. During exam time, stress is inevitable. Students spend a good deal of time on their own studying. They also meet up to share experiences and offer help to one another. Class social networks can offer a valuable informal support service at exam times in particular. With AS, you may miss the benefits of the informal support system. Be alert to joining any exam study groups.

In advance of the exams spend time finding out if the class is setting up study groups and attach yourself to the one with the most able students. One way to work your way into a group is by offering to help produce a study schedule for the group. Always offer your skills to people if you need them to reciprocate with their help.

If you become tuned out of class activities, studying on your own can become very tedious at times. Knowing what the class is doing, or at least knowing what the more competent class students are doing, can help enormously in resolving course questions you may have.

If you find yourself in a panic over a topic or because you feel you haven't done enough with a particular course, stop panicking. Write out clearly the points you have covered and look at what remains to be done. You may surprise yourself. If you still feel adrift, then assess how much time you need to complete the topic. If the time needed is time that you must take from other topics, then you need to assess if this is realistic. If it is realistic, go ahead. If it is not realistic, then stop. Consolidate what you know of that course and continue with your schedule for the other courses. Finally, if you are uncertain, talk to the course lecturers and the course mentor about your predicament, before talking with the student counsellor. The academic staff may give you tips on what to concentrate on. In any event, if your schedule is going awry, then it may indicate that your planning was too late. Assuming you pass the exams, you have learnt a lesson for the next year and begin exam study planning earlier.

If you find that your studies are not progressing at a rate that you find acceptable then think about discussing your progress with others. The others can include a friend, counsellor, course mentor or therapist. When you feel under pressure or in despair, then talk about your situation with someone responsible. Do not keep despair within you.

Asking for help

There are three sources of help that you can explore during exam preparation. These are your classmates, the academic staff and finally the student counsellor. Occasionally you may need help with a specific topic in a course. The best source of help here will be the tutorials or else a direct approach to the course lecturer. Use email to clearly describe your difficulty. Difficulties in comprehending academic qualities of courses are best addressed by the academic staff. If the difficulties persist then you might involve the student counsellor or your therapist.

However, if you have social contacts within your class, then consult with them on your difficulties with course topics. Perhaps someone in the group has had the same difficulties and overcame them. They may well help you as well. Knowing how to approach someone in your class for help can be tricky. If you feel more comfortable with email, perhaps email them first with a request for help. Introduce yourself and ask if they can help you understand whatever the particular course problem is. Suggest a time to discuss it, but be flexible. Remember you are the one asking for help.

Approach the student counsellor or your therapist if you find that your exam preparation schedule is not working out, despite your best efforts. Also liaise with your course mentor. You may find yourself panicked at this point, but try and remain solution focused. If you find yourself unable to study or are hopping from topic to topic aimlessly, then an approach to the student counsellor for some support is worth considering. Always keep an eye on your schedules. When persistent deviations occur, then it is time to look for outside assistance. Learning to ask for assistance in order to pre-empt a crisis is a sign of tremendously mature judgement.

Responding to requests for help

Weaker students may seek your advice and help because of your abilities and focus. When you receive requests for help, respond to them graciously. Avoid sounding vain and self-important. If you are willing to help someone then set time limits on your assistance. Only assign time to people that you can afford to assign. If the person you are assisting wants your time then you have to ask yourself is this person my friend? Has he ever come to me before? Has he abused me, or excluded me socially before? If he or she is a friend, then you might want to say: *I can spend 20 minutes with you on this topic but then I have to get back to my work.* Be realistic in assessing what you can offer. Always remember that your first priority is to make sure that *you* pass the exams, not someone else.

If the student looking for your help is an acquaintance, you need to ask yourself the same friendship questions. You might have to say: *I can't go over that topic now, as I am still trying to understand other areas of the course. I wouldn't want to give you inaccurate advice. Why don't you talk to the course mentor?* Giving people the 'brush off' is not easy, but sometimes it is unavoidable and the correct action. If the other person simply wants to take advantage of your knowledge, but has never shown any friendship towards you, you need to protect your intellectual capital. Avoid exploitation around exam time.

Using the library

Using the library when you first arrive in college can be stressful outside of exam time. Get the foreknowledge. Trying to become familiar with library routines and practices near exam time is not recommended. Use the library regularly through the year to get an understanding of its routines.

As Jim's case above conveyed, accessing and using the library facilities around exam time can be anxiety provoking. Ideally, you reach the library early in the morning to forestall any problems in getting a seat near the shelves for your topic area. If it turns out that you cannot get a seat or your favourite seat is taken by someone else, you need to fall back on one of your alternative strategies. Almost certainly there is a classroom or lecture hall you can use. If that option is not viable then return to your accommodation and study there.

If you are short of textbooks you may find yourself disadvantaged at exam time. Most libraries cannot carry all the books that are needed by the student body. The simplest solution is to purchase the course books rather than rely solely on the library. The library should be used for consulting secondary source texts and journals. You should really have bought the primary texts at the beginning of the college year.

Donal was not diagnosed with AS until mid-way through college. He sought assistance after seeing a television documentary on autism. One of the stories Donal recounted to his therapist involved the college library. When Donal first came to college, he dutifully used the library to read books and research papers. However he avoided borrowing books because that activity required interaction with the library staff. He was uncertain how to interact with staff and anxious that some part of the interaction would go wrong. As a result he never borrowed any books in his first year. At exam time, he was worried that some books he needed would be borrowed by other students. Consequently, he needed to be in the library very early in the morning, and would be one of the last to leave at night. This routine, caused by his interaction anxiety, put him under

> tremendous pressure during exam time. Fortunately, in his subsequent years, some classmates helped him learn the interaction process. With practice and patience, he was able to borrow books reasonably comfortably.

The lesson to be drawn is to know the library early, and understand the processes and routines that define the library. Spend time discreetly observing how the staff do their jobs. All of this intelligence gathering will build up your confidence. If an unexpected event occurs, such as a book you desire is unavailable, redesignate your needs and focus on an alternative positive action.

Recommendations

We have covered a huge range of activities and responsibilities in this chapter. We have emphasized and re-emphasized advice on schedules, planning, organization and redesignation strategies. We have emphasized that foreknowledge is valuable for minimizing stress. Schedules can encapsulate foreknowledge, but you need to commit to enacting schedules. Documenting your performance and measuring it against the relevant schedule will help you monitor your needs and identify gaps that have to be filled. All college activities must be ultimately assessed in terms of how they support your learning needs. Antisocial or distractive behaviours must be addressed and remedied early in their emergence.

We have described how to look for help from various grades of staff, and how to interact with and react to the same staff. Fellow students, your classmates, are also sources of support. However, learning to distinguish between friend and acquaintance is a difficult process, and some trial and error is inevitable. Social engagements are very pleasant, but sometimes they are unpredictable.

Exam preparation through study schedules has been explored and again the focus is on thorough preparation to minimize stress and anxiety. We touched on several strategies that are useful in managing domestic and social responsibilities, proper preparation and planning for activities being essential in these areas. There are many good study guides available. Check the internet bookstores for a highly recommended guide. Other brain-and-mind improving books might be useful. For instance, a book with the intriguing title of *Mind Sculpture* explains how education and the environment mould the brain, and offers good tips on how to make the most of your abilities (Robertson 2000).

In addition, we examined how you might construct flexible plans which allowed for alternatives. This is not always possible, but where the examinations of alternatives are possible they should be explored. Accept that the unexpected can occur. No one has a copy of tomorrow's newspapers. Finally, remember that you are a bright intelligent person who can– and will–triumph over moments of stress.

5 Working with Student Support Services

Behaviour is a measure of how we feel

In this chapter we describe several guidelines about when you should see the student counselling services, and what you should report to them. A more detailed look at general mental health issues that may be beyond the scope of student services is given in Chapter 8. In particular Chapter 8 gives a detailed look at stress and anxiety-related behaviours and their management.

A person's behaviour gives us a good clue about their mental well-being. In college you will be largely responsible for reading your own behaviour. Of course reading behaviour is not easy at times, especially for someone with AS. In this chapter we will not focus on reading other people's behaviour but talk about you reading your own behaviour. If you can learn to read your own behaviour, in certain contexts, it will help you cope with stress and upsets. Sources of stress in student life usually arise from academic and social communication demands. When your stress levels are very high, your ability to meet the demands of both these areas of your life can deteriorate. The problem facing most people with AS is determining safely in advance that the deterioration is affecting their mental well-being. The facts are that persistent stress has a bad effect on academic performance and also on social participation.

However, to be fair we must admit that, first of all, no one is perfect and that stress, as we said before, is inevitable.

Talking out one's problem is still good advice. In the college environment, as in life, close friends can be very understanding and worth confiding in. But you must be sure that these friends are truly your friends, and are discreet. The other point to bear in mind, if discussing personal issues with your peers, is that they are your peers. In most cases your peers will be aged between 18 and 24 years old, with limited life experiences and unlikely to have the insight of a professionally trained counsellor or therapist. Your peers are probably fine to advise on issues that do not threaten your mental or physical health. For serious issues, you should seek more professional advice from the student support counsellor, course mentor or your therapist (these being the most suitable authority figures in whom to confide). In most cases a mentor will refer you to the counselling services anyway. In any event, if you feel anxious, tense and upset for more than a few days you should consider speaking to one of these people.

A question that frequently arises during therapy is: *How do I know I am stressed out?* When someone asks this question he or she is really asking a more important question: *How do I know that I am so stressed out that I need to see someone?* Unfortunately, when humans are dispirited and stressed there are few extraordinary outward signs. We do not turn bright green, grow a third arm or develop a flashing message box on our foreheads. In most cases, reactions to stress are measured by an initially slight but increasing fall-off in attending to routines. Where the stress and anxiety are in the 'normal' range, most affected people will correct their behaviour and continue meeting their commitments. If the corrective action does not occur, then there is cause for concern.

Departures from routines

In previous chapters we emphasized the importance of maintaining diaries for recording adherence to plans and commitments. Departures from routines are often the only early indicators of stress. If you find that your capacity to meet your daily commitments – be they academic, social or even personal hygiene – is shrinking over one to two weeks, then you should consider discussing your situation with the student counsellor or your therapist. A classic indicator of being too stressed, and having difficulty coping, is the gradual collapse of personal hygiene. If you have difficulty sticking with your personal hygiene schedule, try to assess how you feel. Has anything occurred that you ignored at the time, but is actually continuing to arouse your anxiety levels? Whether you identify a 'cause' or not, consider having a chat with the student counsellor or your therapist. Remember that bad hygiene will produce negative reactions in your peers towards you.

Missing classes in favour of staying in bed or hanging around your room is to be strongly resisted. When departures from legitimate routines such as class attendance become established over time, returning to legitimate routines becomes more difficult. These situations are never very 'comfortable'. Usually the tension between what you ought to be doing and what you are actually doing increases anxiety. As time passes the tension can worsen. The most worrisome outcome is often the development of a social phobia, which translates literally into a fear of social contact. Do not let these changes in routine behaviours go unchecked. Any radical change in behaviour which violates normal daily schedules should be discussed with the counsellor or your therapist.

Anger resulting from stress

When people are feeling under a lot of pressure, their judgement about the appropriate way to behave and react to others is often impaired. They are unsure how to react and unable to interpret other people's reactions to them correctly. Someone with AS frequently encounters this predicament in daily life. When stress persists, one's behaviour can become very volatile. If you had tantrums in school, then you already have an understanding of what we mean by 'volatile behaviour'. It is not a pretty sight and alienates people whose natural instincts are supportive.

Volatility caused by stress often results in feeling very angry and really not being quite clear why you are so angry. It is a confusing experience which may lead to aggressive behaviour, and outbursts of rage and tantrums. The initial outburst may relieve some of the tension. However, it also leaves you feeling very bad and upset. Remember that outbursts of anger affect other people. You may be able to forget the episodes, but others may not be able to forget the impact of the anger on them. Anger is a definite hurdle to forming social relationships.

In school many of the angry pupils may have been bullies. They may have had friends, in the sense of henchmen, who were scared of being picked on. College is a more mature environment and the prevalence of bullying is very low compared to school. Consequently, there is a very low tolerance of people who display angry outbursts. Anger is a very alienating experience for other people. Anger is not socially acceptable and the social conventions of the adult academic world are not receptive to outbursts of anger. Outbursts of anger should be recorded in a diary. Most importantly, record your apologies to the affected people and their reactions. Outbursts of anger, even infrequent outbursts, should be discussed with your counsellor.

Using a daily diary to record anxiety

We talked earlier in the book about documenting your schedules and timetables, writing out your plans and assessing their viability, and generally keeping an electronic diary of your daily routines. We will add a little more detail to this practice now by suggesting that your diary should have a 'How Has Your Day Been?' section. We suggest that you have a satisfaction scale for each day. The scale is: (1) very satisfied, (2) slightly satisfied, (3) slightly dissatisfied, (4) very dissatisfied.

Recording this information is much easier with a computer. We know of one student with AS who wrote a computer programme based around a spreadsheet application to record his social 'highs' and 'lows'. Being able to computerize his schedules and social calendar enabled him to review his own progress over any given period of time with ease. He also brought progress reports to his therapist for assessment. The other advantage of the computer over paper diaries is that your personal thoughts and commentaries remain secure with password protection and encryption.

No matter what media you choose for your diaries and schedules, allow yourself space to record any incidents that were particularly enjoyable or very stressful. Try to avoid recording only negative experiences, but record what gave you pleasure. This is particularly important if you choose to document satisfaction with your leisure time. If in any two-week period you find yourself making mostly reports of being very dissatisfied, then consider talking to either the student counsellor or your therapist about your sense of dissatisfaction.

Panic attacks, or feelings of panic, should definitely be recorded, as these are invariably related to anxiety in people with AS. You can record these easily. If you felt very anxious in a situation during the day – listening to students in the locker room, for instance – to the point where you felt unable to function very well, then record this event and mention the phrase: *felt panic today*. Later on, in discussions with the student counsellor or your therapist, you may be given additional advice on how to record these events for discussion with them.

Interview with a student counsellor

AB has been involved in student and adult counselling since the early 1970s. When she first entered counselling, her work was focused around students with learning disabilities. Over time, she became more aware of problems with students who were not learning disabled. Quite the contrary, many of these students were exceptionally able. Their main difficulties related to not coping very effectively with social expectations. Interviewer is John Harpur (JH).

JH: When did you first come across AS?

AB: I first heard of AS in the UK in the late 1980s. I was involved in a number of projects supporting learning disabilities. When I look back on those years, it is quite likely that I was encountering people with AS but trying to fit them into a learning disability model.

JH: Are counsellors more informed about AS now, in your opinion?

AB: Speaking only for myself, I can say that I am more informed now than I was 15 years ago. Over that time, there has been a general rising in awareness of autism and autistic disorders. I would be surprised if student counsellors were not informed about AS. Certainly

Tony Attwood's book on AS has been enormously helpful in filling an information gap.

JH: I know that people vary considerably, but what is your approach on first meeting a student with AS?

AB: A lot depends on whether they were diagnosed before coming to college or while in college. If they have been diagnosed before coming to college, they will have had time to accept and explore the diagnosis. In these cases, we can get right to the point when discussing anxiety, stress, interpersonal problems, academic concerns and such like. Students that are diagnosed in college tend to need more time and more support while they accept and explore the diagnosis. In most cases both sets of students will have some contact with private therapists or psychiatrists. Consequently, a student's support needs are spread between the professionals.

JH: What categories of problems are you likely to hear about?

AB: Where they slip is in their social life. Anxiety and depression are among the common problems. Students with AS do want to fit in and have friends, but they have difficulties assessing where they are at in these activities. They can be exploited as well. A kind of 'I'll be your friend if you loan me money' arrangement occurs. It is despicable, but not uncommon. Mixing with members of the opposite sex is another huge area of uncertainty.

JH: What concrete suggestions do you make to students with AS?

AB: Group work can be very helpful. Students can make partnership arrangements to help and support each other. The group can provide a source of 'buddies'. The counsellor is merely the facilitator. In the past I have been a temporary 'buddy' to several AS students with a view to helping them make their own friends. Student societies offer outlets for interests and the opportunity to make friends. However, you have to work at remaining in the society and not giving up after the first meeting.

JH: Finally, what does the student need to know about the student counsellor to make a successful connection?

AB: AS is a complicated condition to understand. It has many subtleties. The student needs to be assured that the counsellor has an understanding of AS. If the counsellor needs more time to come to terms with AS, then the student will need to spend more time with an external therapist.

To see or not to see the support office?

Get to know the support services as soon as possible. If coming to college for the first time, arrange to meet the service staff out of term and get a tour of their workplace. Ordinarily, there will be a leaflet describing their work. Take a picture of yourself with the support staff as a means of recording the space. Foreknowledge is important in these situations. Finding out about the services offered by the student support office in advance of visiting the counsellor can take much of the anxiety out of the initial meeting.

Apart from the reasons mentioned earlier for contacting the student counsellor, you may also feel bad because a relationship has broken up, or a personal tragedy has affected someone in your family. Work with the college services before looking for an external therapist. If you have moved from one city to another, finding a new external therapist can be stressful. In these cases, the student counsellor will be your most appropriate contact, and he or she may also identify an appropriate external therapist if you should want one. Usually external therapists are not as accessible as the student counsellor, which is something to consider.

Many people have difficulty talking about their emotions, especially when the emotions are related to experiences with the opposite sex. A common belief is that your problem is so personal that it would be too difficult to reveal to the student counsellor. In practice, there are few new problems, and counsellors will have encountered most of the common problems faced by students.

If you do not have an external therapist monitoring your performance and offering support, then the student counsellor is a good ally in helping you manage your college responsibilities. The effects of not working with the counsellor may include exam failure and eventual departure from college. Of course, the most serious consequence is that any deterioration in your performance may not be picked up in time to help you. If you find the demands of college, especially the social demands, very stressful, then regular meetings with the counsellor are recommended.

When to present oneself

If you were diagnosed with AS before coming to college, then hopefully you will have made arrangements to see the counsellor regularly during the first year. It is critical that the counsellor is familiar with AS. After the first year, your needs can be reassessed and possibly a different schedule will be discussed. If you have been diagnosed in college, then you may require more frequent contact with the counsellor. More than likely you suspected something was 'wrong' and the diagnosis is often welcome. However, it still takes time to accept the diagnosis and this can be both a period of immense highs, as you gain some insight into your condition, and a period of immense lows, as you also gain some insight into your condition. You may need additional support to keep you focused on academic commitments during this period of acceptance. Make a point of seeing the counsellor regularly if you are depressed, prone to depression, or feel too stressed.

Every person's situation is slightly different and there are no fixed rules about frequency of attendance. The only rule to follow is that once you agree a schedule with the counsellor you must stick to it. Remember, if you miss sessions you have deprived others of that time with the counsellor and that is wasteful of college resources. If at any point during the term you are unable to cope with normal daily demands and are considering leaving college, then a chat with the counsellor should be undertaken before you make any definite decisions. The counsellor will probably have discussed 'time out' of college options with many students. In certain cases, a temporary break is very useful, and in other cases there is no need for a break but just a redesignation of priorities. There is no escaping the planning. A counsellor can advise on planning and reformulating your schedules.

Another time to consider approaching the counsellor is if you are not getting along with other people. This experience can be very distressing. The counsellor will not have a magical solution to this problem, but he or she may be able to direct you towards other groups in college that might share your interests. Student societies are the obvious first choice, but in many colleges the counsellors may be assisting support groups for people with social difficulties. A counsellor will generally try to find a 'buddy' environment that will help you meet other people.

If you have had a romantic relationship with someone and regrettably it is now over, you may feel depressed and upset. These are common reactions. If you find your days continually 'clouded' by these reactions and they are not diminishing, then you may benefit from talking through the experience of the relationship with the counsellor.

Finally, remember that no matter how bleak you may perceive your situation to be, the support services are there to help. Attending the counsellor is not an admission that your situation is hopeless, but an indication of the strength of an intellect that knows when to muster additional resources to solve a problem.

Asking about interviewer obligations

Asking the counsellor, your interviewer, about his or her obligations towards you is another way of asking: *What are my rights in this situation?* After all, here you are pouring out your thoughts to a complete stranger, so it is not unreasonable to ask about your rights. You rarely have an absolute entitlement to rights. For instance, your right to confidentiality during counselling does not preclude the counsellor reporting you to the police for a serious crime. However, leaving aside extreme cases, you should ask about your rights in relation to (1) the college authorities; (2) your family; (3) any external medical or therapeutic agency. Colleges may differ in their interpretation of confidentiality agreements, so it is useful to discover if your understanding of confidentiality and the college's understanding coincide.

In simple terms you should ask the counsellor at your first meeting: *How much of what I say to you will leave the room?* In other words how much of what you say to the counsellor will be reported to other people. Ordinarily, nothing that you say will be reported to anyone else without your permission. Ask about your rights to confidentiality. Unless you have committed a crime, are a threat to other students, or your health and behaviour are causes of concern, your interviews will remain completely confidential. If you are also attending an external therapist, either or both may seek your permission to communicate with each other about you from time to time. Give your permission in these circumstances; it will help you get a better quality service.

The role of the counsellor is to provide assistance and support. The college authorities, or at least your course mentor, will need to be contacted if you need special tuition arrangements or you are falling behind in your work and need an extension on the submission of coursework. Unsurprisingly, if you are planning to leave college, the counsellor will need to liaise with the college authorities on how best to respond to your choice.

Exam time is stressful for everyone and getting appointments with a counsellor can be difficult. Try to arrange your appointment schedule so that you have an extra appointment at this time. If you fail to turn up for an exam, contact your course mentor as soon as possible and then try to make an appointment with the counsellor.

If a counsellor is seriously concerned about your health – mental or physical – he or she may ask your permission to contact an external medical agency or therapist. If you think about this request logically, the counsellor is indicating that outside help is now in your best interest. It is wise to be guided by the counsellor's judgement.

What to present

Avoid telling the counsellor how to conduct the sessions. You may very well have views on how you want the sessions to develop. Indeed, you may have studied a whole bundle of therapeutic theories. You are entitled to voice your opinions. However, a counsellor is not obliged to accept them. Generally a counsellor will develop a long-term plan of how the therapeutic relationship should develop with you. Give the plan a chance to develop, even if this takes many months rather than a few weeks. Building a relationship with a counsellor takes time. Trust is not arrived at immediately.

Counsellors generally follow an interview format; usually this is not obvious to the untrained observer. You should ask the counsellor whether you should prepare any material in advance for each session, and what format to follow. Write out a report if necessary and bring it along. Even if the counsellor has not explicitly requested a report, you can still read from it. The report should give a brief description of an event or a series of events that you have found distressing. You should conclude with questions you want to ask the therapist. If you find that the therapy sessions are overwhelming your capacity to record everything relevant, ask the counsellor for permission to tape the sessions for playback later. People with AS can wander from the point during therapy sessions. You may find yourself spending much of the session discussing events and issues that are really not related to your problems. The counsellor will do his or her best to keep the session focused. However, the distractive tendency is difficult to control, so we recommend that in advance of any session you spend time identifying issues that are causing you anxiety and distress.

What you present to the counsellor will very much depend on the problem of the moment. By and large you will be presenting difficulties related to social interactions. For instance, you may be feeling down because of friendship difficulties. It is likely that a persistent sense of being misunderstood will bring you into contact with the counsellor. You may have had difficulties with a member of the opposite sex. It can be hard to communicate about these issues and distresses. The counsellor will help you communicate.

BEHAVIOUR, THOUGHTS AND FEELINGS

Your counsellor will be interested in your behaviour, thoughts and feelings. It is important to report these as clearly and simply as you can. Your daily diary and schedule adherence notes will form the basis of much of what you will report. Obviously if you have stopped using these aids that is very significant behaviour in itself.

You are likely to be questioned about any alcohol consumption and drug taking. At a more mundane level your eating and hygiene habits will be noted. If you are in a relationship with another person, this will also be discussed. Your academic performance may also be discussed and the counsellor may look to corroborate your accounts with the records from the academic mentor.

Behaviours, verbal or nonverbal, that lead to violence or ridicule should be noted for reporting. Any thoughts about leaving college or doing harm to someone else should also be reported. Thoughts about self-harm should be noted immediately for reporting to the counsellor. Expressing anger is a behaviour that will draw negative attention from other people. Counsellors are always interested in how people manage anger, so be prepared to discuss anger.

How you handle everyday events, in terms of the skills you deploy, is usually a reasonable predictor of how you would cope with a crisis situation. If your handling of everyday events is deteriorating, the counsellor should be told.

When Thomas first came to the student support services he had already been diagnosed with AS in his teens. Thomas was of average academic ability and worked consistently in college. Before arriving in college he notified the support services of his diagnosis. Initially he had weekly meetings with a counsellor. As he gained in confidence, these meetings became monthly for the rest of his three years in college. Thomas's main liaison with the support services revolved around difficulties he had in his social life. Thomas found making friends quite difficult. He was involved with a number of college societies but failed to attend meetings on a regular basis. Thomas was interested in girls but needed help to frame appropriate requests. He participated in a group outside college specializing in role play and with help from the student counsellor was able to transfer some of these skills to the college environment. Thomas was issued with a format for each session which he returned completed to the counsellor just before each session. It took the counsellor several months to develop an individual questionnaire for Thomas. However, the effort made the sessions much more meaningful for Thomas and certainly assisted him in completing his degree.

DISCUSSING TIME-OUT OPTIONS

Under certain circumstances taking time out of your course of study is the right choice. However, try to reach this decision with input from the student counsellor, course director, your therapist and your family (if acceptable). The common circumstances that justify time out may involve bereavement when someone close to you has died. However, the amount of time required will vary from person to person. People with AS can be very resilient in the face of bereavement and may take only a limited time to return to college.

If an academic course is going badly for a sufficiently long time, or you have concluded that another course would be a better prospect, some time out may be recommended. Changing courses usually means changing degrees and such options are never to be undertaken lightly. Get advice from the academic staff and take time to reach a decision. You may need to consider a break from college for a few weeks or even a few months to help you assess your real ambitions. Your counsellor can help considerably here by discussing the implications of each option with you.

It is always useful to maximize your options. If you are planning to leave a course, try to leave with your year's exams completed successfully. You then have the option of returning to that course in the future. More importantly, it means you are changing course on the back of a success.

The other major occasion when you will need to consider time out of college is when stress overpowers your judgement and undermines your daily living skills. In common parlance, we are talking about a nervous breakdown. After a breakdown, you will need time out. Depending on your resilience and your therapeutic supports, recuperation time will vary. Student counsellors and academic staff are very sympathetic to people in these circumstances.

Do not view taking time out as some type of personal failure. In fact it is usually a much more sensible option than trying to push your interests and resources in a direction that you do not actually want to go. Counsellors are used to discussing choices with students. Often they will put in place strategies that will allow exploring choices in discussions without you having to take time out of college.

DISCUSSING SCHEDULE ADJUSTMENTS

Before deciding to leap from one course to another, it is worthwhile exploring whether a different schedule arrangement will better meet your needs. If you followed an individualized education plan (IEP) in school, college can come as a bit of a shock. However, many colleges offer modular degree courses which mean that you can 'pick and choose' the courses that make up your degree, subject to certain minimum conditions. The modular degree course is probably the nearest colleges come to offering IEPs.

Modular degrees offer some flexibility about the courses you take, but not with their timing. If a course is scheduled for spring, it is unlikely that the college will reschedule it for autumn to suit the needs of one person. More achievable schedule adjustments are around your participation in laboratory sessions. In first and second years, colleges usually duplicate lab sessions because of the volume of students. For instance, this means that if your lab is stressful on Mondays because of the antics of some people, you may be able to get a place in the same lab later in the week. Your course mentor and student counsellor are best suited to advise you about schedule changes.

Ultimately there is some flexibility in college schedules that you can use to your advantage. In any event, if you need a more flexible arrangement you should make a case to the counsellor and discuss a joint approach to the course mentor. You will lose nothing by asking for a more individualized schedule. However, be prepared for disappointment.

Listening

Interacting with the student support services can be very rewarding. To get the most value out of these interactions, learning to improve your listening skills may be necessary. Hearing, however, is not listening and we need to distinguish between them. Listening implies actively paying attention to something with your hearing skills. This could be a car engine, a singer, or your favourite computer games. Active listening is purposeful listening. Interacting with any counsellor or therapist requires good active listening skills. To test your skills, ask yourself: *Did I follow everything that was said? If I didn't, did I ask an appropriate clarification question? Can I reconstruct our interaction with high accuracy?* Active listening is covered in more detail in Chapter 6.

A key component of active listening is paying attention to what the other person is saying. Let the other person speak. Let them finish their sentences, and repress any impulse to sudden interruptions. One strategy to check if you have understood what has been said is to rephrase the other person's last exchange before responding. You might want to say: *If I understand you correctly you are saying …* These are not easy skills to pick up, but they are good skills for people with AS. They help minimize distractions by keeping you focused on the interaction of immediate relevance.

CHOICES HAVE CONSEQUENCES

One outcome of any counselling will be recommendations for behaviour change. This means you will be asked to do some things differently, stop doing other things and possibly pick up new things to do. For instance, you might be asked to change your morning routine to ensure that you have clean clothes available every day. You might be asked to stop staring at girls in class after they have complained. Finally, you might be asked to join a few college societies that offer weekends away on cultural tours as a means for making new social contacts. Depending on resources, the counsellor may accompany you for a period of the day to help you adjust to the changes and to assess your reactions.

Disclosing that you have AS is a very personal and sensitive issue. However, if your classmates know that you have AS and have some instruction in how to behave towards people with AS, then the quality of your social life can improve substantially. It is highly probable that the counsellor will raise this issue with you for discussion. No single solution will work for everyone and it is important to discuss the implications of disclosure very thoroughly with your counsellor (and usually with your therapist and family).

Every choice has consequences. When a counsellor suggests changes in behaviour or change in routines, he or she does so in the hope that the consequences will be positive. However, understanding what the counsellor is suggesting, and implementing the recommendations, are very different activities. Try to implement the recommendations as best you can. You may not succeed in all cases, and the changes may need much time to come about. If you are unsure about any of the recommendations, ask the counsellor for a logical justification for it. In any event accurately record the counsellor's recommendations.

Returning with feedback

It is likely that the counsellor will request that you return with feedback to each session. If the recommendations allowed for contact with the course mentor, the counsellor will have been given some feedback from the mentor. Feedback means reporting your experiences in trying to implement the recommendations. Your experiences will vary depending on the recommendation. Some routines are easier to change than others. Some changes will cause less stress than others. Some activities may bring more satisfaction than others. Irrespective of your reaction to the recommendations, make sure to record your experiences and satisfaction ratings. If you find the tasks stressful, resist any impulses to phone or email the counsellor continually with queries and worries. Try to work within the agreed schedule.

You may find yourself reporting that you were unable to enact most of the recommendations. Do not worry if this is the case. It is a common occurrence. You can only try as best you can to effect change. No one can expect any more.

Moving beyond local support

Sometimes the local support services are limited in what they can offer when someone becomes severely depressed. In these circumstances you may be requested to see a psychiatrist. For example, the student counsellor will not be in a position to advise on medication choices and schedules. Moving beyond the local college support services does not necessarily mean that they have failed you or that you have failed them. It is usually in recognition that more specialist support and assessment skills are needed. If the counsellor is concerned about your mental and physical well-being, he or she will probably suggest liaising with a psychiatrist. The psychiatrist will take over from the counsellor until such time as the counsellor's resources and skills are again appropriate. Most people with AS have attended a psychiatrist at some stage (many may have regular psychiatric sessions).

The role of psychiatric liaison

When anxiety and depression become severe and persistent, daily living commitments can be undermined. At this point a psychiatrist can play a significant role. There is always the risk that persistent depression will provoke suicide. There may be a need for medication in these circumstances but that judgement needs to be made by a psychiatrist.

A psychiatrist may be invited to help with support and assessment, when a counsellor believes that more progress might be possible with a different approach. However, sometimes a counsellor, depending on their knowledge and experience, may have unrealistic targets and a psychiatrist may be a much better source of support for someone with AS. If the range of behaviours is 'too odd' by the counsellor's standards, then he or she may request that responsibility for dealing with the student's needs be shared. Depression can produce behavioural extremes in people.

Of course a student may simply refuse to work with the counsellor and, in the absence of any other counsellor, referral to a psychiatrist is a reasonable option. Occasionally the relationship between a student with AS and a counsellor may become dominated by oppositional demands. This may arise because of personality friction between both parties. It is impossible for any therapeutic relationship to work if there is unresolved personal friction between the two people.

Some problems that may be encountered

The main problem that may be encountered in dealing with a student counsellor is the counsellor's lack of preparedness for AS. Lack of knowledge is still a problem among professionals, but it is a diminishing problem. Next to lack of a basic understanding of the syndrome, a counsellor may try to 'treat' someone with AS with a social skills intervention programme not based in AS research. This can create unrealistic expectations in both counsellor and student. Both parties become frustrated when their expectations are not met. Over-enthusiastic interventions may exacerbate depression rather than improve it.

After an individual assessment, group therapy, involving role playing within groups, is a popular strategy for helping people with social anxieties or phobias. You may not want to be introduced to a large group of strangers. If possible persuade the counsellor to introduce you to one person in the group before meeting the rest. You may become very dependent on the counsellor for support. In fact you may come to see the counsellor as your 'buddy'. Bonding with the counsellor is healthy, but remember that you are one of a number of students requesting support. If the counsellor has occasionally to decline to see you immediately to discuss an issue, try not to perceive the counsellor as selfish or rejecting. The counsellor has a broad student agenda and everyone who requests attention must receive it in turn.

Recommendations

The counsellor's knowledge of and experience with AS are the crucial factors in determining the value of a counselling relationship. Make sure you enquire about the support services' previous work with students with

AS. If no previous experience is reported, then you may have to rely on an external therapist until such time as the college services become better informed.

Reporting as accurately as possible your behaviour, thoughts and feelings and any persistent interaction difficulties you have will help the counsellor provide better quality support. This process may be difficult and it is not uncommon for very little to be said in sessions. However, over time a great deal gets said, so stick with the appointment schedules.

Finally, try to work through any recommendations from the counsellor that may direct you towards 'buddies'. Social skills groups and friendship groups are growing in popularity and you may find one that suits your interests and social desires. College societies should always be explored and consultation with the counsellor about your choices may be helpful. If you are taking any medication for mood management, the best person to refer your concerns to is your prescribing psychiatrist or other medical doctor. It is important to inform the counsellor if you are taking medication. In the final analysis, the student support counsellor can offer you very valuable support. In times of crisis, this support can be precious so try to remain within agreed schedules with your counsellor.

6 Communication
Getting Along with Others

In this chapter we will describe some of the most important skills we use in everyday life, our communication skills. This chapter is a *hinge* around which the recommendations in the other chapters turn. There is a slightly more technical flavour to the text here, but as we are preoccupied with communication strategies and skills, that is inevitable. These skills help us pull our social lives together. They help us get along with each other and they are everywhere. The question you may ask is: *How does all of this affect people with AS?* In the first place, social interactions are probably confusing from time to time. Comprehending the point of requests, the verbal innuendos, indirect asides and body language of other people is confusing. During a conversation with another student you may wonder: *What does he want of me?* Understanding what other people expect of you is far from trivial. It is hard to achieve consistency in your own understanding of other people's behaviours. Yet, second, we must acknowledge that without making some effort to understand these behaviours much of ordinary social interaction will pass before our eyes unnoticed. Finally, 'quality' social communication revolves around the participants valuing the relevance of the various contributions. A conversation is more than an information-sharing exercise – I tell you something and then you tell me something in exchange. It is also a means of getting to know someone and letting him or her get to know you. The big question is: *Can someone with AS reasonably apply the basics of quality communication skills?*

Realistically, there are no miracle answers. In nearly every case any progress is made through prolonged trial and error interactions. Your approach to understanding social communication skills has to be rooted in observation of others' behaviours and interactions. Your observations are then followed up by experimental interactions. Before you understood something of AS, you may have tried imitating personality traits in other people as a way of 'mastering' communication, with uncertain outcomes. As you get older you will want to develop a stronger sense of self, and that requires intellectual effort. This is a common theme in the autobiographies of Temple Grandin, Liane Holliday Willey and Gunilla Gerland. Communication is also about creating an identity and managing it. Rather than relying on instinct to guide social interactions, you will apply your intellectual skills to making progress in this area. Of course communication can be tiresome. You feel like 'erupting' at times due to the pressure of having to talk to one or more students. Practising the relaxation exercises described in Chapter 8 will help you manage your feelings in these situations. Practise combining both communication and relaxation skills with a social skills group, a support group, a counsellor or a student peer that is supportive.

Phone text messaging, email and internet chat are forms of textual communication. This means that you form your messages using some type of keyboard. Textual communications often have their own conventions. Email, for instance, has a collection of emotion icons to indicate the mood of the sender. Typical 'emoticons' are ☹, ☺ and ☻. These, respectively, indicate a sad or frustrated mood, a happy or playful mood, and a neutral or indifferent mood. People use emoticons to convey to the reader how the message should be interpreted. Text can be very literal and the emoticons help us convey intention. For example, a student might email home to report that his exam performance was as he expected:

1.   The exams went as expected ☹.

2.   The exams went as expected ☺.

3.   The exams went as expected ☻.

The text remains the same but the emoticon conveys the *real meaning* of the email, what the sender really wants to get across to the reader of the email. In (1) the student is conveying that he did not expect to perform well in the exams and that is what happened. In (2) he expected to do well and the emoticon conveys that he is pleased that he met the expectation. The third example is harder to interpret as the emoticon conveys a neutral attitude to the exams. The student is conveying an uncertain attitude to his exam performance.

The value of the emoticons (and there are many more than we have shown) is that they act as nonverbal signals in the message. Without the emoticons above, the literal meaning of the message would say something like: *I was not surprised by my performance in the exams.* There is nothing wrong with this message, but it does not tell us anything about the student's own appraisal of the exams. Attaching an emoticon to the message tells us much more about how the student felt about his performance.

A great deal of ordinary social interaction uses nonverbal behaviour a little bit like emoticons are used in email. The mood of a person as they do or say something will often convey the real meaning behind the action or speech. Their gestures, such as pointing and hand waving, will often communicate a lot of information about their interest in the topic and the audience. We must not, however, ignore the crucial importance of sound in conveying a message. One of the huge limitations of textual communication is the difficulty of indicating 'sound effects' in text. Typing in uppercase letters is considered shouting, and that is largely the closest we come to a text sound effect. Why is sound so important? Well obviously speech is sound. Sentences are merely the written versions of spoken speech. Traditionally the spoken sentence is called an utterance to emphasize its oral origins. The tone of voice can change the meaning of the same piece of speech from a joke to a threat depending on the occasion and location. Even emphasizing one word in an utterance can change its meaning entirely between one occasion and another. It is not easy to 'get at' this meaning. The human versions of emoticons are incredibly varied and sophisticated.

Nonverbal communication skills, unlike text icons, are demonstrated in face-to-face conversation. They are not textual creations. These nonverbal behaviours can include facial expressions, eye glances, hand gestures and body postures. In fact, a huge range of body movements can be involved in nonverbal communication. Everyone has problems grasping the significance of non-verbal behaviour from time to time. Parents and grandparents frequently complain that they cannot understand the meaning of many behaviours of the younger generation. People from one culture become confused about the meaning of gestures in another culture. In Europe, for instance, people do not bow to one another when they meet, yet in Japan bowing is a respectful greeting.

Conversation is primarily a verbal form of communication. For instance, phone conversation between two people is a form of verbal communication. Conversation, talking to one another, is an activity that involves purpose and direction. If conversation was just a case of one person making sounds in his throat and then another person making sounds in her throat, we would not be communicating. The heart of conversation is the *exchange* of meaning and the construction of new meaning. In any exchange there must be turn taking. You say something and then I reply to you, and so on. For example, Daniel talks to Miriam in the expectation that Miriam will understand him. When Miriam takes her turn, she expects Daniel to understand her. And so on. Often we use non-verbal behaviours to augment these conversational exchanges.

In college, conversations with the academic staff are generally focused around getting specific information, making requests, arranging appointments, reporting difficulties, and so forth. These types of conversational interaction are usually focused on tasks that derive from academic courses. More often than not the conversations are formal in nature. This means they are tightly rule guided, perhaps rigid even. These are conversational contexts where the participants base their communication around a particular topic, rather than themselves. In these contexts it is appropriate to discuss a course topic, such as properties of frictionless planes, but not to enquire into the private life of a staff member or reveal details of your own private life. For instance, you would not enquire into a professor's eating and drinking habits, his religion, or his family background. It is best to focus solely on the course content in these situations. A simple strategy is to email the lecturer your question and topic in advance when making an appointment. When you arrive for your appointment, bring your email and simply restate the question and topic. Keep conversation focused around the topic. A major comforting factor in formal conversations for someone with AS is that they are generally devoid of small talk.

Frequently student conversations will involve more than two people, so where we mention speaking to other people below, you can interpret 'other people' to mean either one or more persons. Conversations among students are mainly informal, good humoured and frequently involve small talk. What is small talk? Briefly this involves a number of topics being rapidly turned over in conversation, most relating to the casual aspects of daily life. Unlike formal conversations with academic staff, student conversations will often contain references to personal experience, gossip, sexual liaisons, parties, coursework, food, accommodation, music, sport, etc. In fact the topic list is practically endless. The very nature of informal interactions means that the rules are 'more' beneath the surface than in formal student/lecturer interactions. Participating in small talk can be a problem if you are out of touch with the interests of your peers. Read the newspaper for current affairs but also read at least one story each on sport and entertainment (movies, music, plays or literature). Many newspapers are available on the web, so 30 minutes per day should give you a good knowledge of what is topical. This will hugely improve your capacity to integrate.

The challenges

The vast majority of people with AS are as keen on making friends as anyone else. However, past upsets in friendship attempts can sometimes force a withdrawal from peers. The first thing to recognize is that everyone has experienced friendship attempts going badly at some stage, especially when interacting with the opposite sex. The second thing to note is that learning from mistakes is the only way to move forward on these fronts. No matter how many books, manuals, role-playing classes and so forth one has ingested, there comes a point in time when social experimentation is essential. The final point to retain is that most people are not supremely socially skilled. Consequently making mistakes in social interactions is not uncommon, contrary to what television and film dramas may suggest.

College is a time of immense change, much of it continuous. Even when friendship has been established it may not last beyond either the context of the time or the shared interests. Friendships that become firm in one year may weaken in the following. Someone that you may have disliked in first year becomes a reliable friend in final year. Early adult-hood is a time of intense developmental change. Young adults are exploring new freedoms and responsibilities and regularly testing their limits.

Sometimes in the course of a friendship or an intimate relationship, one person simply 'moves on' and there is nothing one can do to stop him or her. This can be very confusing and upsetting, especially if you are accustomed to factoring this person into your plans. Even the best conversationalist in the world cannot stop these changes. You may have been friends with someone in school or college and within what seems like a short period of time he or she has left your company and is in the company of others. It can be hard to accept, to 'swallow', since it implies rejection. However, this happens to everyone. Good friends can grow apart during the process of maturation. It's life and, yes, sometimes it is not very nice, but we need to accept it and move on ourselves. An acquaintance or friend may want an understanding from you that you cannot give. Reading the social signals in these circumstances can be difficult. They can be unclear and ambiguous, but you need to ask what does this person know or what has he experienced that has caused a change in behaviour? Is this change temporary? These are often not easy questions to answer, irrespective of AS. Quite a number of these challenges are experienced by nearly everyone. What is important is your capacity to face and overcome these challenges and to accept that some are inevitable.

Talking is important

Richard had difficulties grasping non-literal meaning from an early age. He had only learned to process requests such as *Can you pass the salt* as indirect requests to pass the salt in his teens. When he started college, he experienced difficulty understanding indirect communication again. On one occasion after a two-hour tutorial, the tutor got up to put his coat on. He said to Richard, *You are obviously not stuck for time.* Richard said he had plenty of time, clearly failing to grasp that the tutor wished to leave. On another occasion, Richard was introduced to a student leader who was described as another Ché Guevara. Richard asked him whether he had met Fidel Castro.

Richard has had a number of miscommunication events, but prior to attending college his parents had ensured that the college staff were supplied with information on AS. By patiently working through a list of likely indicators of indirect requests (can you, could you, etc.) he has been remarkably successful in identifying the actual request. Richard is the first to admit that he 'gets things wrong' on occasion. He now asks for clarification if he is in doubt about the real meaning of a request.

Any person with AS will find oral communication –conversation –stressful from time to time. This is a challenge as conversation is necessary in making friends with peers, both male and female. Conversations that are academically focused are information driven. One person is exchanging information with another; similar to how you might build up a mathematical proof. However, nontechnical and nonacademic conversations are the main student preoccupations, i.e. typical conversations.

Conversation is a means for defining oneself socially. We use conversation to introduce *who we are* as individuals and *how we relate* to others in the world. It is not an exaggeration to say that our social world is formed from our capacity for typical conversation. Learning to initiate, maintain and repair conversation is of great long-term significance. However, we should distinguish between typical conversation and *phatic* conversation. In the former we talk to communicate, tell stories and pass the time pleasantly. There is a purpose, perhaps not a very lofty one, to our conversation. In phatic conversation we are simply passing the time politely but indifferently. For instance, you may find yourself having several exchanges in a bar with other people while waiting for students from your class to arrive. These exchanges could be about the weather (a favourite topic of phatic conversation) as this example shows.

Barman:	Nice weather isn't it?
You:	Yes.
Barman:	Not as nice as last week though!
You:	No, not as nice.
Customer:	They say it will pick up next week.
You:	Really?
Customer:	You never know about weather.
You:	I'm going to sit over here. I have a few friends coming in. Nice talking to you.

In the case above, you are passing the time politely while waiting for your drink. You do not want prolonged conversation with the strangers. You politely conclude the conversation by thanking them for the interaction and signalling that your social group is arriving soon. Only then do you remove yourself from their proximity. Phatic conversations are commonplace, especially in bars or restaurants and on buses or trains. It is impossible to avoid them. This does not mean that every conversation with a stranger will be a nonspecific exercise in politeness, but many will be. Be aware also that generally people in service positions are used to making small talk with the public. If they bring up the subject of the weather, they are not expecting anything more than a few nods and pleasantries in response. They do not want a lecture on meteorology. What all this means is that in certain circumstances you do not need to take an intense interest in everything another person utters, but merely a polite interest. Of course, you have the right to feel bored in these circumstances, but avoid expressing your boredom. Make a polite excuse to move to another part of the bar (if you are in a bar). A useful tactic – again let us return to fore-knowledge – is that once you have arranged to meet someone in a bar or restaurant, bring a newspaper to read while waiting for them. The newspaper is a means of deflecting phatic conversations.

Typical conversations are more specific and usually involve people talking about themselves in terms of experiences they have had (or more often wish they have had) and ideas that they have about the world. Conversations among young adult males often contain both sports and sexual content, and male students are no different in this respect. Young adult females will tend to have more psychological content in their conversations but matters of sexuality are also expressed. These observations do not imply that sexual interests dominate typical conversations, but they are topics of interest to both genders. Do not get drawn into crude or vulgar conversation. Many young people with AS have engaged in vulgar talk because it got a laugh from their peers. But were the peers laughing with them or at them? It is hard to know, isn't it? Avoid vulgarity and avoid the uncertainty.

As we mentioned earlier, participation in typical conversations helps each of us carve out a social identity. Correspondingly, participation in academic conversation, where the topic of interest is academic, helps us define our academic identities. Exams are really textual assessments of one's academic identity. Unfortunately there is no such convenient assessment of one's social identity apart from the reactions of peers, and their willingness to engage with you in conversation. Learning to talk to others is a critical skill. Unlike the academic sphere, the rules for success in the social sphere are not as clear. Occasionally social interactions can seem like playing a game of cards wherein everyone but you appears to have grasped the rules.

The rules of typical conversation at not easy to grasp and will vary depending on whether you are talking to friends, acquaintances or complete strangers. Furthermore there is a gender component to using the rules which is subtle. For instance, two males discussing the same topic may have a very different conversation than a male and a female about the exact same topic. To complicate things even further, certain topics are 'off limits' to men when in conversation with women.

Kevin was a physiology student who was diagnosed with AS at age 16 years. He commuted to college daily from his parents' home. He had managed to become part of a group in his class and was happy with his social circle. During his course, he became fascinated with the mechanisms of female reproduction. This academic interest began to intrude into his social conversations. On several occasions he asked female students to discuss their menstruation cycle with him. Understandably they were reluctant and when news of Kevin's interests reached the dean the matter took a more serious turn. Eventually Kevin's therapist explained the nature of AS to the relevant staff and Kevin agreed to limit discussion of sexual biology to his tutor. The difficulty was resolved satisfactorily and Kevin successfully completed his degree.

Talking at peers vs. talking to peers

Despite all the restrictions and warnings mentioned above, talking is essential in the effort to seek out and maintain friends, both male and female. You will make good friends with people on the basis of shared interests (astronomy, computers, etc.), but sustaining the friendships over time may require moving beyond the original common attractors. Conversation is a rewarding mode of human interaction and turn taking is crucial to determining the satisfactory nature of the interactions. In reality, turn taking is an ideal to which many of us aspire. Certainly in the case of young adults turn taking is not perfected and its usage in conversation can be uneven. Young people tend to interrupt and talk across one another more frequently than older age groups. This behaviour produces less effective communication, but part of human development is learning that this type of behaviour needs monitoring.

In an ideal context one person utters whatever they have to say and then another person responds with whatever he/she has to say. So the conversation continues. The skill is in recognizing when your turn begins and when it should end. There are many guidelines to consider. Do not interrupt. Do not talk for too long. Do not be terse. Do not shout over people. Give enough information, but not too much or too little. It is not easy to put all these rules into practice. The clever thing about conversation is that we generally do not put all of these rules to equal use. Many conversations contain little corrective moves and utterances to stop someone talking too long, to extract more information from them, to slow them down, speed them up or simply rebuff them. We do not expect every conversation to begin with demonstrations of tremendous social skills, but merely that each participant will allow themselves to be corrected by the conventions of conversation. When someone is talking too long, he or she will allow themselves be cut off by whatever nonverbal or verbal signal is required. It would be great if everyone was so good at self-monitoring that we did not need to run the equivalent of signal flags up and down in a conversation, but that is not the case in the real world. We will have more to say about this in the next section, but for now let us look at turn taking as an example of a simple but powerful convention.

Conversation would be impossible without turn taking. It allows the construction of larger units of meaning between people than simply their individual utterances. Turn taking has to allow for the introduction of new topics or changes in emphasis when staying with the same topic. Of course when people disagree, which is not uncommon, turn taking is often put under strain and rude interruptions may result. Irrespective of the difficulties, if you do not engage in some form of turn taking you will be perceived as talking *at* your peers rather than *to* them. Conversation has to be understood as a participative activity wherein everyone can contribute something.

Taking turns may involve verbal and nonverbal components. In many cases a simple nod of the head indicates to a speaker that you are actually listening to him. It is not enough to allow someone a turn to speak; you must also show that you are interested in what they have to say. When dealing with peers it is very important to indicate to them that you are 'tuned in' to what they are talking about. Head nods combined with go-ahead phrases such as *Yeah, Really, I see* and *That's an interesting point* make all the difference between being well received by other people and being marginalized. A go-ahead nonverbal signal or a verbal phrase tells the speaker to continue speaking and that you are interested in hearing more. Bear in mind that student life has a rich communicative flavour, exemplified in debates and the exchange of ideas. Appearing not to listen to other people is definitely not well received. Signal to others that you are listening. Experiment with head nods and go-ahead phrases above until you develop your own pattern or style. An existing social skills group or appropriate college society such as the drama society can really help here.

In terms of friendship building blocks, turn taking is often presented as necessary (1) to allow others to speak and (2) to avoid boring other people. In addition, turn taking is also a means for bringing yourself into conversation. People experience a mild amount of frustration when they feel that their conversational efforts are being rebuffed. People with AS may unwittingly find themselves cast as conversation killers on just these grounds. If the pauses between what one person says and your responses are too long, then the first person will reason that you are not interested in listening to him. How to you deal with this problem?

We recommend that you ask yourself: *Do I really want to talk to this person now?* If the answer is yes, then you must listen hard to what the person is saying and try to respond as he or she finishes a point. If you are worried about how to respond, then you can sometimes buy yourself time to think with a question such as: *You said X, why do you think X?* On the other hand, if you do not want to speak to this person now but have no other option (except being rude, which is never an option), limit yourself to at most three exchanges and announce that you have to do something else now. In any event, if you are not entirely comfortable in either context, or feel the conversation is confusing or draining you, consider making an excuse to leave such as: *Will you excuse me? I have to go to the bathroom (or make a phone call, or meet someone elsewhere).* You are not obliged to listen to everyone who speaks to you, but be polite at all times.

Effective turn-taking skills develop from good listening skills. To develop these will require experimentation – trial and error. You can improve your listening skills by applying some foreknowledge. If you know a little about the other person's interests, try to build a conversation around these and limit your interactions to a set time. Do not be afraid to set time limits on your conversations. If you are getting to know someone then an open-ended conversation (one where you are not sure when it will end or what topics will be covered) can be stressful. However, open-ended conversations are impossible to avoid, so allowing yourself a participation time limit of five, eight or ten minutes may be the best strategy until you become more comfortable with the company.

Ian was a graduate who attended fortnightly social skills sessions with a group. As a teenager Ian found social company very stressful and anxiety provoking. With the support of his therapist, he had learnt over time that company was necessary, especially in college when he required the assistance of other students from time to time. Even though Ian found company difficult, he persevered with social gatherings on the understanding that the long-term goal of building a circle of friends would be worthwhile. During this time he gave his therapist fortnightly, and eventually monthly, briefings on how his social life was progressing. For his initial year in college he attended frequent social gatherings, sometimes only speaking once or twice in two or three hours. However, as he became more comfortable with his class he gradually participated more in social activities. In his final year he had a circle of friends and acquaintances and was never stuck for a weekend social activity.

Ian's case is not remarkable, but it does show that being goal focused and willing to work to a plan can pay dividends. In Ian's case he spent a considerable amount of time practising active listening skills and learning to use knowledge of his peers' interests to give him some 'leverage' in conversation. Ian was willing to practise and engage in trial and error interactions with the support of his therapist. He did not find this easy, but he persevered. Crucial to his success was early acceptance that his social identity could be improved if he improved his communication skills.

Conversation as a language game

One of the first questions someone with AS will ask when small talk skills are mentioned is: *Of course, I want to get an understanding of small talk, but what do I talk about?* In other words, how do you go about making conversation? College life imposes few restrictions on conversational subjects, which is a definite advantage over life outside college. In this context, the difficulty faced by students with AS is the likelihood of talking too much about too few topics. Typical students will talk about their favourite topics and hobbies, but they will also talk about other topics. On the way to managing a tendency to talk solely about your own interests, it is also useful to make a note of what other people are interested in. Enter these into your computer diary. You can then raise these interests later, but impose a time limit on your interactions until you get to know the other person (or people) well. In Chapter 3 we recommended joining college societies as a stepping stone towards developing a circle of friends. The communication advantage to you is that college societies and their activities can provide stimulating and humourous common conversational topics. Membership of the societies creates a common platform on which to meet students with similar interests. Furthermore, society activities logically provide interesting and relevant conversational topics. Society activities create shared memories that can be discussed with other students and thereby help form a bonding between you and your peers around relevant common interests and experiences.

Recognizing that certain activities and interests can help you improve your conversational skills is part of learning to treat conversation as a language game. If you have ever played chess then you know that you need to plan the moves very carefully. You are aware that you need to make deliberate moves. In conversation, typical students will respond almost as if they are on automatic pilot to gibes, questions and ripostes. Rarely in typical conversation do people plan the next move deliberately. However, you will need to consider what you have to do to make a conversational interaction effective (successful). This is a level of conscious thinking and planning that most people have internalized at an early stage (not perfectly admittedly). The person with AS must be more aware of what is happening in a conversation than his typical peers. We have already emphasized the importance of being alert to turn taking.

Unlike other games you have encountered, the language game is a lot more subtle. Most of the rules are not mathematically precise. Conversation is inherently ambiguous and everyone makes miscommunications from time to time. Unlike other games, the outcome of a conversation is not a set of points or scores. It is difficult to know if you have 'played well'. No one will approach you afterwards to list your successes and failures, unlike the coach for a team. How do you know if you have successfully taken part in the game? There is no obvious prize, though some people believe that if they dominate a conversation then they have effectively 'won'. This is a mistaken belief, of course.

The real prize in a conversation is the willingness of people to speak with you again. Conversation, especially among your student peers, should be viewed as a process. One conversation lays the ground for another. The goal for you is to become more comfortable with this process and use it to develop a social identity. This does not mean that you must strive to be the greatest conversational wit on earth, but merely that you are delivering less miscommunications and more relevant communications than before.

Jim was a philosophy student with a major interest in mathematical philosophy to the exclusion of all other schools of thought. As a postgraduate, he alienated many of his peers by constantly disparaging their areas of interest. Everyone acknowledged that Jim was incredibly bright, but he was also not very socially skilled. Jim told his therapist that he was beginning to feel socially isolated. Shortly afterwards, one afternoon, having rowed with several of his peers, he was in a lift with another postgraduate. Jim was expressing his opinions about the other student's area of interest, when the other student turned to him and said, *The problem with you Jim is that you never listen to anyone else.* Jim was so stung by this comment that over the next few weeks he asked several of his peers whether it was true. He eventually returned to his therapist and they discussed ways of improving his communication skills. Central to this strategy was Jim allowing other people to make their moves in conversation without being drawn to challenge them.

Jim's case is interesting because it shows that he was unaware of the impact of his 'not listening' on his audience. To overcome this tendency Jim had to become more consciously aware of other people's moves in the conversation and give them time and space to state their opinions. He also had to learn that rejecting other people's views needs to be balanced against respecting their articulation of them. These principles were not easy to grasp but within a year remarkable progress had been made. However, Jim still has to apply conscious awareness to conversation to control any domineering traits.

Practising 'wrong way/right way' analyses of conversation can help understand conversation expectations. If possible practise these with another student (a friend), and the student counsellor or your therapist. These analyses are a useful way of capturing the game aspects of conversation. Remember that the prize is getting along with people. We look at a few examples below.

You enter a study room and find a group of students admiring a book just bought by Joan, another student.

1. You see the book and say: *That book is complete crap. It is a complete waste of money. I would not read it under any circumstances.* The group ignores you or tells you to shut up.

2. You see the book, wait for a break in the conversation and say: *Looks like it could be an interesting book. Has anyone seen any reviews of it?* The group acknowledges your comment, and accepts it as sensible but neutral.

In the case of (1), *the wrong way*, you have interrupted the group and made arrogant offensive statements. The likely reaction of the group is to keep you at a distance from now on. In the case of (2), *the right way*, you have made positive comments and raised a question about the value of the book in a neutral, non-arrogant way. The likely reaction of the group is to invite you to comment on any review you have read.

You are asked by another student to proofread his project. He offers to proofread yours also. However, you are not keen on this arrangement.

1. You decline and say: *I haven't time to read your project. I wouldn't be interested in it. I do not think much of the area you are interested in. Find someone else to proofread your project. Mine doesn't need proofreading.*

2. You decline and good-humouredly say: *Thanks for that offer, but I'll pass this time. I am not very good at proofreading and I wouldn't like your project to suffer because of me.*

In (1), *the wrong way*, you are blunt and block any possibility of re-establishing a social relationship with the other student at a future time. In (2), *the right way*, you point out that you are pleased to have been asked but the responsibility for his work is something you prefer not to take on.

The game component here is to interact with others so as to present yourself as polite and cooperative but firm in your views. It is well worthwhile experimenting with your own lists of 'wrong way and right way' scenarios. You will learn a lot from analysing how a conversation flows and what type of moves and interruptions block or divert it.

In presenting conversation as a game of moves, we are explicitly asking that you develop a conscious awareness of what is happening in the conversation. This requires you to understand *what* has been said, *why* it has been said and *how* best to respond. You will also have to take into account figures of speech, which can often interfere with your comprehension of the what, why and how components of utterances. Most people with AS find figures of speech problematical, as their meaning and significance seems to depend on something way beyond the context of the conversation. An example such as *You are pulling my leg* is a metaphor meaning *You are not being serious with me, you are being humourous.* Metaphors are phrases used to convey a meaning that is not immediately obvious from the surface meaning of the phrase. Most metaphors only apply within a particular culture. The only sensible approach to understanding these items is to make a list of common ones you hear (see your student counsellor or therapist for assistance) and buy a book listing modern colloquialisms. You could waste a huge amount of time learning off lists of metaphors and figures of speech, but we recommend that you know a dozen of the most common and learn to ask your peers for clarification after that.

You will encounter mimicry of television or media people among students, especially their catchphrases and gestures. Despite the fact that your peers will laugh and joke about the person doing the mimicry, you can be sure that the point of the mimicry is not immediately obvious to many of them most of the time. Figures of speech and mimicry play a role for people in conversation, the conversation game, by either helping them to confirm their social identity ('I'm cool, man') or else helping them redefine it. However, mimicking *speaking Klingon* may work in one context, but be resoundingly awful in another. In general, unless you are a confident entertainer, avoid mimicry.

THE GREAT GAME OF POOL

One of our strongest recommendations in learning to initiate and maintain conversation is that you learn to play pool. Pool is a gender neutral game. It is also a reasonably short game to play. Obviously, you can only play pool in certain settings, but since you will find yourself with peers in the student club, playing pool is a distinct possibility. Pool has so much to offer people with AS as an aid to learning conversational skills, that we are tempted to call it the Great Game of Pool. The many advantages of pool are that it allows you to:

- participate in a conversation and yet be legitimately removed from it while either awaiting your turn to play or playing

- interact with your opponent without large amounts of eye contact being required, yet you can still have a conversation

- initiate communication with pool-playing members of each sex without becoming anxious over how to approach the person – an utterance as basic as *Do you fancy a game of pool?* will suffice

- award yourself a certain social esteem for playing a conventional game accepted by all your peers

- observe and process various degrees of social sophistication among your peers without immediately having to involve yourself

- build occasional social outings around pool, offering to make the necessary arrangements, and invite other students along

- learn about alcohol consumption – if the pool table is in a bar then people will be drinking around it.

If you have an interest in physics or mechanics, pool provides a practical and playful opportunity to observe the dynamics of collisions and to 'reason' visually using table angles for certain shots. Pool will add another topic to your repertoire of interests. It is also enjoyable to win, but remember to balance your interest in pool against your academic commitments.

We are not discouraging card games by the way; just avoid those that involve gambling. Bridge is a useful game for getting to meet people through tournaments. However, it is likely that more of your peers will play pool rather than bridge.

INITIATING MOVES

We mentioned that the prize in conversation is getting people to want to talk to you again. In the sections that follow we will look at roles that typically occur in conversation. First, we look at the conversation starting role, the initiating role. Next we look at a responding role, the acknowledging role. Finally, we will look at a maintenance role, the go-ahead role. These roles are fundamental player roles in the language game. During the course of a typical conversation you will find yourself swapping these roles around, depending on turn taking and the stage which the conversation has reached. One word of advice about these roles: clinical experience suggests that young people with AS often find themselves overwhelmed by multiparty conversations. Consider setting time limits on your participation in any conversation until you become more comfortable, more secure with the people. This needs to be done discreetly. You cannot pull out your watch without causing offence and declare: *Sorry, I must go now, I only allowed myself ten minutes with you.* It is far preferable to look at your watch and announce a few minutes in advance that you have to leave: *This is interesting, but I have to go in five minutes.* You may only need a temporary time-out. Perhaps five or ten minutes in another part of the building (e.g. the restroom) will suffice before rejoining the conversation. In any event, if a conversation is becoming confusing and stressful, learn to exit early rather than later.

In order to start a conversation, you have to say something. You could nod and signal with your hands that you are interested in starting a conversation, but to initiate conversation you must utter something. Getting the attention of the other person (or persons) is the first task. This can be as simple as calling their name, pausing while they respond (acknowledgement), and then beginning the conversation proper. A successful initiating move allows for the acknowledging response of the other person.

You want to ask John several questions about a project. He is working at his computer.

1. You go up to John and say: *I want to compare notes from the last lab exam with yours. Have you got yours here? Are they in your locker? Can you get them for me now?* John might say: *Go away. Can't you see I am busy?*

2. You go up to John and say: *Hi John. When you are ready can I ask you a few questions?* Wait for John to acknowledge your initiating move. He may say: *I'm busy now. Will this take long?* You then respond with your request: *I'd like to compare my lab exam notes with yours, please.* John says: *OK. Can you come back in an hour, as they are in my locker?* You conclude by confirming the appointment and thank him: *That's great John, thanks. I'll see you in an hour.*

In (1), *the wrong way*, we see clearly an ineffective initiating move as it kills any chance of the conversation starting and helping you achieve your goal. In (2), *the right way*, John is asked to acknowledge your request politely and given time to respond. It is a much more effective initiating move.

In almost all cases, initiating moves will begin with some form of greeting, usually followed by the person's name. Examples are: *Hi, Hi Ruth, How are you Dan?* After that, a pause is allowed for the person to respond. The pause will rarely exceed two seconds. If it does then you may need to repeat your initiating statement. If an acknowledgement is still not forthcoming, ignore the other person and assume that he or she has something on their mind. When you get to know someone well, you can shorten the initiating utterance to just their first name.

During the course of an evening out with other students, you will not need to rely on initiating moves as outlined above. Once you have established a presence in a group or with a friend, you can initiate conversation by either asking questions or making statements. Of course in both cases you should get the attention of the others before beginning the conversation. For instance, during a lull in the general conversation you may want to tell the others about a new laptop. You might say: *What do you think of the new laptop technology? I read a review of it last week.* Wait for the others (and it may be just one other) to acknowledge your utterance before delivering your views.

Remember that initiating moves help us begin and restart a conversation. You need to practise these moves in order to become familiar with them. While practising listen carefully and look at other people's reactions. You may need to refine your initiating skills over time. If you are lucky, a social skills group on campus may already have been set up by the student counsellor. This group can help you to practise the relevant skills and provide constructive feedback. A drama society is really very useful here, since acting and the delivery of lines very much depend on precise timings.

ACKNOWLEDGING MOVES

An acknowledging move in a conversation is a way of indicating to the other person or persons that you have received and understood their message. Let us look at an academic example first. In a tutorial situation many issues come up for discussion, generally following a question-and-answer format. Both the tutor and students are free to ask and answer questions. Now picture yourself in a tutorial class. The tutor comes in and says: *I'll take questions on the principles of spectrometry today.* You raise your hand and ask your question. At the same time several other students also ask their questions. Would you feel frustrated if the tutor continually asked for more questions from the class but never even looked in your direction? Of course, you would. Why? Because the tutor is ignoring you. He is not acknowledging your attempt to participate. When you acknowledge someone in a conversation it is a way of giving that person a role, and respecting that role. Failure to acknowledge the participation of others in conversation is a common cause of communication breakdown.

Acknowledging moves are also the means by which we move a typical conversation along. For instance, if Daniel requests Miriam to explain her shopping list, he has a reasonable expectation that she will comply with his request.

Daniel:	Miriam, I can't read the shopping list that you wrote out. Can you read it back to me please?
Miriam:	Sorry Dan, I was in a hurry at the time and scribbled it down. Give it to me and I'll read it back to you.

If Miriam ignored Daniel's request, or declined to clarify the list, then further communication would have been impossible. However, Miriam is cooperative and acknowledges Daniel's request. In fact, whenever we make a request or issue a polite order, we have a reasonable expectation that the hearer will respond as expected. For instance, if one of your housemates asks you to take your feet off the table while he begins to set out the dinner, he has a reasonable expectation that you will acknowledge his polite request. Likewise if you ask someone to turn off their mobile phone in the library, you have a reasonable expectation that he or she will comply.

There is a possibility that people with AS may believe that they have given an acknowledgement to a speaker, even though they have not explicitly uttered an acknowledgement. This is a tricky area to understand and advise on, but it is crucial in conversation to make sure you are acknowledging the participation of others. A few simple guidelines follow.

If you are asked a question, give more than a yes or no answer. Straight-to-the-point responses, terse responses, may suit you and seem quite logical. Conversation requires more than terse answers to be fluid and satisfying to other people. For example, if a student asks: *Are you going to use the lab later this evening?*, then an answer such as no is barely acceptable. It is too terse. However *No, I will not need the lab tonight* is better as it clearly acknowledges the content of the other student's question. Moreover, short answers may suggest to the other student that you are not interested in a conversation anyway.

If you receive a polite request, acknowledge it and indicate whether you will comply or not. Suppose the classroom is very humid, due to an air-conditioning problem. A student asks you to open the window beside you: *Hi. Can you open that window beside you?* You know that the rules state that windows must not be opened, but it is hot: *I would like to open the window too, but the rule is that windows must stay closed. If you want to open the window, I'll swap places with you.* Of course you could have muttered a no, but would that have been as helpful?

Another type of acknowledging move involves affirmation or agreement with the speaker. Suppose a student in your class says to you: *I found that class on applied dynamics tough going this afternoon.* Is he simply making a statement? Yes, he is making a statement but he is also expecting you to respond with your own reaction to the class. People frequently use statements as an indirect means of asking your opinion. A critical point here is that when people speak to you they routinely expect you to reply; to acknowledge that they have said something. In the case above, if you think that the student is just making a statement, then the communication will break down. He is making a statement but he is looking for an acknowledgement in the form of your opinion. Of course, it would be much easier if he said: *I found that class on applied dynamics tough going this afternoon. Did you think the class was tough going as well?* As a guide when people make statements that do not immediately appear to be questions, either ask them if they are asking a question or else affirm some of what they have said. You could reply to the original assertion with: *Applied dynamics is a tough subject. I'll have to work hard at it.* Notice that you are not agreeing with all that he has said but at the same time you are not denying all that he has said. Learning to use neutral affirmations as acknowledgements will require practice.

Remember also that people expect conversations to yield closure at the end. It is a way of indicating that the topics have been wound up and the conversation is over. These end-of-conversation acknowledgements are not easy to identify. People with AS need to practise closing off their participation in a conversation, and also recognizing acknowledgements from others that the conversation is winding up. Again, if a social skills group is available on campus use it to test and develop acknowledgement strategies. This will require trial and error, but that is inevitable.

GO-AHEAD SIGNALS

Go-ahead signals act like green lights on traffic signals. They tell a speaker in a conversation that he may continue talking. Typically, when someone is telling a story such as recounting the experiences of last weekend, we use go-ahead signals to tell him or her that they may continue. Why are go-ahead signals important to AS? Well, go-ahead signals are an important way for an audience to communicate either their boredom or satisfaction with an unfolding conversation. In one-to-one or one-to-many conversations, go-ahead signals include head nods (affirmative) and short utterances such as *Yeah*, *Really*, *I see*, *Can you tell me more?*, even *Go ahead*, and so forth. These signals are uttered where there would normally be natural breaks in the conversation. The speaker uses the signals from his or her listeners to guide the pacing and content of their delivery.

When go-ahead signals are absent then the other person, the listener, is signalling that he or she wants the conversation to end, or that they are bored and want the topic to change. Everyone has bored someone at some point in time. The trick is to recover sufficiently and learn not to do the same again. It is worthwhile remembering that a conversation can only be a conversation when there is an agreed topic. The verbal and non-verbal methods that people use to signal topic agreement are instinctual in typical cases. However, you may need to use more explicit techniques to introduce, maintain and change topics. Go-ahead signals are part of the repertoire of topic-handling 'tools'. The usual way of introducing a topic is by way of a question.

Daniel: Did you see the television programme on gene therapy last night? [*pause*]

Miriam: No, I got home late. Was it any good?

Daniel: Yes, it was really interesting. [*etc.*]

[*Several exchanges later.*]

Miriam: I do not watch enough science programmes. I am quite busy with the drama society most evenings.

Daniel: (1) You should always make time to watch science programmes. There is one on tonight on the Big Bang. I saw a preview and it will be fantastic.

Daniel: (2) I watch a lot of science programmes, but I haven't kept in touch with the drama society. Can you tell me what you are doing in it currently?

Notice that Daniel pauses for an acknowledgement from Miriam before further presenting the topic (the gene therapy programme). She responds with an explanation for not seeing the programme, but then gives a go-ahead signal to Daniel with a request for more information. Daniel's next interaction allows him to maintain discussion of the topic. After several exchanges on gene therapy, Miriam signals to Daniel that she would like a change of topic. She is now introducing a topic of interest to her – the drama society. If Daniel replies as in (1), *the wrong way*, what will be the consequences? Well, if we examine (1) it is clear that he has ignored her attempt to introduce a new topic. In other words (1) is not a go-ahead signal to Miriam, and she will leave the conversation and Daniel. So (1) is the wrong way to respond.

In the case of (2), *the right way*, Daniel still affirms his interest in science programmes, but acknowledges Miriam's desire to introduce her topic. He responds appropriately with a go-ahead signal. Consequently,

(2) is much more likely to produce a successful conversational outcome. Miriam is more likely to feel positively towards Daniel if he sticks to (2). The lesson to be drawn is that taking an interest in another person's topic is important not just in building conversation, but also in building friendships. Using and recognizing go-ahead signals is most important in achieving these goals.

Developing active listening skills

We touched on a distinction between *hearing* and *active listening* in the last chapter. As you spend your day, you will hear many sounds in the environment. The sound sources may be traffic, canteen voices, the wind in the eaves, rain on the window, elevator motors, keyboard clicks, and so on. There are so many sources of sound in the environment that you may wonder how on earth you get through your day successfully with so many auditory distractions. The reason you manage so well is that you have learnt to filter out certain sounds as background noise. In the movies background noise is used to create atmosphere in scenes. The ambience of a scene is conveyed through appropriate sounds. For instance, if you see two actors in a coffee bar, you expect to hear the sounds of cups clinking, stools being moved, water running, and so forth. Now when you go into a coffee bar with some students you will hear similar sounds, but yet you have learnt to block them out in order to concentrate on the conversation. You focus your attention on the conversation. From time to time a sound may be so loud or distracting that focusing on the conversation is hard. Few people can continue to converse over the noise of a percussion drill, for instance.

However, people are not the same as background noise. Being with people requires active listening. At the level of academic goals, you already know that daydreaming during a class will interfere with your uptake of the material. You may misunderstand a topic or only partially grasp an argument if you daydream. If the tutor or lecturer suddenly asks you a question, you could be stumped for an answer. From his point of view, you have not paid attention. *Active listening is purposeful listening.* It is listening with your attention switched on. Everyone appreciates being listened to and it is important to other people that you are actively listening to them when they speak. More importantly, poor listening skills will not attract any friends.

The main purpose behind active listening is that you get to understand what someone says. This includes using your ears to listen and your eyes to pick up nonverbal signals. Using ears and eyes together in active listening will require practice. The activity entails a commitment to listen and learn from others. It does not mean that you accept everything you are told but that you are at least able to absorb and process other people's arguments. If there is a social skills role-playing group on campus then join it. Otherwise devise practice sessions with the student counsellor, your therapist, friends or family.

Active listening essentially is about paying attention to what is said and indicated by others. Listening is a learning experience. Treat it as a stimulating activity. The task is to apply your intellect to become a very effective listener. Acknowledge other people in conversation. Put yourself in a position to hear clearly what is being said. If the conversation is at the front of the classroom, go up there to listen. Ask for clarification if you do not understand something: *Excuse me. I think this is what you are saying. Am I right?* Try to suppress any tendency to anger due to your reaction to the speaker, or something being said. Process and evaluate what has been said before rushing to a judgement. Is it scientifically plausible? Is it logical? Is it believed by many other people? Above all else, keep trying to improve your listening skills. They are very important in learning to evaluate other people and making friends. Students with AS will benefit greatly through using active listening in the college environment. These benefits include:

- minimizing distractions
- focusing on the present
- curbing tangential topics
- blocking daydreaming
- helping to build friendships
- accepting criticism
- suppressing interruption tendencies.

It is easy to become distracted and let your attention drift away on to something else, something that seems more interesting. By engaging active listening, you will minimize the opportunity for distractions to intrude. Active listening also compels us to focus on the present, on what is happening here and now. This is very helpful in the learning context of college. It is especially important to pre-empt tangential topics emerging in your conversation. Likewise active listening is a method that will deny daydreaming an opportunity to develop in inappropriate circumstances. People will respond well to you if you show that you are interested in their conversation. This requires active listening. It does not require you to agree with everything said, nor does it require you to challenge what is said. While it is important to make judgements about other people's contributions to conversations, hasty judgements are unwelcome. Listen actively before making a judgement. If you are criticized in conversation, listen carefully before judging the worth of the comments or the speaker. Remember there is always tomorrow, and sometimes insisting on resolving all disputes immediately can only bring more problems.

Interrupting without jarring

We mentioned already that interrupting without jarring is important in social conversation, but is difficult to achieve consistently. What does it mean to interrupt someone anyway? Surely you might ask: *Am I not entitled to express my opinion?* When you interrupt someone who is speaking, you are inserting yourself into the conversation in a way that prevents him or her from completing the expression of their point of view. In other words, you are cutting off his or her conversational turn. Occasionally, when you interrupt someone who is talking it may well be for good reasons. For instance, if you are in the student canteen and notice that another student is talking and not paying attention to filling his cup with coffee, you might interrupt politely and say: *Excuse me, but if you are not careful with the coffee you may burn your hand.* This type of interruption, where the goal is to preserve the safety of another, is permissible. It is a *positive interruption.*

Positive interruptions are permissible and are recommended. They can be beneficial in that other students will thank you for looking out for them. However, do not walk around actively seeking opportunities for positive interruption. You have to presume that outside of direct health and safety threats, interruptions are taboo. Suppose you were with two of your classmates and one was talking about something or other. Now if this was near the kerb and you noticed a car veering dangerously towards the group, it would be right to positively interrupt with: *Get out of the way, a car is coming this way!* Why is it acceptable? It is acceptable because your primary concern was not to make room for yourself in the conversation but to preserve the lives of the others. As a guide, you should connect positive interruptions with health and safety issues. Picture yourself in a campus bookshop where the shop assistants are busy discussing orders with customers. You notice someone stealing books. Should you interrupt? Yes, most certainly. Again you are protecting the rights of others.

However, if two students were talking to each other in a café you would not interrupt to say to one of them: *I like your coat. I have one just like it. It was given to me as a present.* This type of interruption would be a *negative interruption.* People will perceive interruptions as negative if they believe that you are interrupting with the sole aim of getting your point of view heard. Unlike positive interruptions, which are motivated by health and safety concerns, negative interruptions are motivated by your need to express yourself and be heard. Negative interruptions are 'me focused' and involve violating someone else's turn in conversation. When a negative interruption occurs, people think to themselves: *Hey, this guy does not want to listen to anything being said.* Unsurprisingly, negative interruptions are frowned upon and seen as markers of bad conversational manners, bad conversational style. If you practise active listening you will control tendencies to interrupt. If there is a social skills group off campus, you can practise with them. Otherwise you may need to practise with the counsellor or your therapist. It is very important to monitor any interruption inclinations you might have as they can interfere with building friendships and relationships. When you interrupt someone, you are effectively denying them the right to speak, and no one likes that. So only interrupt when it is a positive move.

Every now and then a conversation has run on and you have not been able to find a space for yourself in it. This is very frustrating and you might say to yourself: *Why won't the others make room for me? I think I'll interrupt straight away.* This is a natural reaction, but sometimes conversations will run on without you having the chance to contribute. This does not just happen to students with AS, but to everyone at some stage. The difficulty arises because, despite the emphasis we place on politeness and conversational turn taking, we are not entirely consistent in applying these principles. If you have difficulty getting into a conversation, this may have more to do with the bad manners of the other speakers than you. On these occasions having an interruption strategy on hand is vital. If you are with a group (or even one other person), you will need to say something like: *Guys! Guys! I'd like to interrupt if that's OK? I want to say that I think X and Y.* Notice first that you must get the attention of the others before continuing. We have already covered the importance of getting a person's attention before speaking. Next you need to clearly state what you have to say. You may be tempted to criticize the others for ignoring you, but avoid this temptation. Concentrate on the topic. Finally, notice the reactions and responses of the others to your interruption. If you have acted reasonably, they should respond respectfully. If you have acted reasonably and they are abusive or attempt to shout you down, then consider leaving their company.

Most people find interruption skills very difficult to master. The effectiveness of the skills is often dependent upon the politeness and good manners of the other speakers. It is fair to say that most people have difficulty in this area well into adulthood. However, all you can do is observe, practise and learn from people's reactions. There is no shortcut.

Nonverbal skills

We mentioned earlier in the chapter that people in conversation often use nonverbal behaviours to help them get their messages across to one another. Nonverbal behaviour that helps us with communication is also referred to as nonverbal communication behaviour or nonverbal communication. Consider the following circumstances and let us look at several scenarios.

Two students (boyfriend and girlfriend) are just leaving college to go to the cinema for the evening. Another student, Ben, rushes up and says: *If you are going to the pictures, I'd like to come too.* The boyfriend knows Ben and does not want him to come along, but also does not want to hurt his feelings. The girlfriend is adamant that Ben should not join them, but she does not want to say this openly to her boyfriend, which might cause a row and hurt Ben's feelings.

Ben: If you are going to the cinema, I'd like to come too.

Boyfriend: Er ... We are going to the cinema.

Ben: Great. I'll come along.

The above scenario is the bare verbal scenario. It lists a possible conversation. Now remember that the couple were keen to be on their own and also to avoid hurting the other student's feelings. Let us look at the scenario again and instead of speech we will list the 'thoughts' that might be associated with the students.

Ben: [*Thought*: Daniel and Miriam look like they are going to the cinema. I would like to go too. I'll ask to make sure.]

Boyfriend: [*Thought*: Oh, it's Ben. I do not want him to come to the cinema with us, but I do not want to hurt his feelings.]

Girlfriend: [*Thought*: I do not want to go to the cinema with Ben, but my Daniel is too kind hearted to tell him we want to be alone. I will have to let Daniel know what I want but without causing a row or unduly hurting Ben's feelings.]

Ben: [*Thought*: We will have a nice time at the cinema.]

If we compare the speech and the thoughts we see that the couple do not want anyone else to accompany them to the cinema. They want to tell the other person that they want their own company, but they want to be polite. If they wanted to be impolite and rude then we might get something like this.

> Ben: If you are going to the cinema, I'd like to come too.
>
> Boyfriend: No! You can't. We want to be on our own tonight.
>
> Girlfriend: Get out of here, you dork. I can't stand the sight of you. Go away.
>
> Ben: OK, OK … I'm going home. You have really upset me.

Of course we totally reject the above interactions because rude and impolite conversation is hurtful and harms relationships. However, using nonverbal communication skills we can achieve much of what is in the 'thought bubbles' without insulting the other student, Ben. He may still be disappointed, but at least the matter has allowed everyone to keep their dignity and remain friends. A version of the interaction using nonverbal skills is below.

> Ben: If you are going to the cinema, I'd like to come too.
>
> *[Ben runs over with a smile and waves.]*
>
> Boyfriend: Er … We are going to the cinema.
>
> *[Boyfriend glances at girlfriend slightly dismayed. Raises eyebrows in a 'what can I do?' gesture. He pauses for a few seconds before replying hesitantly. He glances unhappily at Ben. Boyfriend glances again at girlfriend.]*

Girlfriend: [*Remains silent. Barely acknowledges Ben. She stares fixedly at her boyfriend with her lips pursed and a tense frown on her face.*]

Ben: OK. I see you two want to be alone. I'll head off now. Have a nice night.

             [*Ben waves goodbye and heads off with a slightly disappointed look.*]

Couple: Bye. Have a good time.

Notice that the nonverbal elements in the conversation are very useful for conveying what people really think and believe. They have a very forceful impact on the whole conversation. The content of the communication between the couple and Ben is almost completely shaped by the gestures, facial expressions, body language and eye gaze of the couple. In fact these nonverbal components compel Ben to back off and change his plan.

Tuning into and decoding the nonverbal components of a conversation is very difficult for people with AS. Even in a focused academic conversation with another student, you may be confronted with a wide array of nonverbal skills. The problem has two aspects. On the one hand, recognizing nonverbal skills being used by others would help you understand their contribution to a conversation that much better. On the other hand, you would like to have a range of nonverbal skills better to improve your communications and improve relationships.

Recognizing the purpose behind other people's nonverbal skills can be very frustrating. You can study movies and television dramas as part of an attempt to understand them, but the entertainment media are very stylized and the behaviours may be 'too perfect' compared with real life. A supplementary tactic is to list what people can do with movement of the head, eyes, mouth and hands. Ask the counsellor or therapist to help you here. Even composing a shortlist will move your understanding on a little. You may never produce a very rich or complete list, but working towards developing some insight is a worthwhile goal.

'PLEASE DO NOT STAND LIKE AN UPRIGHT FREEZER'

Face-to-face communication typically has some element of nonverbal skills. In fact a lot of casual contact and communication among people is facilitated by nonverbal elements. In a shop, for example, it is not always necessary to get the shop assistant's attention by saying clearly: *Excuse me, miss, but I would like your attention please.* Mostly people will try to catch the other person's eye. This means that they will try to get the attention of another person by using eye contact. However, managing eye contact correctly can be extremely challenging.

Beyond eye contact there are other nonverbal skills that can be developed more easily. In a restaurant, you might try to get the attention of a waiter by slightly raising up your hand from the table. In an exam you will raise your hand to get attention if you need to leave for the bathroom or require extra sheets of paper. If a tutor asks you across the room whether the coursework is going well, you may simply nod yes or no in reply. You can shrug your shoulders to communicate to another student that you do not know the answer to a question (do not shrug your shoulders with academic staff). So there is a range of nonverbal skills that you can master.

It is important to assemble a collection of nonverbal skills. Even a small but functioning repertoire is better than none at all. For instance, shake hands with people in authority if introduced to them. Do not shake hands with your peers (under normal circumstances). In the absence of some minimal set of skills, you will find integrating yourself into conversation somewhat tricky at times. To collect these skills requires observation, practice and refinement. There are no easy routes, but again if there is a social skills group on campus, use it. It is important to remember that people use nonverbal skills to present their emotions. Undoubtedly these can be difficult to decode.

Leaving emotions aside for the moment, nonverbal skills are also used to add attention and emphasis to points in a conversation. Now this is something you can identify and practise. For instance, short nods of the head are used to signal agreement with another person's point of view. Chopping the air lightly with your hand adds emphasis to a point in a discussion. Having your arms unfolded in a discussion indicates openness to other points of view. A fuller selection of skills needs to be worked out with the student counsellor or your therapist, however. Remember that the skills as physical behaviours mean nothing. So learning the behaviours is of little benefit if you do not grasp that they have a purpose in communication. Anyone can nod his or her head or chop the air with their hands, but it is doing so with the right purpose that is difficult to grasp.

Recall some of our earlier comments on planning and goals. Conversation is not simply about trading information but on defining yourself as a social person. Consider setting yourself the goal of using nods to emphasize agreement with another person or to acknowledge another person's role in a conversation. Use active listening as a means of establishing cues for using the nods. Identify a conversational setting where you will try it out. Put a plan together for the occasion and set yourself a time limit. While participation in social skills groups can be very useful, a more natural setting is a student society meeting. All of this will require practice, but you have the intellectual skills to make it work. Keep with a 'small steps' approach – one step at a time. Do not try to master a range of nonverbal skills but focus on deploying one skill before deciding on others. One further setting for exploring nonverbal skills is the student drama society. This is an excellent venue for experimenting with nonverbal communication. It will be a challenge, but if you find the prospect of the drama society even mildly interesting you might discuss this option with the counsellor. It is important to make sure that you are not adopting skills which make you feel uncomfortable.

People are not very kind or understanding towards others who have a different mode of communication. A student with AS was told by one of his housemates: *Please do not stand like an upright freezer.* Typically people tend to notice communication deficits and, in the absence of knowledge about AS, they will not understand that they are with people who have a different mode of communication. Educating people about the communication issues in AS is easier said than done, but if you are experiencing a lot of distress due to nonverbal communication failures with your peers, you may need to discuss this option with the student counsellor. However, if you can manage conversation verbally using the conversation moves described earlier, this will help compensate greatly for any short-comings in nonverbal skills.

LOOKING WITHOUT STARING

Learning to use and maintain eye contact appropriately is extremely diffi-cult. For a start, how does one distinguish between looking, glancing, staring and gazing? Eye contact is all about timing and direction. Staring is simply looking at something or some person for a period of time longer than a few seconds. Glancing is looking at something or some person for a second or less. Eye contact is important in communication because it helps us attract the attention of another person. When we look across at someone in conversation, eye contact also signals that we are interested in what they are saying. Finally, we use eye contact in turn taking as a way of starting a new turn and handing over a turn to someone else. All of these aspects of eye contact help with building relationships. Now some people with AS have good eye contact while others are less able in this area. However, reiterating the point made in the section above, using eye contact without the correct motivating purpose is similar to pushing a car rather than driving it. The car will get from place to place but you are not using the car effectively.

With the exception of telephone calls, in any conversation you have to look at who is speaking at least some of the time. In theory you could have a conversation with another person during a pool game and never engage in eye contact. However, for sit-down conversations a degree of eye contact is desirable. Doing anything else is not an option if you want to build friendships. On occasion when you look at another person in conversation with you, he or she may think that you are staring at them and feel uneasy. This is not the outcome you want. One way to avoid this outcome is by gentle nods every couple of seconds. Nodding will move your head (obviously) and the line of sight between you and the other person will be momentarily disrupted. You are less likely to be perceived as staring as a result. Using this tactic effectively will require practice along the lines of the advice given earlier.

Using limited eye contact is one issue, but recognizing other people's eye contact and what it means is an entirely different challenge. Most people with AS experience difficulties in understanding facial expressions, especially where the eyes are involved. One way to improve these skills – and it is not foolproof – is simply to spend time observing other people and trying to tie what people say to their facial expressions. A great deal of practice is required to make progress in this area and most definitely membership of a drama group can be a considerable benefit.

The expressivity of the eye is largely a function of the movements of the eyelids, both upper and lower, and eyebrows. Some movements on the face are probably easier to notice than others. For instance, if you are in conversation with another student and his eyelids are suddenly raised, his eyes will appear bigger. This may indicate that he is surprised by what you said (or perhaps afraid of something you said or did). Usually his eyebrows will also be raised. Generally a surprised look will only last a second or two. If the student narrowed his eyes, this would be seen as his upper and lower eyelids moving down and up respectively. His eyebrows would be lowered and may even meet just above the bridge of the nose. The movements are often slight, but narrowed eyes usually indicate anger or suspicion. When eyebrows droop and eyes are looking downwards, you may be witnessing sadness in a person.

The point of the above is not to 'skill' you to read eyes, but simply to highlight that expressions of emotions are understandable in terms of eye muscles. The extent to which you want to explore this topic further will very much depend on the counselling system on campus. We do not recommend that you study eye muscle physiology in an attempt to understand emotional expressions, but recognize that the messages in the expressions are scientifically explicable.

GESTURES

Gestures can include hand, face and body movements. The most common class of gestures is the hand signal. We use gestures to communicate something about ourselves and our needs. For instance, when greeting someone in authority, it is customary to extend one's hand for a handshake. Have you ever held a wet piece of fish? Think about it – a damp, limp and flaccid creature about the size of the human hand. If you are shaking hands with someone, do not offer them the equivalent of a wet fish. A handshake should be firm, purposeful and convey a welcome to the other person. Say *Hello* or *It is nice to meet you* at the same time and remember to look at the person.

Handshaking is uncommon among students, so avoid doing it with your peers. However, if you are meeting students from another college after a match or a college society meeting, then an introductory handshake is not out of place. Shaking the hands of one or two people in a room is usually sufficient. Do not go around the room shaking everyone's hands. It is not practical and you will not have an opportunity to develop a conversation with anyone in particular.

Hand gestures that signal hello are very commonly used by students. Mostly this consists of raising one's hand up to chest height with the palm facing outwards. The exact procedures may vary from culture to culture, but hand raising in some form is invariably linked to hello gestures. Head nods are also used as hello gestures. Most people with AS find gesture communication difficult, not because they cannot manage it but because of uncertainty about its outcome. This is very understandable. Making a gesture is one thing, but knowing whether it has been understood is another. Worse is when you make what appears to be the right gesture, only to experience hostility or rejection.

Sean had been attending social skills classes in college since being diagnosed with AS in his first year. In college he became involved in the hill walking society and would volunteer to help arrange weekend trips. Sean enjoyed hill walking and the company of the other students. However, he often did not grasp the impact of some of his gestures. He tended to attempt to lead the group and would make huge sweeping gestures to call attention to the direction he wished to follow. After hill walking, the group would relax briefly in a bar. Sean would move from person to person, offering comments on their performance that day, usually interrupting conversations. When food arrived he would signal that he wanted condiments by clicking his fingers and shouting *Here, here*. Women complained that he tended to slap them on the back as if he was introducing himself into the company of men.

Sean was using conventional gestures but either using them too frequently or not in appropriate contexts. He was aware that gestures were important, but had difficulty understanding the impact of his gestures on others. More importantly, he had difficulty processing the feedback from his peers. When these issues were raised again during a visit to his therapist in his third year in college, she advised that he stop multigesturing and focus on using and understanding one gesture at a time. Backslapping women was completely banned. By altering the frequency and range of gestures, Sean could concentrate more on perfecting one gesture and thereby gradually understand the rules for using that gesture from context to context. By the end of that year, Sean's interactions with the other hill walkers were much calmer.

Gestures are important. They add value to our communications and enable us to convey complex messages without needing to speak. However, they are difficult to master and often a very small but working set of gestures is much preferable to a large and trouble-provoking set. In the context of college life, students often use fashionable or 'cool' gestures that define the youth culture of the time. It is important to try to recognize which are the 'in' gestures of the moment. You do not have to use them yourself. Using your computer you can make a list of gestures and what they mean for reference. Occasional reviewing of the list will help you better understand your peers and hopefully encourage you to experiment with gestures yourself.

The vexed question of emotion detection

Recognizing how people feel is a very important aspect of getting along with them. Emotion recognition is not an on/off skill in the typical population. Some people are very emotionally tuned in and others are not. There is a sliding scale of emotion recognition abilities from excellent to weak throughout the population.

You might ask: *Why is emotion recognition important?* Well, it is important in grounding many friendships, and especially relationships. If people are of the opinion that you are indifferent to their emotional states then they may not want your company. We know of one case where a young farmer with AS turned up at a neighbour's funeral only to inquire of the bereaved family if they would be selling the farm soon. While the young man's reasoning was impeccably logical, his approach to the family was very poorly timed.

Developing good communication skills requires some support from emotion recognition skills. In conversation people can convey how they feel through a combination of voice tone, actual speech content, gesture, nonverbal behaviours and body postures. You have a lot to keep an eye on. If you are sensitive to other people's emotional states, then you are likely to be popular. Certainly if you are insensitive you will not be popular. There are no immediate remedies to improve emotion recognition. One recommendation is that you spend time studying collections of facial expressions. You may already have a scrapbook of facial expressions conveying different emotions. Otherwise compile one and discuss it with your counsellor or therapist. It definitely helps to study newspaper photographs of people while trying to relate how they look to the story. By concentrating your analytical skills you will effect some improvement in emotion recognition. Even though progress will be slow and somewhat patchy, it is important for the long term to persevere with recognizing at least the basic emotions such as anger, fear, surprise, disgust, sadness and joy.

DO NOT KID YOURSELF: COMMUNICATION IS EMOTIONALLY LOADED

In college you will be among young people who are still honing their emotional skills. This is advantageous as it means that almost everyone, certainly among the males, is still refining their own emotion recognition skills. To be fair, most will have a good grasp of anger, fear, surprise, disgust, sadness and joy as emotions expressed by other people. These are very much key human emotions and found scattered throughout our communications. It is worthwhile remembering this basic list of emotions, and adding other emotions to it once you comprehend the basic ones. Not every conversation is emotionally loaded but emotions play a part in communication. They can play a direct part through someone expressing their feelings and seeking support, or an indirect role through the reactions of others to something that has been said or done.

Conversation is a means for announcing to others 'this is me'. Most people want to present themselves as polite and sensitive to others. If they speak in calm respectful tones, we are impressed with their attention to what has been said and to the speaker. On the other hand, if they interrupt and comment negatively on other people's views, we will not be impressed with their manners. In fact they will seem impolite and rude. The first group of people bring harmony while the second group bring friction. In conversation you should aim to bring harmony rather than friction.

How you express yourself often conveys more than what you say. It is easy to be literal and convey the information in a manner that offends others. The situation is recoverable if you apologize in time, but this relies on spotting that the other person is offended. People have an expectation that they will not be insulted or offended in conversation. Being strictly logical in your interactions with others will not encourage people to come forward and communicate with you. People expect that a conversation will produce some kind of understanding or rapport between the parties, even if temporary. If one person is exploring emotional issues and you are responding with logical analysis, rapport may be impossible to achieve. Emotion recognition is influenced by conventions governing the appropriateness of emotional expressions in various contexts. In other words, we have expectations about how people will express themselves emotionally in given contexts. Our young farmer interacted completely inappropriately given the occasion. The difficulty that people with AS face is that understanding other people's feelings can be mysterious and confusing. It is helpful to distinguish between recognizing feelings and responding to them. Recognizing that another student is grieving does not necessarily require that you understand grief, but it does require that you have some understanding about responding to grief. For instance, you need to say something sympathetic such as: *I am sorry to hear your bad news. Sorry for your troubles.* Likewise, if a student announces her engagement and is laughing and happy, you need to recognize the signs of happiness and respond appropriately. This can take the form of an utterance like: *That's great news. You must be delighted. I am really happy for you.* The gain in responding appropriately is that you are likely to be more popular by doing so than by not doing so. As we emphasized above, this can only help build friendships and relationships. Admittedly, the emotions above are at two extremes – sadness and joy – and extreme emotions are easier to identify. The basic emotions will be easier to identify most of the time.

For 'intermediate' emotions, which lie in some sense between the basic emotions, one tactic is simply to accept that other people have feelings and to monitor your interactions so as to minimize offence. This requires the use of active listening. It is inevitable that you will have doubts from time to time about your understanding of other people's feelings. We reiterate that all you can do is continue to practise emotion recognition and responding, whether in a social skills group, a college society, with your counsellor or therapist, or simply by cautiously experimenting with your peers. Trial and error experimentation must be guided by the reactions (the feedback) of others, but you have the intellectual skills to make progress in this area. Many people with AS do develop a working model that enables them to meet partners and marry. It is a matter of perseverance and critical analysis of one's own performance.

A final feature for mention here is tone of voice. It is no secret, but how you say something, in terms of the tone of voice you use, can have a remarkable impact on how people perceive you and receive your message. If you read any of the speeches of great orators (Churchill being one example), you will notice that the speeches are sometimes less inspiring than the oratory that delivered them. The oratorical power that a person brings to bear on a written text transforms it from something mundane to something electrifying. Now, we are not suggesting that you should address other students as a great orator would address a crowd. We are simply saying that tone of voice is important to getting your point across. One thing to watch is that you do not speak to others as if you were addressing a crowd. Monitor the pitch of your voice and try not to sound the loudest in your group. People associate shouting with the emotions of anger and aggression. Avoid shouting in company. When you are speaking about your favourite interest, your enthusiasm may burst through and you will have difficulty monitoring your own voice. However, remember that you want to get your point across and build social relationships, so you should monitor your tone at all times.

BODY POSTURES: THE ROLE OF BODY LANGUAGE

Body language refers to the messages that are given off by one's body postures. For instance, if you went into a lab and found a student sitting back in chair with his feet propped up on a bench, you might wonder why he was not working. In fact you could reasonably conclude from his body language that he was not interested in attending to any academic commitments. Why? Well, if he was working he would be standing at the lab bench busy with an experiment. Later on that same evening you head over to the student bar and notice one of your classmates talking to a girl. He notices you, but as you get nearer he adjusts his position. You end up looking at his back. What is he doing? Well, he is sending you a body language message saying I do not want your company just now, I prefer to be with this girl.

Body language is another complex collection of nonverbal behaviours, a kind of bigger version of gesture communication. Understanding the rudiments of body language conventions is very important in social settings, especially if both men and women are mixing. You may have heard the phrase 'sexual politics' used to refer to the kind of interactions that take place between men and women around relationships, physical intimacy and sexual intercourse. These negotiations are not usually very explicit. Not everything relevant is verbalized. Nonverbal communication of feelings and attitudes is also prominent. For the person with AS, it is this implicit understanding within relationships that is often mysterious and puzzling. No one party lays out a schedule of arrangements that is the basis for a relationship agreement. You are unlikely to encounter a partner who says: *If you do everything on my list, I will go out with you.* The convenience of such an explicit contract is undeniable, but rarely achievable. If in any doubt about the body language communication of a friend, ask for clarification: *I see you have your legs crossed (arms folded, back to me, etc.). I am not good at reading body language. Can you tell me what that means?* Asking strangers to clarify their body language should be postponed until you have met and spoken with them on at least half a dozen occasions and they are no longer strangers.

Some pieces of body language are context dependent. If you go to the library, you expect to see people hunched over their desks with intense concentration in evidence. The general demeanor of a student studying is 'do not interrupt me please, I am concentrating at present'. Likewise during a lab practical session a student should exhibit body language that says 'I am busy with the lab tasks now'. Notice that he does not need to verbally state that he is busy; his behaviour tells you that. Recognizing how people communicate through their body postures is part of knowing how to read body language.

Recognizing the significance of body language takes practice, and even the most socially skilled person is often uncertain. Body postures are notoriously ambiguous. For instance, you might think of approaching a student sitting on a bar stool only to see him spin around with his back to you. Is his posture saying go away or has he simply changed his posture because he was uncomfortable? Likewise you see a girl in your class whom you are friendly with at the bus stop. As you approach she glances at you and then turns and runs in the opposite direction. You ask yourself: *What have I done?* Has she run off because she cannot stand your company or is she deeply upset or embarrassed? Hard to tell unless you speak to her the next day. Even when the body language appears obvious to the typical eye, people with AS may be confused. We know of one student with AS who did not understand that when his classmates put on their coats at the end of the night in a bar they were signalling that they were about to leave. Frequently, one of the classmates would tell the Asperger student that they were now leaving and he should also put on his coat.

Despite the ambiguities, there are areas of body posture that students with AS need to bear in mind. One of these, and a very important one, is proximity. You must be mindful of your distance from other people, especially members of the opposite sex. Proximity refers to *nearness*, and people like to maintain a distance from others based on how well they know them. If you meet a stranger, he or she will expect that you keep a reasonable distance apart. An arm's length is a useful distance to keep between yourself and strangers (including acquaintances). When you know someone for a longer time and they treat you as a friend, then you can reduce your distance to half an arm's length. Obviously if you have a girlfriend or a boyfriend, you will eventually become intimate and both of you will enjoy much closer proximity. When dealing with people in authority, however, try never to break the arm's length rule (travelling in lifts or on buses and planes does require a relaxation of these rules, so be flexible).

Other aspects of body language fall under the rubric of *social etiquette*. Many of these have to do with good manners when eating food, and being in the company of others. Conventional table manners are important as this personal story illustrates.

Franz moved straight into a research position with a pharmaceutical company having completed his PhD. Franz had been diagnosed with AS during the second year of his postgraduate studies. One day the managing director of the company visited the staff canteen for lunch. After lunch the managing director summoned the personnel officer and informed him that under no circumstances was Franz ever to be promoted to a position that could bring him into contact with either the public or clients of the company. The managing director had witnessed Franz's lack of table manners. The personnel officer knew something of Franz's history and explained AS to the managing director. Eventually they agreed that Franz needed help with certain aspects of his nonverbal behaviours. The company engaged a therapist to work with Franz over the next year. There was a marked improvement in his behaviour as a result.

This case history shows how harshly people can judge those with AS without any knowledge of the condition. Equally important, it also shows just how much people value conventional demonstrations of nonverbal behaviour in certain contexts. People have expectations of behaviour. They expect a degree of conformity. While you are in college, conformity rarely comes top of anyone's list of priorities, but college life is also a foundation for life after college. How you manage yourself in college is most important to pursuing a satisfying career afterwards.

Some solutions: a repertoire of moves and phrases

Speaking practically, all you can do is monitor your behaviour as best you can and work on your social skills development with the assistance of the student counsellor or your therapist. At the risk of seeming obsessional, we again recommend that you use any social skills group or a college society to help you practise and refine your skills. You will only be able to discriminate between what works and what does not, what brings you positive social attention rather than negative social attention, by mixing with people. You have the intellectual skills to make progress in these areas, but interaction with other students is absolutely essential.

Susan has been a speech therapist for nearly 15 years in the USA. In the past 12 years she has devoted a lot of time to developing social skills groups for adolescents with AS. Interviewer is John Harpur (JH).

JH: I will not ask you whether social skills groups are beneficial, but instead can you tell me what do social skills groups need in order to be beneficial?

SK: First of all, there needs to be a facilitator to structure the group and assign tasks. This may seem self-evident, but people with AS like structure and they feel reassured when they know it is in place. Second, the activities have to contain basic and advanced items. Basic items are the skills you need to get through the day. This can range from asking someone the time or looking for attention in a classroom, through to noticing that someone is injured from an accident. The advanced skills depend on the age and gender mix in the group. Ordinarily we would try to introduce boy–girl issues at that stage. Finally, a group is only as successful as the external follow-up allows. If there is no attempt in the external environment to help reinforce the skills learnt in the group, then the individuals involved will not benefit as much.

JH: Your point, if I understand it correctly, is that a social skills group is a start, but practice is much better. Can you tease out the issues here?

SK: It is a bit like learning to drive a car. If you just take the driving lessons and do not practise in between lessons, it will take you a lot longer to learn to drive than someone who has been practising intensively between lessons.

JH: Who should take responsibility for the in-between-lessons practice?

SK: If the people in the group are not legally adults, then their parents and schools have to shoulder that responsibility. If we are dealing with adults, then ultimately they must take responsibility for managing their own practice.

JH: That is a big responsibility. Is it too big a responsibility?

SK: For certain individuals it may seem like too big a responsibility initially. However, we emphasize the importance of taking small steps in using social skills. Trying to learn too many skills at once is not practical. The aim of social skills programmes is to help the individual identify the purposes behind social skills and how to use them reasonably well. There is no option but to practise in the real world.

JH: What do you recommend as essential to social skills training?

SK: The essentials are to spend time observing how people interact and how people react to other people. In a conversation we emphasize *observation* followed by *waiting* to take your turn. The latter also involves using initiating tactics to get into the conversation. Finally, we emphasize the importance of *listening* to what others say, listening for their reactions. These operations involve timings that individuals with AS find hard to get right. Conversation flows because of the timings used by participants. Practice is absolutely essential to learn how to time participation in a conversation.

JH: Thank you.

You may have to grit your teeth from time to time, but persevere. It will be worth it to you in the long run.

Assembling a collection of stock phrases and conversational moves that you have learnt to use successfully is a very useful strategy. Success builds on success, so you can keep adding to your stock as you encounter new phrases and moves that meet your purposes.

Realistic expectations: you cannot pull it all together

> Humpty Dumpty sat on a wall.
> Humpty Dumpty had a great fall.
> But all the king's horses and all the king's men
> Could not put Humpty together again.

The Humpty Dumpty nursery rhyme has been a favourite one for generations. Children love it because it has a taste of realism. A train set breaks and is never 100 per cent again. Someone treads on your favourite remote control car; it is repaired but is still not 100 per cent. Humpty Dumpty in fact had two problems. First, he slipped off the wall, and being a giant egg that was not a logical vantage point. Second, he had an expectation that if all the resources of the state (the king) were devoted to his plight then he would be perfectly restored. A very unrealistic egg indeed. Now we are not going to spend our time dissecting the merits of Humpty Dumpty's faith in eggshell repair processes, but let us learn from him that sometimes one's expectations are too optimistic. In fact, sometimes we have to compromise and settle for a state of affairs that is short of what we would like, but is the best that can be achieved under the circumstances.

The same is equally true of social skills programmes. When you undertake a social skills programme in college or join a social skills group, you need to be realistic about what can be achieved through the programme. Certain difficulties pertaining to facial expression and emotion recognition may be reduced, but they will not disappear completely. Some residual challenges are inevitable. This is not a pessimistic conclusion by any means. We have consistently pointed out that you have the intellectual skills to make huge strides in managing your academic and social life in college. You have also got into college and that is quite an achievement. The key to success is continuous assessment of your social performances until you reach a level with which you are comfortable, and which is respected in the reactions of your peers.

Attending to verbal and nonverbal communication, gesture and body language interpretation requires a degree of multitasking that is very difficult to achieve. These are complex skills to synchronize. If you are over-ambitious in your social targets, you leave yourself open to being overwhelmed by failures. You need to adopt a small steps approach to minimize the risks to your own goals.

When Kevin became involved with a college society he found his life improving quite rapidly. He had been diagnosed with AS in his teens and attended a number of social skills groups over the years. He lived with his parents while at college. His mother noticed that Kevin had developed the habit of ringing other members of the society very frequently. Generally the phone calls were to confirm trivial details but few seemed to add new information. Kevin then began intervening in disputes between society members, placing himself in the role of arbitrator. This produced even more phone calls. Eventually, many people stopped taking calls from him. He became very depressed as a result. His therapist advised that he take control of events by limiting the number of calls made to any one person in a week and only ringing if he had information that the other person would not have. The aim was to get Kevin back to monitoring the impact of his interactions on others.

Kevin's enthusiasm is marvellous. We should also be proud of the enormous progress he made in social communication. However, once he achieved a certain level of performance he became ambitious for a more socially controlling role – a domineering role. The net effect of this on Kevin is that he ceased to monitor the reactions of others. A slippage in active listening had occurred. Kevin, however, had the intellectual skills and experience to recover from the situation and re-establish a more durable social identity.

COMPROMISE ARRANGEMENTS AND STOCK PHRASES

You need to remind yourself that, in reality, communication skills are distributed on a continuum among your peers. Social communication skills are distributed somewhat like the distribution of athletic skills. Some people will be very good, some will be good, most will be mediocre and some others will be weak. There are few exemplary communicators. Factor this into your self-assessment exercises. There is room for compromise arrangements which play to your intellectual strengths and fence in your weaknesses. The recommendations in this chapter describe the scaffolding of just such arrangements. The strengths of a student with AS are intellectual, which means that they are primarily cognitive and verbal. Focusing on developing clear modes of verbal expression is something to prioritize. Move away from any mumbling tendencies and speak clearly after collecting your thoughts. This will take practice and time.

A young Swedish woman, Gunilla Gerland, has written a book about her life as a person on the autistic spectrum (1997). In the book she describes a process of development and maturation from her teens into adulthood which led to an improvement in her social interaction skills. She was also helped by regular therapy over a number of years. The improvements she charts are also described by Liane Holliday Willey (1999) in her life story. What's more, Temple Grandin (1996), in her autism life story chronicles improvements between adolescence and adulthood. What is inspiring about these authors' stories is not just their remarkable tenacity and desire to improve, but their common recognition that improvements only come about slowly and through conscious analysis of one's social performance. A final aspect of their lives to reflect upon is the amount of planning that they are willing to put into social communication and social engagements. Implicitly they are using the Foreknowledge Principle to manage their lives. Planning helps with goal achievement, which is an outcome you want in the friendship stakes. Also planning affords you a measure of control over your social interactions.

In simple terms, what the above authors have in common is the recognition that what they do not have instinctually, they will have to capture cognitively. In more ways than perhaps they even realize, they are cognitively computing their daily social interactions and effects. You can do the same, and this chapter outlines principles and procedures that you will need to use in this task.

From time to time your understanding of other people and their emotions will break down. In fact emotion recognition will be very difficult on many occasions. We have pointed out, however, that the business of recognizing emotions and responding to another person's emotional state need to be separated. If you are unsure about how someone is feeling or unclear whether they want some understanding from you, then you need to ask clarifying questions. For instance, use an initiating stock phrase followed by a slight nod, such as: *I hope you do not mind me asking, but are you feeling OK?* If you are rebuffed, so what? You've done what you could to take an interest.

If a student tells you that she is upset, you do not need to grasp the extent of her upset to respond with an appropriate comment: *I'm sorry to hear that.* Responding with a bland but conventionally acceptable comment is preferable to making a tangential comment. This means that you may have to suppress the comment you want to make and substitute the one you should make. Saying what is on your mind is often interpreted as bluntness. Being blunt is not a good strategy for gathering friends. For instance, suppose someone criticizes you and you are fuming. This is the time to distinguish between what you would like to say in response and what is wisest to say in response. We are promoting a degree of self-control here that is difficult to use in the face of provocation. However, there is always tomorrow.

If a student tells you that she is pleased with some coursework or an exam result, you can respond with something upbeat such as: *I am glad for you. That's a great result.* You do not have to mimic her ecstasy or react in an extreme manner. This is true for many expressions of emotion. Remember that sometimes all you can do is take an interest in what a person says, since discerning his or her emotions and intentions may be too difficult at the time.

Use your active listening skills. If you find yourself in conversation with another person and the topic is your special area of interest, you need to monitor your interaction carefully. Use a stock phrase that will cue the other person to help you with this monitoring: *I am inclined to go on a bit about computers, so will you stop me if I am boring you?* College life does not have a high degree of unpredictability, and sensible stock phrases can be honed for various settings. Working with either the student counsellor or your therapist will help assemble a reasonable set over a period of time. One student would rock and mumble to himself in lectures. His behaviour was a distraction to the other students. If told to stop, his response was to say sorry but within a few minutes initiate the distracting behaviour again. Saying sorry was clearly not enough to satisfy the demands of his peers. In fact, saying sorry but continuing with the behaviour served to alienate him still further. A better strategy was to use a stock apologetic phrase: *Sorry. I am not good at monitoring myself. Please tip me if you see me starting again.* This was a much better strategy as it involved peers in helping provide a solution.

The advantage of stock phrases is that they help insert you into a conversation without violating social conventions. However, a conversation cannot be driven by stock phrases. Once you position yourself within a conversation, you must rely on your knowledge of current affairs, fashionable topics and specific student topics to continue your participation. We emphasized earlier that some knowledge of current sport and entertainment topics is very useful. You are not required to have the same enthusiasm as your peers for these topics but even a shallow familiarity is usually better than none – especially at student parties. Over time you will become comfortable with these phrases as your conversational skills improve. It is at this point that you will want to experiment with your own set and gradually adopt a set which seems natural to your ears.

A potential disadvantage of stock phrases is that they may appear fake if overused, or used inappropriately. If the phrases appear fake, you may appear insincere. You can guard against this by having a large repertoire of such phrases. A small number of failures are inevitable, and you may even be taken to task occasionally for your social etiquette. In these circumstances all you can do is apologize and learn from your mistakes. Using stock phrases does require a conscious effort and this can be draining. You are effectively computing responses to interactions that typical people take for granted and appear to produce with ease. People with AS have a much greater conscious workload imposed on them in a conversation than is generally realized. Consequently being intellectually able confers a huge advantage.

At the end of the day, all of these strategies call for experimentation. Trial and error with processing of other students' reactions is necessary. If you have access to a social skills group or a drama group, then so much the better. The student counsellor or your therapists are there to help support you should you become overwhelmed by particular miscommunications.

Even after their support, you still have to pick up the pieces and continue your experimentation.

Review and recommendations

This chapter has quite a lot of detailed content. The focus on dialogue analysis and emotion recognition is important to understanding just how deep typical expectations are of conversation participants. These expectations are foreign to many people with AS, but one needs to be aware of them nevertheless. You cannot ignore communication skills, as they are essential to getting along with other students. Practising wrong way and right way exercises will help you grasp some of the fine details.

Membership of social skills groups is definitely to be encouraged. If you can afford the time and commitment, a drama society is an excellent vehicle for exploring a huge range of nonverbal skills. Not everyone is ready for a drama group, but keep it in mind. You will also gather friends through these groups. One-on-one games (such as pool) that are played in a social environment are valuable for developing social contacts and practising conversational skills.

Conversation can be seen as a sort of game with a variety of moves. We presented a very limited set of moves, but they are key ones nevertheless. A more complete overview of moves is found in Eggins and Slade (1997). Understanding the face and eyes as emotional beacons is very problematical. A good technical description of emotional expression based on the face can be found in Ekman (2003). He also has an interesting collection of photographs for testing emotional recognition skills.

Earlier we recommended the autobiographies of Temple Grandin and Liane Holliday Willey, particularly because of the college-relevant material. However, equally fascinating insights into mixing in broader society can be found in Gerland (1997) and Lawson (2003). We would recommend you read these books and note strategies that the authors found successful.

In the final analysis, practice moves one towards perfection. Social communications skills are the bedrock upon which most friendships are based. You can garner these skills by experimentation within familiar settings and among your peers. The end result may be a succession of compromises, but that in itself will be a great leap forward.

7 Interacting with the Opposite Sex

Sex and Sexuality

Exploring human sexuality is an endless source of fascination and pleasure for most young adults. As adolescents we pass through puberty with a large injection of hormones that prime our sexual development. Along with all the bodily changes that result go strong and at times almost overwhelming feelings of sexual desire. Most teenagers tend to be very sexually aware and want to experiment with their sexuality. Many in high school (and college) begin to express their sexual interest in others by flirtatious behaviour and some by making provocative but humourous remarks. Others quietly store strong unexpressed feelings towards the objects (people) of their desire. In college you will meet some students who have a lot of dating experience and some who have none. A tiny minority of students find partners early in their course and get married. Another minority go through college both as undergraduates and post-graduates without a partner, only to develop a stable relationship later in life. Some people will never wish to marry. Temple Grandin, in her auto-biography of a life with autism (1996), explicitly states that she did not wish to marry as she wanted to avoid the complications of relationships. Yet she has had a remarkably successful and fulfilling life. Between the two ends of the scale, there is the majority that will have a few relation-ships, some serious and some casual. These relationships are fitted in around their coursework. Movie presentations of students as gregarious, sexually confident groups of vivacious young men and women are simply not truthful. Most students experience relationships as a bonus when they occur.

A good basis for a relationship is to let it grow gradually. A slow build-up of contact gives you time to get to know the other person and also slowly to integrate your own feelings and reactions together. A good stable relationship is one where both people feel comfortable with each other, where both people can talk to each other and be helpful and supportive to each other in dealing with problems. Both people should experience the relationship as protective of their self-esteem. Relationships between men and women are not driven along rapidly and smoothly by logical reasoning, which can be a severe test for people who like logic, order and predictable routines. In reality most relationships evolve slowly. Feelings are complicated for people with AS and from time to time managing one's emotions can be very draining and overwhelming. Expressing feelings is an equally complicated business. The difficulty lies in the expectations of one's partner that verbal expressions of affection and emotion are produced with spontaneity and sincerity. A conversation with a student peer must have a different tone from a conversation with your prospective boyfriend or girlfriend.

To become involved in a relationship it is necessary to work out how to convey to another that you find him or her attractive and how to gauge whether this attraction is mutual. Getting along with someone is necessary before moving towards dating. Before dating a girl or boy, you have to convey to that person that you enjoy their company. This can be done simply by using any number of initiating moves. After a class you might say: *I like the way you argued your case over coffee yesterday. I enjoyed that discussion we had earlier in the week. You really have a good grasp of theory X, I wish you could help me learn it.* Do you notice anything about the above? Well they all include a compliment. That is an important point to retain. When you want to signal to someone that you enjoy their company and are interested in them, always begin with a positive complimentary statement.

All young people, by trial, error and often a lot of heartache, have to learn how to control the expression of their feelings of attraction to others and how to make socially acceptable overtures to them. It is equally important to be able to recognize if others are making romantic overtures to you, to decide if you find them attractive, and then to decide how you want to respond. People you find physically attractive may not have nice personalities and could be abusive to you, or even exploit your feelings for them. It is important for your self-esteem and well-being to avoid relationships with people that show this type of behaviour towards you or others. If someone behaves badly towards others, you can be sure that some day he or she will behave badly towards you.

Young men with AS often ask: *What are the rules for successful dating?* This is one of the oldest questions known to humankind. Earlier in the book we introduced the idea of planning for occasions, identifying your goal, the resources you need and the actions you will have to take. This idea is equally relevant to dating and relationships. You must be more flexible and have a range of alternative plans to cope with disappointments. Every young person is anxious about dating. In truth, whether one has AS or not, dating is a challenge to one's confidence and self-esteem. When people talk about the dating game, they are really talking about the social and emotional plans necessary to get a successful date while at the same time enhancing one's self-esteem. Though they may not mention it explicitly, they are also talking about empathy and its role in relationships. We say that someone has shown empathy when they demonstrate that they can understand another person's point of view and are sympathetic to it. The term 'sympathetic' is revealing here. It indicates that empathy is not just about understanding the logic of another person's point of view, but also understanding the person's associated feelings.

We have already looked at some of the basic strategies for getting another person's attention and conversing in the previous chapter. Understanding that other people's feelings often influence their communication is most important in decoding what they 'really mean'. People with AS have difficulty with emotion recognition and emotion communications skills, which can affect their capacity to be empathic and sympathetic to others. Trying to fix empathy deficits by simulation through the use of stock phrases and carefully planned communication strategies can be very successful. Working hard at being a good active listener and good verbal communicator will help a lot in minimizing any effects of an empathy deficit. The work will be gradual and will involve trial and error, but you will make progress if you are sufficiently motivated to succeed. The most important action or tactic is taking an interest in the other person's interests. Finding some common ground that is not exclusively related to your academic course is highly recommended. This could be reading the same type of books, listening to the same music, having similar hobbies or memberships of college societies. Common interests open up the possibility of sharing relevant mutually enjoyable experiences. These in turn are good foundations for a relationship.

Most of the examples in this chapter focus on male students with AS interacting with typical female students. The statistical distribution of AS justifies the male focus. The bulk of the advice equally applies to female students with AS interacting with typical male students. We have very little to say specifically about gay and lesbian students with AS. Hopefully some of the more general advice will be of use to them.

Casual and romantic relationships

At the outset, it is important to distinguish between having casual sex and being in a relationship. It is easy to get the two activities confused as both involve intimacy. In most relationships, intimacy between the two people proceeds slowly. The emphasis is on getting to know and trust one another. In a typical relationship, as understanding increases between the couple, intimacy will normally increase. The progression may follow a pattern leading from petting, necking, intimate kissing, and mutual masturbation through to full intercourse. However, many stable and satisfying relationships among young people do not result in full intercourse. In any relationship, only do what feels right and comfortable to you and only what feels right and comfortable for your partner. If you and your partner are genuinely attached to each other, each of you will respect each other's right to decide not to go any further until you know one another much better.

Casual sexual relationships between students are not uncommon. Casual sex means just that – the one-night stand. Casual sex is unplanned sex based on a random encounter with no promises of further dates or long-term commitments. While people enjoy sex with their partners, casual sex is often less satisfying than is popularly acknowledged. It is also very unsafe behaviour, carrying a high risk of contracting or transmitting very serious sexual diseases. The movie presentation of casual sex is completely unrealistic, so do not model your behaviour on actors that have rehearsed their simulated sex scenes perhaps several dozen times. Movie characters are always strikingly confident and in control, and very unlike real people. They never worry about knowing what to do next, being able to perform sexually, being rejected, contraception, sexually transmitted diseases, or unwanted pregnancy. In contrast, responsible people in the real world have to think of these possible outcomes.

While casual sex can be a release from frustration, it is a risky and unsettling practice. The aftermath of casual sexual counters, especially for women, is that the experience is rather 'empty', devoid of any emotional intimacy. The attractive vivacious person you went to bed with last night can be a thoroughly deflated wreck the next morning. Someone with AS may not understand that the other person was only interested in a one-night stand and may become confused and upset when his or her requests for further dates are rebuffed. The other thing to bear in mind is that casual sex often occurs after a party where alcohol or drugs have been consumed. We raise a *danger* sign here. Judgement is impaired after drink and drugs. Under their influence, you could be pressurized into doing things that you should avoid, and engaging in risky practices that could threaten your health and well-being.

Apart from the challenge of learning to say the right thing at the right time, behaviour and self-presentation have a huge impact on one's appeal to the opposite sex. For instance, a girl who uses vulgar language and has poor personal hygiene will be a much less attractive partner than a girl who takes pride in her presentation, appearance and personal hygiene. No matter whether a casual or steady relationship is your goal, first impressions count a lot in the dating stakes. You can spend a long time trying to recover from making a bad first impression. The time spent doing this is wasted when you could just as easily have put some planning into creating a good impression in the first place. This includes our hygiene recommendations made earlier in the book. Shower regularly, brush your teeth, keep your hair tidy and wear clean clothes. Second, always introduce yourself and demonstrate that you are actively listening to the other person. This shows that you are taking an interest in him or her and that you want to get to know the person. Do not neglect to develop your conversation skills in these settings. Third, avoid vulgarity and sexual slang when in mixed company. A sexual innuendo is an indirect comment about someone, suggesting something sexually rude. Sexual innuendo can be a very powerful force in a conversation between two people of opposite gender. However, it requires a great deal of communication skill and judgement to use sexual innuendo humourously and avoid offending a person's morals. We advise someone with AS to avoid mimicking the use of sexual innuendo.

Do give compliments, however, but limit yourself to one per day until you become comfortable with gauging people's reactions. Everyone likes positive statements to be made about themselves. As a general rule, compliments should be given privately and preferably only to a potential date or your actual date. Examples of compliments are: *It is nice to see you again. You are looking great today. That's a really nice dress you have on. Is that a new hairstyle? It really suits you.*

Be cautious and be alert

Relationships and their development are often confusing and complicated for people with AS. So much is left unsaid that is crucial to the relationship prospering. Within limits you can learn what you should do and say, but it is more difficult to learn what you should not do and not say. You have to be careful experimenting with different strategies, especially those involving body language, lest you end up being seriously misunderstood. It is strongly recommended that you explore nonverbal communication strategies in a local social skills group, whether on or off campus.

Whatever the nature of the relationship, casual or more settled, respecting the rights and entitlements of members of the opposite sex is extremely important. When one student tells another student that he or she is not interested in dating, then this decision must be respected. The person has reached a decision and, no matter how disappointing this is, one has to accept it. If a girl tells a boy that she does not want to date him and the boy persists in asking her out and paying her unwanted attention, then the boy could be charged with harassment. If that happens, his college career is interfered with and most likely his employment prospects will shrink greatly. We single out the male here, as harassment is usually practised by men against women. It is not a political judgement, but a statement of fact. Males with AS need to be careful that the attention they pay to females is not misread as harassment. Accept a woman's decision when she says something like: *No, I do not want to date you, thanks all the same.* Touching without the other person's consent is a mistake. If a girl tells you not to touch her, do not touch her. Remember our comments about empathy? Express yourself in a way that is consistent with empathy, which means showing that you respect the other person's wishes. If she tells you not to phone or email her, then do not call or email her. We cannot emphasize enough how important it is to respect the decisions of the opposite sex in this regard.

Figuring out whether you are doing the right or wrong thing in showing an interest in another person can be a source of uncertainty. People are not like traffic lights turning red or green to signal whether you should stop or continue. They may appear to you to be stuck on amber most of the time. There is a common thread running through the experiences of young men with AS, which is illustrated in Ben's story.

Ben is a male student. He hangs out with a group of students. Ben has AS. A girl in the group has caught Ben's attention. He is very attracted to this girl and finds being around her very exciting. Ben makes frequent efforts to be near this girl and talks to her about his interests. He waits for her before classes and walks out with her after classes. From Ben's point of view everything is fine. What Ben does not know is that the girl does not like him being near her so often. She feels he is crowding her. He interrupts her frequently. She is beginning to feel uncomfortable around Ben. In polite tones she has tried to discourage Ben's interest in her, but she believes he is not listening. Eventually, she has a huge row with Ben. He is completely crushed and confused. What did he do wrong? The group sees the girl's side of the story. They see Ben as harassing and stalking the girl. He is rejected by the group and has to look for company elsewhere.

Ben has to come to terms with rejection, but he is also bewildered. What on earth did he do that was wrong? He never touched the girl or spoke suggestively to her, yet he is now an outcast. Ben's experience is not uncommon. He has difficulty working out what the girl is really saying to him, what she really means. Perhaps Ben was polite enough to ask her whether she minded him sitting beside her at every lecture. She may have said something like *Oh no, not at all* or *You can sit where you like*, or any of umpteen other replies. She may have believed that she was making it clear to Ben that she did not want him to sit beside her. She assumed he would 'get the message' and leave her alone. Ben, however, did not pick up that understanding from what she said, nor from her nonverbal behaviour, her body language. Communication, when indirect and not logically precise, causes just this type of misunderstanding. Alas, it is also very common.

What should you do to avoid similar unpleasant outcomes? You need to learn caution in pursuing your attraction to a girl. First, you should note in your diary that you are attracted to this girl. If you are worried about someone else reading your diary, you can devise a code of your own for romantic notes (or encrypt it on the computer). Next you should consider placing a limit on the number of times you will meet the girl in a week. This is hard to manage precisely, so be flexible. You should also set a time limit on these meetings. Combining these recommendations together will respect the girl's personal space. It will also give you more time to integrate and manage your feelings. However, at some point in time you will have to figure out if this girl is interested in a romantic relationship with you. This is the big question: *Does she like me enough to date me?*

You have to be alert for signals that show whether the girl is positive towards you or negative. This is a very difficult skill to acquire. Even the most socially able are tripped up here. Anyone can misread these signals. Sometimes the person sending the signals is not a very good communicator, which can add to the ambiguity. Because people are often not very explicit about their feelings, it is easy to mistake an ambiguous signal as either positive or negative. There are some simple pre-condition tests however. If a girl does any two of the following consistently then you could reasonably infer that she is not romantically interested in you. The pre-conditions for a romantic relationship are not in place if a girl:

- avoids looking at you or talking to you
- makes no effort to include you in conversation

- does not respond to your initiating moves
- turns away from you in conversation
- expresses negative comments about how you dress
- ridicules your views
- invites another person to make fun of you.

However, a girl may do none of these things and still only like you as a friend, and have no interest in having a sexual relationship with you. A person with AS has to be exceptionally alert to these signals. The final move that you can consider is simply asking her out on a date politely and with a calm voice. Obviously, you only do this if you are satisfied that the pre-conditions exist. It is essential that this not occur in a group setting.

Making a date: a sample plan

Asking someone for a date is an act of intimacy, an act of special familiarity. You can build up to asking for a date by inquiring about what types of music and movies the potential date likes. Music is a very important part of the private and social lives of students. If you show a familiarity with some aspects of contemporary music, making small talk will be much easier. You can then talk about your favourite music and movies (but limit your enthusiasm to a few sentences). If you plan on asking your potential date to go to the cinema, ask her at this point what types of movie she prefers. If she hates all types of war movies, do not ask her to a war movie. If you plan on asking her to a music venue, try to ascertain what music she likes before you invite her out. A combination of active listening and careful planning will help you put your best case forward for a date, but remember she (or he) still has the right to decline.

When you ask someone for a date you are telling that person that he or she is in some way special, a friend that you would like to spend more time with and potentially confide in. You are also offering to be a special friend to the other person. You need to show the other person that you respect him or her. Feelings about relationships are private and should be expressed privately. If you are in a café with six other people, it is not appropriate to ask for a date across the table. You should find a space, perhaps after class, where you can speak with the girl (or boy) privately and introduce the idea of a date. A public space is probably preferable as long as you are out of earshot of others. The best way to go about looking for a date is to build on some foreknowledge. Ask yourself: *Have I spoken to this girl before? Did I like her responses? Has she interests in common with mine? Has she an existing boyfriend? Am I attracted to her for the right reasons?* The last question may seem odd, but it is easy to become attracted to a person's random features such as their clothes (she dresses in black), or their hair (I like blonde spiky hair), or their shoes, and so forth. Ask yourself whether you would still find the person attractive if she wore different fashions or a different hairstyle.

> Simon was a new undergraduate student with AS. He was infatuated with a girl in his class who always wore black clothes. Her peers would have described her as a 'Goth'. He never approached her for a date, however, as he found her somewhat intimidating. After the summer break, she returned to college wearing jeans and a T-shirt. She had abandoned her Goth fashions. Simon later told his therapist that he was shocked at the girl's change in appearance and completely lost interest in her.

Answering these questions helps you establish whether the pre-conditions are in place. You need a plan for your 'get a date' goal. A plan will help make explicit some aspects of what is typically implicit. When you put your plan into action you will evaluate her responses to each step in the plan. The sample plan outlined here has five action steps:

1. Make small talk about some aspect of the course or student life: e.g. upcoming music events, new movies, enjoyable aspects of the course/college, interesting college society events.

2. Compliment her about her work (or the way she dresses): e.g. *Your hair looks very nice today. That dress looks good on you. You performed really well in the lab yesterday.*

3. Mention how great it is to unwind at the weekend: e.g. *I really enjoy relaxing at the weekend with a trip to the movies* (or music venue or museum or new restaurant).

4.   Ask her if she would like to go to the cinema with you: e.g. *There is a new movie opening next weekend. It is directed by X and the reviews are very good. I am planning to see it. Would you like to come along with me?*

5.   (a) If she says *yes*, make arrangements to meet her at the cinema or travel with her to the cinema.

(b) If she says *no*, say something like: *That's fine. I just thought I'd ask. Let me know if you change your mind. I have to go to a class now.* Wave goodbye. Remain calm.

All this time you must actively listen to what she has to say in response. This is a logical strategy where you move from discussion of a topic of interest, to expressing an interest in the person as a person, to leisure time, and then to the possibility of a date. She may decline or she may accept. Whatever response is given, you have to accept it calmly and politely but you should have acquitted yourself well. A plan like the above does not guarantee success but it can help control anxiety. Paying a compliment to a girl is a special kind of move in a conversation, telling her that she is nice and attractive in specific way. Compliments are so special that you should restrict them to dating situations.

If a girl declines a date with you, you will feel disappointed. Indeed your emotions may sway between anger and anxiety because your goal has not been achieved. You have been rebuffed, even if very politely, and handling rejection may not be one of your strong points. You have two choices. First, you can go into a solitary rage (not in public please) and end up feeling even more dejected. Second, you acknowledge your disappointment but move on. You learn from the experience. What do you learn? You learn to improve your assessment of someone else's interest in you. Treat the experience as a positive learning exercise. Do not dwell on failure, but learn to improve your chances the next time around with a different girl.

If a girl agrees to go on a date then a bit of foreknowledge should be gathered about the cinema (or whatever venue) to which you are going, the nearest transport points, and where the nearest café is for a coffee afterwards. Planning the evening in advance will reduce your anxiety, but remember to adopt a flexible planning approach should the unexpected occur. Make sure that you have enough money to pay for both of you. If you are using an electronic diary or your computer, make sure to enter in the arrangements of the date. Access these just beforehand to refresh your memory.

COMPUTER DATING

Trying to secure your first date can be a bit nerve-wracking. The body language of other people may be too hard to read and you are being frustrated and confused during interactions. After a few unsuccessful attempts with dates, you may be tempted to give up. In these circumstances, is there an argument in favour of computer dating? On one level, computer dating lets you choose your date on the basis of fairly rigid criteria such as brown hair, chemistry major, interested in stamp collecting, and so forth. These are criteria chosen by you, so you have a large degree of control over your potential date's profile. This can be very helpful in screening for likely partners. You will also define your own profile for the dating service and you should emphasize your strengths. Avoid posting a photograph immediately. Be cautious with computer dating. Do not arrange to meet anyone in a secluded place. Always pick public places such as restaurants for your first couple of meetings. In college, with so many people around, the option of computer dating must come last over face-to-face interactions. If you are using computer dating, get to know your contacts through email first. The bonus from email, as we know from earlier in the book, is that it delays face-to-face discussion, which puts off having to deal with the body language issue. During the 'email only' period both people build up cognitive models of each other. If one person decides to pull out of email then the other will probably cope better with the rejection than in face-to-face settings. All of these features of computer dating are positive supports for those with AS. Definitely building up email communication before dating would be useful. However, there will come a point in time when you will have to meet your computer date, and then social communications skills will be required.

Is there a particular type of person that suits someone with AS? Would you be better trying to find people of a particular type to date rather than 'browsing' the typical majority? Most certainly there are partners out there for people with AS. College is ideal in providing access to a broad range of people with varying interests. However, there is a case to be made that some people with AS may fare better romantically when involved with someone from outside his or her culture. There are definite advantages when a couple does not share the same first language. The cultural nuances and nonverbal subtleties of communication are not as important to the relationship. Communication can be more explicit and direct because of the language differences. Does this mean that a student with AS should join a foreign language society in the college? Well, it may be worthwhile. Try it and see for yourself.

Observing personal space

There are a number of simple rules about personal space. Do not stand too close to a member of the opposite sex unless you are in a relationship with the person. Apply the arm's length rule. Above all do not touch any part of the body of a member of the opposite sex without their permission. This rule must be strictly followed. Do not handle their books, bags or clothes without explicit permission. Always ask for permission to borrow something before picking it up. Obviously you also expect people to respect your space.

A common complaint of women is that men are too presumptuous and do not respect their personal space sufficiently. Men often presume that their date is willing to go further in sexual contact than she indicates. Most males with AS may in contrast present as being possibly too reserved and polite. Being too pushy is not a good strategy as you may have difficulty reading the 'back off' signs from a woman. Our advice is that you take courtship slowly. Try to work to a plan, but allow for the unexpected. There is great uncertainty in dealing with another person. You cannot predict their every choice and action. It is all right to feel confused at times. Also it is all right to be a bit reserved. Better to respect your date's personal space than upset her. Over time, when you become more comfortable with the other person, that reserve will diminish.

Interacting with the opposite sex is strongly rule bound. Nonetheless politeness is a universal pre-condition, especially in speaking with women. We have briefly classified behaviour into four categories in the next section. You will find it useful to reflect on the distinctions between each category and if possible do some role playing in a social skills group.

Types of behaviour

In social settings people will judge you by your behaviour. Behaving politely and without giving offence is very important. Politeness is tied to social conventions and someone with AS will have difficulties grasping at least some of these conventions. Those conventions that are explicitly stated are easiest to learn and put into practice. For example, when you meet someone in authority, offer to shake hands, or say hello to strangers and tell them your name. You have learnt many of these rules in school.

There are many other rules. The less obvious conventions, those that are known but not said, are more difficult to comprehend. For example, if someone sees you approaching and turns their back to you, this means you should not talk to that person now. If someone is crying that means they are upset and will not want to hear about your project work. If a girl tells you she has a headache and cannot talk to you now, then you do not enquire into why she has a headache. One reason why these conventions are less easy to grasp is because you may not understand the other person's point of view, perspective, or judgement on your behaviour. A social skills group is ideal for experimenting with the unwritten conventions. Outside of the social skills group, as we mentioned earlier in the book, you must observe and plan trial-and-error experiments. Everyone behaves unacceptably from time to time, but the trick is in learning not to repeat the behaviour. Correcting offensive behaviour relies on monitoring the reactions of others.

INAPPROPRIATE BEHAVIOUR

Students tend to hang around in groups. Students with AS are initially not keen on groups, often due to bad experiences in high school, but in college there is no escaping group conversation. One just has to accept this and make the best of one's skills. A group can be a fairly loose association of people, but if you offend one person in the group you could lose friends quickly. This is something to reflect upon in male–female interactions. The same is true of official student societies. Inappropriate behaviour refers to actions (verbal and nonverbal) that are not suitable for the context or situation.

When you are attracted to another person, you will be enthusiastic and excited in his or her company. Sexual arousal is a normal response, but its expression needs to be channelled appropriately. The fact that you are aroused does not logically entail that the girl (or boy), the object of your interest, is equally aroused. The following equation is only intermittently true: *I like you = You like me.*

Suppose you encounter an attractive student in your favourite college society. You need to monitor your interactions with him or her. If you demand this student's attention too enthusiastically, he or she may complain to the society's board. A complaint like that could see you ejected from the society. Monitor your enthusiasm and use active listening to infer what the other person is saying and whether any comments particularly include you. It is useful to set time limits on initial contact to help you manage your emotions. People with AS can find this area of social etiquette very confusing. Comprehending whether the other person wants or does not want your company is not easy at times. When your emotions are aroused it is less easy to see yourself acting inappropriately.

One young man with AS would wink at girls that he liked. He understood this to mean that they knew he was attracted to them. He did not understand that they did not like his nonverbal communications. In fact, it was only when a complaint was made that he began to grasp that the girls did not want his attention. His behaviour was inappropriate, but it was not dangerous or threatening.

If you have a very strong attraction to another person, an almost obsessional attraction, then try to restrain yourself from telling him or her how obsessed you are with them. This will make them feel uncomfortable and definitely destroy your dating plans. It is not appropriate to do or say anything that will make another person uneasy and afraid.

ABUSIVE BEHAVIOUR

There are different forms of abusive behaviour. You can verbally abuse someone by shouting at them in anger. You can abuse someone by calling them names or making hurtful comments about their appearance, abilities or family. More often than not, you may be unaware that your behaviour was abusive. Hitting people is physically abusive. Any form of touching or fondling of another person without their consent is abusive. Any form of touching or fondling of another person that causes them offence or distress is abusive. You can also abuse someone, for instance, by putting one of your hands on parts of his or her body without consent. This can be both physically and sexually abusive.

People with AS are rarely physically abusive. However, giving offence verbally, verbal abuse, can occur unintentionally. As a rule female students do not like sexual slang. They do not like parts of their bodies identified or spoken about in public. If you tell another student who is not your steady girlfriend, that she has a 'nice arse' or 'good tits' she will not like that comment. It is extremely important to avoid sexually explicit terms and phrases when conversing with, or commenting on, other female students. We know of one young man with AS who thought it was 'cool' to refer to women as 'bitches' due to the frequency of use of the word in certain types of music. He was reported to the college authorities for calling to one female with the phrase: *Hey bitch, did you get your lab report written up over the weekend?* The entertainment industry can easily mislead you into thinking that vulgar, uncouth behaviour is acceptable, but the industry uses this behaviour to stimulate public interest in their products. Suppress any inclinations to be vulgar.

Also do not comment on the physique of other students, particularly female students. If you meet a girl who is overweight, do not say things like: *You are quite fat. Have you thought of a diet?* Also if other students, male or female, have any noticeable physical characteristics such as prominent ears, short stature, bad skin, birthmarks or any physical deformity, do not comment on them. These comments are terribly offensive and could easily get you into trouble with the college authorities. One student with AS was reported to the Dean of Discipline after telling a girl with a prominent birthmark that her face had the same colouring as a slice of bacon. He was just making an observation, but had no comprehension of the girl's sensitivities about her birthmark.

Are people with AS open to being abused? Most certainly the social openness and naivety of many people with AS does put them at some risk of abuse in certain types of relationship. People with AS can be abused verbally, physically or sexually. You should not allow anyone to abuse you in any way. If they do you should tell them: *Stop. I do not like you doing that. I want you to stop right now.* Real friends do not abuse each other. Use the friendship tests to decide whether a person is the right company for you or not.

If you become obsessed with another person, you could find yourself accepting a lot of abusive behaviour from him or her just so that you can continue to be near the person. This behaviour could include anything from nasty ridicule to physical beatings. The Swedish autistic writer, Gunilla Gerland, describes herself clinging to one relationship, even though she was being beaten on occasions and ridiculed as a 'piece of furniture'. Abusive relationships do not happen just to those with AS, but if you are uncomfortable in a relationship, document your discomfort and bring the documentation to the attention of the student counsellor or your therapist. Shrugging off an obsession can be very difficult, but the main advice here is to get out of relationships where you experience any kind of abuse or humiliation.

DANGEROUS BEHAVIOUR

Behaviours that are dangerous in male and female interactions are those which could bring you to the attention of the police. Dangerous behaviour is brought on by a combination of attraction, passion and fixation moving beyond your control. The most common form of dangerous behaviour exhibited by people with AS is sexual harassment, manifested as stalking. Following a girl around campus when she has indicated that she does *not* want your attention, or has never indicated that she wants your attention, is stalking. Look at your daily diary and if you find yourself following one girl around, try to redirect your interests and consider strongly a discussion with your student counsellor or therapist. All forms of touching driven by sexual arousal are thoroughly dangerous without the consent of the other person.

Liam found polite interaction with girls very difficult. Liam had been diagnosed with AS in his teens. He tended to become almost instantly attracted to any girl who said hello to him. He became very aroused and uninhibited, 'loose', after a few drinks in the student club. He would make vulgar comments to girls. On many occasions in company without any attempt at small talk, he would lean across a table and ask the girl to come back to his room for sex. This caused great offence but he would simply move to another table. Liam's behaviour worsened. He asked a girl for sex, and as she turned away he put one of his hands between her legs. Eventually he was charged with indecent assault. He was suspended from college for a year. During this time he was given intensive therapy and social skills training. When he returned to college he was required to 'check in' his feelings on a daily basis with the student counsellor. Eventually Liam was able to manage his emotions better, but it took considerable effort.

If you are very intensely attracted to someone, consider keeping a diary of your encounters and their frequency. Being fixated on someone often prevents you from seeing the rest of the world clearly. Your outlook on the rest of the world is influenced by your passion. Commonly you wake up in the morning thinking about the person you desire, spend the rest of the day daydreaming about him or her or contriving to be near them or in situations where you will be noticed by them. However, if you have strong sexual impulses towards another person you need to think through thoroughly the consequences of acting on them; not just the consequences for you but for the other person as well. Try to redesignate your attention and focus on something more neutral or more academically absorbing when you feel yourself getting aroused. If at any stage you feel that your sexual impulses are beginning to go beyond your control, arrange to see either your therapist or the student counsellor as a matter of urgency.

APPROPRIATE BEHAVIOUR

Behaviour that your date or partner is comfortable with, and that makes her or him feel safe, is appropriate behaviour. Making small talk is always important. You can restrict this to just what was in the newspaper yesterday. You can begin with more student-friendly topics such as the latest movies or music releases and then move on to topics that are more centred on how the other person looks and feels, and what kind of day he or she has had. Conversation based around the latter topics is empathetic conversation and appropriate to situations that are relationship focused.

Here is an example of typical encounter. If you are attracted to someone, then the next step is to get to know them. This means talking to them, listening to their responses and observing their behaviour (e.g. does he or she move away when you talk, or does he or she remain and continue the conversation?). You will meet girls and boys in your classes, in labs, in the canteen and in college societies. It is hard to avoid people in fact. If you find a particular person attractive, try to get near him or her for a brief conversation initially. This may amount to you just introducing yourself and the courses you are taking: *Hi, I'm Jim. I'm studying Computer Engineering. How about you?* Ask her (or him) simple introductory questions: *Where are you from? Are you a member of any college societies?* Listen carefully to the replies. Look for points of common interest. You might suggest something along the lines of: *I'm going to get a coffee now before going back to class (or study). Would like a coffee too?* Take it easy, and put a time limit of at most 15 minutes on your first few interactions (though five to ten minutes is preferable).

Even a limited sense of humour is always welcome in conversation. It helps 'break the ice' between two people in the sense of dissolving any tension in a situation. It is often assumed that people with AS lack a sense of humour. Our experiences are that they have a sense of humour, but it is different to typical loud boisterous humour. Good examples of AS-inspired humour are in the areas of word games and word puns. This is clever humour but it can still be brilliantly witty and appropriate. Not everyone will be equally good at making and expressing puns, but if you have a talent in this area try to develop it.

Learning to negotiate and accept a compromise is very valuable when you are attracted to a girl. Wanting everything your way is not effective in maintaining friendship. When you have a difference of opinion (especially on a date), give your point of view in a calm voice. Always listen to the other person's response. If you can identify an alternative, offer it up for discussion and explain why the alternative would meet both your needs. Try to reach agreement on the way forward. For example, you want to see the science fiction movie, but your date wants to see the romantic comedy. You do not like romantic comedies. She says that on the last date you chose the film and now it is her turn. You might suggest that you both see another movie, perhaps a war drama, which combines action (your interest) and romance (her interest). She feels that she should choose the movie tonight. What do you do? First, acknowledge her point of view. Accept that it is her turn to choose a movie. As a compromise suggest that she go with you to the science fiction movie another night before it leaves town. Now go in and enjoy the movie, and look forward to the next date. Compromise is not submission, but it is difficult to accept. Stable relationships are based on give and take by both people. Wherever possible, choose compromise over conflict. You will feel more comfortable in the long run and your relationship is more likely to be successful and lasting.

Dating

A date is just a date. It is of course a very important step in social and emotional communication. It is not closure on a relationship, but its beginning. Occasionally, young people with AS get so enthused about a date that they forget all the rules they applied on the way to getting it. Never switch off active listening with a date. Do not talk on endlessly about your favourite hobbies. Avoid crowding the other person on a date until you have met them on your own at least four times and preferably six times. The cinema is a good first date venue for people with AS to consider. First, each person's space is defined by his or her seat. Hence body contact is more restricted. Second, the film will allow you to relax and not become too drained by conversation. It is easy to be overwhelmed by the prolonged company of a person. Take time to ease yourself into the relationship. Finally, the film is a common interest that you can discuss afterwards. The time spent together immediately after the film will allow you to determine whether a next date is likely. You may discover that your date is actually not all that exciting and you do not have much in common. Your date may decide the same about you. No matter what happens afterwards, it is important to respect the other person's space.

We have mentioned the arm's length rule before. As you become more comfortable on dates with the same person, you will relax that rule. For instance, if a date has gone even half well, you will end up kissing the other person on the cheek and possibly holding hands. Do not look for too much physical contact on the first date. Maybe hold hands for a few moments over coffee if your date is agreeable. Ask before kissing or hugging: *Can I kiss you? Can I put my arm around you?* It is sensible in the beginning to seek explicit permission, to show that you like and respect the person. The other person may become uneasy otherwise. In fact in the early stages of a relationship it is wise to touch the other person only after you have asked for permission and he or she has consented.

At the end of the evening, always thank your date for his or her company: *Thanks for this evening, I really enjoyed your company.* If you think it has gone well, ask for another date. Even if you are unsure of the other person's reactions to the evening, you should say: *I have enjoyed this evening. Have you enjoyed it as well?* Most people are polite and will probably say something like: *Oh yes, it was very nice. Thanks.* At this point you need to decide whether to ask for another date or not. You could say: *Would you like to go out again? There is a play on next weekend that you might like to see.* Your date may say: *Sounds good. Let me think about it. I'll call you during the week.* They may also reply: *That's a nice offer, but I have something on next weekend.* They are unlikely to say: *That is a fantastic suggestion. You are the most exciting man or woman I've ever been with.* It is not easy to judge whether someone is saying yes or no to the offer of another date. Sometimes you will have to ask for clarification: *Does that mean we will go out on a date next weekend?* There is often no other option.

It is important to be alert to other people's moods. Few of us are experts at this. People can behave differently from time to time without any apparently obvious reason. For instance, you might have a good friendship with a girl or even the beginnings of a relationship, when without you doing anything to upset her she can get quite short tempered or impatient. Her sudden shift in mood may last a few days and is usually due to premenstrual tension (PMT). If a woman has PMT, she is highly unlikely to share that knowledge with you unless you are in a regular relationship. Remember that not every change in mood or behaviour in a woman is caused by something you did specifically. By the way, it is not polite for men to discuss PMT with women, so now that you know something about its effects, just file it away for future reference. A woman with AS, however, may want to explain any sudden moodiness due to PMT to her date or boyfriend, in the interests of helping him understand departures from routines.

Over time you may find yourself regularly dating the same girl (or boy). Having a steady boyfriend or girlfriend is nice. It is good to have someone with whom to discuss aspects of your life and ambitions and share experiences. Getting to this stage has probably taken a lot of planning and hard work, but now you have to maintain the relationship. At times, people with AS can appear very controlling and domineering.

No relationship can flourish if one person insists on controlling the other. In a healthy relationship no one party should insist on having everything his or her way. A healthy relationship is based on mutual consent about choices and courses of actions. This is not easy to internalize and many people with AS have great difficulty comprehending this principle.

A steady relationship can become like a routine, and if one partner is very controlling then he or she will expect their partner to behave in very predictable ways. However, it is a mistake to believe you have complete control and predictability over a relationship. Do not assume that you can predict the other person's desires, wishes, feelings or behaviour. Once one partner takes the other for granted, then the first partner stops working at maintaining the relationship. Eventually it collapses, usually with much venting of rage.

> Declan had a girlfriend in college for two years. He had been diagnosed with AS when he first came to college, and took several years out before returning. While Declan had very mild Asperger traits, he was very domineering. Near exams he would ask his girlfriend to have sex with him and immediately afterwards return to studying. Eventually she left him and he was devastated. At first he was angry, sad and jealous. He frequently raged about her audacity to leave him. Some classmates became very concerned for his welfare and he agreed to revisit his therapist. Over a few months the relationship was dissected and Declan began to comprehend that he had treated his ex-girlfriend very badly. He had been controlling and intolerant. The real reason for his rage was that his relationship routine was gone, and he could do nothing to put it right again.

Relationships break down all the time. Sometimes the parting is amicable when both people realize that the attraction and affection have gone. More often there are some tears as one party is less keen on the parting than the other. In other cases emotions may be very inappropriately expressed. It may be very difficult to know how you feel. If a relationship with someone you like a lot is unexpectedly broken off, you are likely to have a mixture of upsetting feelings. You will probably feel sad, disappointed, rejected and angry. People with AS may take rejection very badly. They may persist in wanting to keep the relationship going, despite the other person's wishes. This persistence can be injurious to one's mental well-being. When your girlfriend tells you that the relationship is over, she'll usually tell you that she has been thinking about ending it for a while. You will try to persuade her to change her mind, but in the end you will have to accept her decision. Making a fuss over the break-up of a relationship can seriously affect coping with your feelings. You may, however, want to meet the student counsellor or your therapist to discuss your reaction and what life changes you need to consider.

If you choose to end a relationship, plan your moves carefully. Consider whether you still want to be friends with the other person after the break-up. Reassure your now ex-girlfriend (or -boyfriend) that the relationship was meaningful and special to you. However, the relationship has changed and you no longer feel comfortable in it. It can be hard to avoid giving offence unintentionally, so a chat with the student counsellor to help model an approach could be useful.

Sex education: know the biology

Education in the biology of sexual activity and reproduction is commonplace in high school and we will not repeat the lessons here. All we emphasize is that if you are sexually active, be careful. Always practise safe sex. Never allow yourself to be pressurized into sexual activity just because your peers are doing it. Only do what you feel right doing.

Women are reminded to understand their ovulation times as they are most vulnerable to becoming pregnant at these times. As nature intended they are also most sexually aroused during ovulation. However, unprotected sex should be avoided at all times, especially during ovulation. The risk of pregnancy is just too great. Most young people, in particular students without an established career path, are extremely unprepared for parenthood.

Private sexual practices

Despite rarely being discussed in public, masturbation is commonly practised by both sexes to relieve sexual frustration and tension. Masturbation is something to practise in private and is not an appropriate subject for discussion with anyone else. If you masturbate in your rooms, use the bathroom for privacy. It is also easier to clean yourself in the bathroom. In college, masturbating in the privacy of the restrooms is not a good idea as you have less security than you think. For instance, someone may fall against the door of a cubicle or it may swing open inadvertently. More significantly, you might be heard by others outside the cubicle and you do not want to attract a crowd of spectators. If you become sexually aroused during the day, try to focus on something else until the arousal subsides.

People sometimes develop an attachment to items of clothing, footwear or even household objects which they find sexually arousing. They may even bring these things to bed with them. There is nothing intrinsically wrong with a fetish such as this, but in the interests of mature sexual development you should try to avoid maintaining a fetish. If you have such a fetish, you might consider discussing it with the student counsellor or your therapist.

Contraception

The time to think about contraception and sex is long before having sex. If you are a man who has never used a condom before, then for goodness sake do not wait until your first sexual experience presents itself to work out how to use one. Some private experimentation is useful. Trying to reason from first principles about contraception in the heat of sexual arousal is too late. You have already begun to put reason behind you. Leaflets on sexual health and sexual practices are undoubtedly available on campus from student services. Pick up a few and study them carefully. Our recommendation is that sexual activity should always take place within the context of a secure and caring relationship. Always remember that you can have satisfying physical contact without full sexual intercourse. Female students in particular may prefer this approach in the early stages of a relationship when trust is being built and where there are fears of pregnancy. Most people like to take time to create the right affectionate conditions for increased intimate contact. Intimacy should only proceed where there is mutual consent. The emotional security of a caring relationship gives someone with AS a better and more controlled situation within which to make the right decisions about the pacing of these activities.

Contraception is not optional but compulsory for both men and women. Any man who is sexually active should always carry at least one condom around in the pocket of a jacket. This is a precaution. You may be at a party and the opportunity for sex arises but the other person insists on your using a condom. You first need to ask yourself whether having a casual sexual encounter under these conditions feels right. If you still choose to have sex, then do not have unprotected sex. Even if the other person does not insist on a condom, you should. You will be pretty frustrated if you do not have one with you. In fact you will be so frustrated that you may consider risking unprotected sex. Stop there.

Apart from being a barrier to the passage of male sperm, condoms prevent sexually transmitted diseases (STDs) from attacking you. However, on very rare occasions a condom can rupture or tear. Ideally your partner will not have an STD, but he or she may be infected without knowing. With the exception of AIDS, STDs will respond reliably to medical treatment. However, you do not want the hassle and embarrassment of presenting at a clinic for treatment. Condoms are essential to prevent infection with HIV, the AIDS virus. No matter how healthy and clean a potential sexual partner may appear, he or she could be infected with HIV. Do not take risks. Use a condom.

There is an argument in favour of women also carrying condoms. However, a woman has to be confident that a man will use a condom and knows how to use one. If a woman is having sex frequently she will need other forms of contraception besides condoms. The most common forms of female contraception are the contraceptive pill and the 'coil' (an intra-uterine device).

If you are in a regular settled relationship, contraception arrangements should be discussed and planned. Many women are reluctant to use a contraceptive pill as a permanent solution, due to potential side effects. However, if a woman has to rely on her male partner using condoms there needs to be a great degree of trust. In these circumstances the male must behave responsibly, and in addition to condoms some type of spermicidal compound should be used.

Many young people find talks about contraception awkward, but these discussions are necessary to protect health. Proper use of contraception coupled with responsible sexual behaviour could save your life.

Pregnancy

This section is primarily dealing with female matters, but males should also read it to get a sense of the responsibility they bear when having sex without contraception. Sex is enjoyable, but you will need to control your impulses and explore it responsibly. An unwanted pregnancy is a huge burden in any woman's life. It is a genuinely life-altering event. An unplanned pregnancy is psychologically scarring. In many cases the father, the inseminator, is not interested or only interested in parenting on his terms. Young men can cope with the idea of being a father, but not necessarily being a parent. If the mother is in a stable relationship with the father, then he may be very supportive. Marriage might even be considered, though the hard facts are that hasty marriages are often not very stable. Having a child is a huge responsibility. A child is also a lifelong responsibility. Children have to be fed regularly, have their nappies (diapers) changed and generally be looked after 24 hours a day. Your free time, whether you are in the father or mother role, will shrink. If you are the mother, your free time will disappear for the first two years. Many marriages made by young couples do not last, so do not rush into marriage. It is not a solution to an unplanned pregnancy.

What do you do if you find yourself pregnant? Before making any rash decisions, your first need is to get balanced advice. There are many counselling services, both on and off campus, that will help you examine all the options. Your family should also be consulted. Support services vary from country to country. One option is to take a year out of college and return when the child is ready for the campus crèche. If your parents are supportive and nearby that can be a great help. However, as a student you need to assess how practical the various options are before committing to a particular choice. Many colleges are very supportive of student mothers and special timetabling of classes and examinations can be negotiated. It is a good idea to get the student counsellor involved here.

There are no simple solutions to the predicament of pregnancy. This is why contraception and responsible sexual behaviour are so important. Responsible sexual relations are not just issues for students with AS.

Recommendations: important rules

In this chapter we have covered some of the ground rules governing talking to and dating the opposite sex. The main rules relate to respecting another person's personal space and decisions. Violation of these rules can cause you social, emotional and even legal problems. Dating can be managed up to a point with planning strategies. However, large amounts of flexibility are required. Be prepared for disappointment and the unforeseen. Identifying the consequences of one's behaviour is not always clear-cut. One's early experiences with dating may include many errors and rejections. However, treat these less as setbacks than as learning points from which to move forward. There is little doubt that the expectations of the sexes are different in the areas of empathy, emotion understanding and communication (Baron-Cohen 2003). Learning several of the core expectations outlined in this chapter will be of immense assistance.

You can try computer dating if you feel that face-to-face meetings are initially too stressful, but there are so many college societies with potential partners for you that we suggest you use computer dating as the very last option. Young women need to exercise great caution when using computer dating. It is very easy for someone – a predator – to fake a charming identity.

Advice on dating and safe sexual practices is found on many useful websites. Opportunities for sexual activity that is unplanned, random and out of the context of a caring romantic relationship should be very carefully assessed. There are many risks attached to casual sex.

Despite myriad pieces of advice, guidelines and rules, relationships are born out of mutual interests, mutual attraction and mutual consent. However, no matter how much one reads and processes, eventually you have to be confident enough to ask: *Would you like to go to the movies next weekend?* Do not forget the popcorn.

8 Managing Anxiety and Stress

AS and mental health problems

No one is immune to stress and this chapter describes some of the commonest mental health problems that people with AS experience. The chapter builds on the work in Chapter 5. It gives guidance on coping with and minimizing stress, and seeking help. The most important lesson in this chapter is learning that help is available. Sometimes we can be so upset as to believe that no one can help us. That is not true. Believe this.

Stress is a part of everyday life for everyone. Stress is a reaction to pressures, to demands being made on you. Stress is not an abstract reaction, but something that you feel, that your body feels (e.g. increased muscle tension). A small amount of stress can be healthy and motivate people to constructive action and achievement. For instance, completing coursework on time, exam preparation and thesis work will involve some amount of stress. In many instances, this is motivating stress. However, at times when more seriously stressful events occur (e.g. losses, frustrations, failures, rejections, disappointments), these can result in feelings of fear, anger, anxiety, depression, and a sense of being overwhelmed. The coping demands being made on you are too great. Here we have manifestations of stress leading to despair. Bad forms of stress (and anxiety) often result in inertia, and are a topic of interest in this chapter. You definitely want to avoid inertia in college.

People with AS often experience their lives as very stressful. This stress is compounded when there is no friend or confidant(e) to whom they can turn for support and advice. This is a bad stress situation. Unfortunately, many people with AS on the progression from childhood into adolescence will have experienced social exclusion, rejection and bullying. Some of these experiences may recur in college and may compound feelings of loneliness, anxiety and depression. In extreme situations they can result in suicidal feelings and actions. When we combine stress with the lack of social support that is not uncommon in AS, a variety of mental health problems can result.

In general you will get psychological support, understanding and sympathy from family members, friends and individual counsellors. Having at least one person who knows you well and understands your difficulties is a major bonus. This is why friendship and communication skills are so important. One dependable peer is someone to whom you can turn in order to help you cope with overwhelming feelings. However, you can also help yourself. There is a lot you can do to prevent things getting out of control and a lot can be done to make things better. The primary goal should be improvements in social competence. This is a lifelong goal, but every tiny improvement is a step in the right direction. Every improvement will help with stress management and stress reduction. Trying to understand the verbal and nonverbal communications of others, as well as learning how to respond, is a lifelong activity. Understanding the feelings and needs of self and others is very difficult. It may involve a constant struggle, but it is a worthwhile struggle. There are opportunities to develop appropriate skills through courses and books (see box).

Theory of mind skills: understanding the feelings, thoughts and intentions of others.

Empathy skills: emotional recognition in self and others, perspective taking, understanding one's own feelings, the feelings of others and about how to be sympathetic and show understanding of others.

Social skills training: assessing social situations, learning what social behaviour is appropriate, rehearsing it with the group, role playing, and practising in the real world with the group or facilitator. Reviewing progress at the next group is a standard feature.

Accessing these resources may involve some inconvenience. They may not be readily available in your location. However, as worldwide aware-ness of AS increases, more training, therapeutic and support groups are becoming available. The internet is another source of information and support, but use prudent judgement. Avail yourself of information that has been endorsed by your national Asperger organization.

We mentioned this at the beginning of the book as part of college preparation, but given the challenges in your new environment, you should contact the student counsellor to arrange regular meetings either before you start college or as soon as possible afterwards. Find out what other supports are available in the college for people with AS and how to access them. Get this foreknowledge together sooner rather than later. Discover who the college doctor is and how he or she can be accessed. Foreknowledge is power. Ensure that you know how to access the maximum available support. Use the supports to make your college life more enjoyable and successful.

Recognizing and managing anxiety

The world defined by social interaction is often confusing, unpredictable, frustrating and frightening. People with AS are seen by others as socially naive and are regularly subjected to ridicule and harassment. It is quite understandable that you might often be fearful of others. Probably the most commonly experienced emotions by people with AS are fear and anxiety. When the demands placed on you by a situation are repeatedly more than you can handle, stress gives way to anxiety.

Learning to spot anxiety in situations

Some level of anxiety is helpful as a natural response to threats or dangers. For instance, if you were woken at night by the smell of smoke in your apartment block, you would experience anxiety that would motivate you to save your life by escaping the building. Once safe, your anxiety would subside. If you have just narrowly avoided being run down by a bus, you will experience some degree of anxiety. These are upsetting events. Potentially life-threatening events do give rise to anxiety. This is an entirely normal reaction, but over time the feelings of anxiety should diminish. Anxiety becomes a problem for people – a disorder – when it does not subside and when the reasons for the anxiety are nowhere near as concrete as saving yourself from being burnt alive or run over. For example, if you persistently experience anxiety every time you enter the student canteen, a lecture hall or lab, then it is very likely that you are not coping well and are underperforming in college. You may find yourself totally unable to leave for college in the morning unless your bags are packed a certain way, your coat is lying in precise fashion across a chair, and you have checked them sufficiently. You may become very anxious if there is any change in these arrangements (e.g. the coat is at the laundry). These arrangements are so important to you that it is impossible to leave the house unless things are exactly the way you believe they have to be and you end up missing your lectures and other coursework. In these cases, where your anxiety is interfering with your life, you are advised to seek professional help.

Keep in mind that everyone experiences anxiety at times. Indeed, anxiety problems are common in the general population. Everyone has some small set of routines. It is our capacity to cope with alterations to these routines and accommodate the unexpected that is important. Recognizing anxiety traits in oneself is not always easy, but the following sections should assist you to identify whether you have behaviours that should be discussed with at least the student counsellor, or your therapist.

Anxiety disorders in young adults, especially those with AS, take a number of forms, which include (1) social anxiety disorder; (2) panic attacks; (3) generalized anxiety disorder; (4) obsessive compulsive disorder. These conditions are very distressing and disruptive, but it is important to remember that they can be treated.

SOCIAL ANXIETY DISORDER

Many students with AS will have had a difficult time socially in school. They often suffer considerable fear and anxiety. Anyone who has experienced being rebuffed, rejected, excluded or isolated in social situations understandably becomes very afraid and anxious about these experiences being repeated. Consequently you may desire to avoid social situations as much as possible. For instance, you may avoid parties, barmitzvahs, weddings, and so on. Avoidance in turn leads to further social isolation, which can worsen your situation. Social anxiety disorder is a common condition in people with AS. It can become overpowering if not properly addressed.

Edward had been a very successful postgraduate student. He had very little social contact in college and lived at home. His postgraduate research work was singular and he avoided teamwork where possible. He was appointed to a teaching position at another college after his PhD. Edward had tremendous difficulty adjusting to teaching duties. Other staff noticed that he was reserved, and was never seen entering or leaving his office though he was 'about' the place. Subsequently, Edward was discovered entering and leaving his office via a window. The Dean advised him to see a psychiatrist. Subsequently it emerged that Edward dreaded passing through the busy concourse of students on his way to his office. His only logical option (his words) was to avail himself of his window. His psychiatrist eventually diagnosed him as suffering from a social anxiety disorder and AS.

This condition often begins in adolescence. The central problem here is a fear of scrutiny by other people in comparatively small groups (as opposed to crowds). The individual feels he or she will act in a way that will be humiliating or embarrassing. This fear then leads on to feelings of anxiety, hand tremor, blushing, progressing to panic attacks in the feared social situation. In turn these intense feelings of anxiety, if unresolved, result in avoidance of the situation. This avoidance then interferes with one's normal routine and one's academic and social functioning. This condition can result in nonattendance at tutorials, classes, lab sessions, etc. As the avoidance increases so does the anxiety about attendance, with resultant loss of academic credits. When avoidance is extreme it can lead to complete social isolation.

PANIC ATTACKS

Panic attacks are sudden feelings of intense fear and terror. Your heart beats very quickly and may feel as if it is pounding in your chest. Your hands may be shaking and you may be sweating. You feel overwhelmed by fear. You may have a pain in your stomach. You may believe you are seriously ill and about to die. Panic attacks are not uncommon among people with AS. New environments, new routines, and strangers all exacerbate any fear of uncertainty.

Although an attack usually lasts only for a few minutes, most sufferers feel distressed for quite some time afterwards. Panic attacks can occur every time you are in a particular situation. One individual with AS, a woman, would suffer a panic attack any time she approached a particular roundabout in her car. The roundabout had six exits. She was extremely fearful that she would take the wrong exit, with resulting uncertainty. The situation is a trigger. However, panic attacks may happen suddenly for no apparent reason whatsoever. Sometimes panic attacks can occur in other illnesses, for example depression. People who experience panic attacks often have other anxiety symptoms, including obsessive compulsive disorder or generalized anxiety disorder. Frequently these are accompanied by depression.

WHAT CAUSES PANIC ATTACKS?

Panic attacks can be triggered by stressful events such as not knowing what to do in a situation, being ridiculed by others, misunderstanding a social context, relationship breakdown, disappointments, the death of someone supportive, and other stressful incidents. There is some evidence that anxiety disorders also have a genetic component. However, the good news is that panic attacks can be successfully treated. You do not have to put up with them. If you are experiencing panic attacks, even if only once a year, you are advised to seek help from your student counsellor or your therapist.

GENERALIZED ANXIETY DISORDER (GAD)

Communication is pretty much a multitasking affair. Lots of inputs from the environment have to be processed and are competing for your attention. Anyone with AS finds it extremely difficult to consciously focus on what other people are actually saying and on how and what they are communicating nonverbally. Trying to understand what is happening in a conversation, while at the same time having to plan how to respond and remembering turn taking, can be overwhelming in certain contexts. Achieving some measure of social success can be very hard won. A minority of those with AS may be so afraid and anxious about their performance that they will be in a constant state of uncontrollable fear, worry and anxiety. This is a condition called generalized anxiety disorder (GAD). It is a long-term condition which often persists for many years before diagnosis and treatment. GAD is an illness which interferes with everyday life. It will cause underperformance in any job. It has associated physical symptoms, just like anxiety. If you worry excessively about minor things, are tense most days and anxious most of the time, then it is likely that you have a generalized anxiety disorder. When worry, anxiety and tension persist for six months or more they constitute a disorder. Symptoms of GAD include:

- nervousness or restlessness
- poor concentration
- irritable or depressed mood
- muscle tension
- disturbed sleep.

Many people with GAD also feel depressed about life and the vicious cycle of anxiety which is their everyday experience. This condition usually starts in adult life and is more common in women than men.

WHAT CAUSES GENERALIZED ANXIETY DISORDER?

Research indicates that biological factors, family background and life experiences are important contributors to the triggering and maintenance of this condition. The communication difficulties of people with AS make them more vulnerable to developing the condition. The fear of committing a miscommunication can cause immense anxiety. Many sufferers report an increase in stressful positive or negative life events in the months or even years prior to the onset of the condition. This condition often coexists with other anxiety disorders, including alcohol and drug abuse problems. However, again the point to remember is that GAD is treatable, but you will need professional medical assistance.

OBSESSIVE COMPULSIVE DISORDER (OCD)

People with AS do not like departing from routines. Routines are reliable, predictable and in a sense certain. Some people may even develop symptoms of obsessive compulsive disorder (OCD) as a result of their attachment to routines. The performance of rituals is often a feature of OCD. This is a condition which usually begins in late childhood or adolescence. It affects between 1 to 2 per cent of the general population and is not uncommon in people with AS. It is characterized by obsessions and compulsions.

Obsessions are unwanted, repetitive, intrusive thoughts. The commonest are listed below:

- fear of contamination by dirt or germs
- being overly concerned about symmetry or the orderly arrangement of things
- fear of aggressive impulses
- worrying about unusual sexual thoughts
- having doubts about things they know they should not be worried about.

Compulsions are urges to carry out rituals. There are a number of different rituals which people perform. The commonest types include:

- washing and hand washing
- checking

- measuring

- counting

- hoarding

- a need to ask or confess.

A ritual helps relieve the fear and anxiety created by obsessive thoughts. Rituals can be very time-consuming. They can interfere with all aspects of your life. For instance, some people may take many hours to complete all their rituals in the morning before leaving the house. A simple five-minute task may take hours to complete once the rituals are observed.

Martha had been diagnosed with AS at age 14. She had to leave home and travel overseas to attend college. In college she had developed a number of rituals which she performed just before leaving her rooms in the morning. These included repeated hand washing and teeth brushing, counting of her clean clothes, and closing all the cupboard doors and room doors in a particular order. If the order was interrupted by her room-mate, she would start the ritual again. Foodstuffs were stacked in a particular order in the kitchen. She was so frustrated with her room-mate's lack of concern for the 'correct' stacking order that eventually she began storing food in her room. She also had rituals associated with using the library and taking lecture notes. In these last instances, she would only take notes on a certain type of paper and using certain pens for different points. She would only sit in certain seats. If a lecture proceeded too quickly, she would become very anxious as not all of the topics could receive the same amount of attention with coloured pens. Frequently, she would stop taking notes during a 'fast' lecture and simply rock in her seat. Martha's parents had arranged for her to meet the student counsellor regularly. The counsellor realized that Martha was experiencing great difficulty adjusting to her new environment and referred her to a psychiatrist. He in turn diagnosed Martha with OCD, and prescribed medication and worked out a management plan with the student services. The college agreed to provide her with daily access to the counselling services until her symptoms had disappeared.

Martha's OCD is not uncommon. However, her capacity to be an effective student was rapidly disappearing. She was fortunate in that the support was there when she needed it. Among people that like routines, OCDs are not uncommon. However, if obsessions and rituals 'overpower' your life you should seek the help of a medical doctor.

Coping with fear, stress and anxiety disorders

If you are experiencing any of the conditions described above, you should tell your student counsellor (or therapist). He or she will recommend that you approach a medical doctor for help. There are a number of specific anxiety reduction measures that you can use to help reduce your level of anxiety, regardless of whatever form it takes. These include general stress management measures, which are described below.

Practising a number of fear and anxiety reduction strategies on a daily basis takes very little time and can give you huge rewards. You can learn to relax by attending a relaxation class, or you could buy a relaxation cassette tape or CD and listen to it every day. A wide variety of relaxation techniques can help relieve muscle tension and 'racing heart' caused by excessive stress. You could very easily incorporate the following two exercises into your everyday life.

MUSCLE RELAXATION

You can do these exercises sitting in a comfortable chair or lying down. Remember to breathe in and out slowly and evenly. Breathe out as slowly as you can manage (obviously not to the point of discomfort).

1. Tense up your shoulders so they almost reach your ears. Hold them there as you count slowly to ten. Then let go and relax.

2. Pull your elbows into the sides of your body. Bend your arms upwards so your hands touch your shoulders, and then clench your fists as tightly as you can. Hold this position as you count slowly to ten, and then let go and relax.

3. Tighten your stomach muscles. Hold as you count slowly to ten. Let go and relax.

4. Focus on your feet on the ground. Tighten your thigh muscles and curl your toes. Hold tightly as you count slowly to ten. Let go and relax.

5. Concentrate on your breathing. Take in a deep breath. Hold it for a few seconds and slowly let go. As you let go, loosen the muscles on your face and forehead, so your eyes and eyelids feel heavier. Gradually let your jaw slacken. Let your shoulders and stomach loosen. Let your arms and legs feel heavier.

6. Continue breathing slowly and evenly until you feel quiet, heavy and warm.

BREATHING EXERCISES

Breathing exercises can be practised several times per day. They can be used before you go into a stressful situation, and you can continue them while in the situation to help you feel calmer. Taking deep breaths will help you manage panic attacks. The exercises are very straightforward and no one will notice you practising them. If you become fearful in a social situation, it will help if you remember to practise the following exercise in particular:

1. Breathe in slowly and deeply.

2. Count to five as you breathe in.

3. Hold your breath for a few seconds and then slowly count to five as you breathe slowly out.

4. The deeper you breathe, the more you will relax.

5. Do this six times and if you still feel very anxious do it again.

Treatments for anxiety disorders

There are a number of different treatment approaches for anxiety disorders. These include different types of psychotherapy and/or medication. All of these treatments will be enhanced by the regular practice of relaxation and tension-reducing exercises. It is important to seek a therapist who is familiar with nonverbal communication problems.

Psychotherapy services are increasingly accessible. Many colleges will offer or will be able to access these services. If you choose any of these therapies it is essential to find a therapist who has an understanding of autistic spectrum disorders. Behavioural therapy can be useful in dealing with anxiety disorders. Psychodynamic psychotherapy, where there is a focus on the action part of the self, may also be beneficial. Cognitive behavioural therapy can be appealing to some people with AS. However, psychoanalytic psychotherapy focusing on the unconscious is not recommended.

Medication is a very useful treatment for anxiety disorders. Different types of medication are given for short-term and long-term treatment of these conditions. Many people with disabling anxiety problems find that medication makes a substantial difference to their quality of life. The most commonly prescribed medications for these disorders are called selective serotonin re-uptake inhibitors (SSRIs). They have positive effects on anxiety, obsessive compulsive disorder, social phobia and depression. These medications can also be used to help relieve some of the obsessional features of AS (e.g. Prozac and Seroxat are well-known brands). However, all medication must only be taken if prescribed by a medical doctor.

Depression in AS

Depression is a common condition affecting a substantial proportion of the general population at any one time. Unsurprisingly, it is even more common in people with AS (and it is usually a reactive type depression). Depression is a medical condition affecting how you feel, how you think and how you behave. It is different to just being 'down in the dumps' or feeling fed up for a few days. Depression frequently coexists with anxiety problems, which is one of the reasons why anyone with AS needs to monitor their moods very frequently.

What is depression?

Depression is when your mood is low, you have lost interest in life and you are not enjoying regular activities any more. In addition these depressive feelings are present nearly every day and persist for at least two weeks. When you are very depressed, you feel worthless and 'bad' about yourself. Your world looks 'black' and terrible, and you feel your future is bleak and hopeless. As the depression deepens, you may feel most of the time that life is not worth living. At this stage, you may have suicidal thoughts and feel like harming yourself. Depression can have extremely serious effects on every aspect of your daily life. It should never be left untreated.

How do I know if I am depressed or not?

Use your electronic diary to record your daily feelings. This will help you decide if you should talk to the student counsellor. Read through the following list of symptoms (see box). If you have one of the first two symptoms and have five or more of the other symptoms most days over a two-week period, you probably have a depressive disorder. You should make an appointment to discuss these symptoms with a medical doctor if the student counsellor is not available. Do not ignore symptoms of depression.

What causes depression?

Depression in people with AS may begin in adolescence as social communication demands increase. At this stage you may become much more sharply aware of being different from others. You can feel very alone and misunderstood. This can last into early adulthood and even through college years. Stressful situations such as a change of routine, loneliness, job/college problems, financial difficulties and understanding strange peers can be contributory factors in the development of depressive symptoms and depression.

Depression can also occur in AS for all the reasons why people without AS get depressed. These include the loss through death of an understanding relative or close friend. It can occur after relationship breakdown. It can be triggered by a series of disappointments or negative life events. It is important to remember that depression is not a sign of weakness. It is not your fault if you have become depressed. Depression can be treated. If you are depressed, do not keep it to yourself. Tell your parents or family members if you feel depressed, as well as the student

Symptoms of depression

Do you have either or both of the first two symptoms and any other five symptoms most days for most of the day, and for at least two weeks?

1. Loss of interest in things you used to enjoy, including sex.

2. Feeling blue, sad or down in the dumps.

3. Feeling restless, slowed down or unable to sit still.

4. Feeling worthless or guilty.

5. Increase or decrease in appetite or weight.

6. Thoughts of death or suicide; suicide attempts.

7. Problems concentrating, thinking, remembering or making decisions.

8. Trouble sleeping or sleeping too much.

9. Loss of energy or feeling tired all the time.

10. Other aches and pains most of the time.

11. Digestive problems.

12. Sexual problems.

13. Feeling pessimistic or hopeless.

14. Being anxious or worried.

counsellor or your therapist. Depression does not get better by keeping it secret. Seek help and treatment for it.

Ask to see the college doctor if you feel you need to be assessed urgently. Make out a list of your symptoms and bring it with you to show the doctor. Explain to the doctor that you have AS and that you think you are depressed. The doctor will be able to advise you about whether or not you have depression and what sort of treatment you should have. The doctor may prescribe medication for you. He or she may wish to refer you to a psychiatrist. Obviously they will refer you back to the college support services if you do not already have a connection with them.

Treatments for depression

Treatments for depression consist of psychotherapy, medication or a combination of the two. In severe cases psychiatric hospitalization may be necessary. As with anxiety disorders, it is more useful to choose a therapist who is familiar with autistic spectrum disorders. There are different types of psychotherapy, and people with AS are more likely to find psychotherapy that focuses on the action part of the self more helpful. One form of psychotherapy that is useful in mild to moderate depression is cognitive behavioural therapy. Its particular approach can be useful to students. If the student services do not offer this service directly, they can possibly arrange an external therapist. This type of therapy involves weekly attendance, keeping a mood diary, recording negative thoughts, learning to identify negative thoughts, and challenging these negative thoughts. All of this involves learning to correct these negative thought patterns and to substitute them with positive self-affirming thoughts. You should ask your therapist for regular reviews of your progress, to ensure that you are getting some benefit from the therapy. Again, psychoanalytic psychotherapy focusing on the unconscious is not helpful.

Antidepressant medication

Sometimes people may feel so depressed that it is not possible to engage in psychotherapy. At this point, you probably need your doctor to prescribe antidepressant medication for you. This medication is not addictive. You may have to be patient as it does not work immediately. It will help to improve your sleep initially, usually in the first week, and gradually over the next few weeks your mood will lift. You may need to stay on this medication for three to six months or longer and it is wise to be guided in this by your doctor or psychiatrist. The SSRI group of antidepressants not only is effective in relieving the symptoms of depression, but also can relieve distressing obsessional thinking. There are some reports that these drugs also have an impact on the social deficits in AS.

Antidepressant medication and psychotherapy

For many people this combination is the best treatment in the short, medium and long term. In your therapy you can learn ways of coping with and preventing the return of the negative thoughts and feelings that are the hallmarks of depression.

Your doctor may refer you to a psychiatrist. People respond differently to different medications and you may need to be assessed by a psychiatrist to ascertain what is best for you by way of therapy and medication. Of course, you may be attending a psychiatrist regularly anyway.

Other treatments may include admission to a psychiatric hospital. This may be necessary if outpatient treatment was insufficient or if you feel very depressed, suicidal, have made suicidal acts or are thought to be a risk to yourself or to others. It is important to remember that the world of the depressed person is a very different world from that of most of us. On these occasions, depression is like a lens that twists things out of focus. When this happens, the depressed person may not understand that the various services are trying to help.

Self-medication is harmful

There is nothing easier than deciding to put off a trip to the counsellor or therapist to discuss one's moods. The usual refrain is that everything will be better tomorrow. You may also feel unable adequately to articulate what is wrong, and decide that it is better left unarticulated. Often you may feel too embarrassed to look for help and decide, as an alternative, that self-medication is an option. By self-medication we mean medicating oneself with whatever drugs you decide are appropriate. Apart from the implied illegality of any such action, it is also very dangerous. Never take any medication that has not been prescribed for you by a qualified medical doctor.

Alcohol and drug abuse

Some studies have suggested that the rate of alcohol abuse may be very high in people with AS. In college a certain amount of social activity centres on bars and you need to be responsible about your alcohol intake. You do not have to drink alcohol to excess just because everyone else seems to be doing so. Peer pressure is not necessarily beneficial. Some people use alcohol to excess, to relieve symptoms of anxiety and depression. It may give some temporary relief but you are likely to feel much worse later.

Drinking a lot of alcohol regularly will affect your health and be detrimental to your studies. You may also discover that stopping drinking is not easy if you drink regularly to excess. If you want to drink alcohol you would be wise to restrict your drinking to a maximum of two units of alcohol per day and preferably not every day (one unit is a half-pint of beer or a measure of spirits).

There are very few reports of people with AS abusing drugs apart from Gunilla Gerland, whose choices seem to have been due to peer pressure and her desire to be part of a social group. Taking illegal drugs is not a good idea. If you do take them, your ability to study will be affected. You may find it more difficult to attend your lectures and finish your assignments in time and as a result you are likely to jeopardize your academic career. Moreover, the effects of the drugs on your health can vary from mild to very extreme. It is essential to remember that the possession of illegal drugs is a crime and could result in your being charged, convicted and possibly having to leave college.

Suicide: the illogical choice

Suicide may appear a logical choice when you are so overpowered by negative depressive feelings that you no longer wish for a future. This is a point of utter despair. However, you should always bear in mind that no one has a copy of tomorrow's newspaper. You cannot predict how things will be in a month or a year from now. You can have strong beliefs about the future, but you cannot know it. Suicide is therefore always an illogical choice.

SUICIDAL THOUGHTS AND ACTS

Suicidal thoughts are not uncommon in people with AS. Some people, from a young age, have reported thinking a lot about death and having suicidal thoughts. If you have suicidal feelings or if you are thinking about suicidal acts you should tell someone you trust. You should seek professional help immediately. Many people who have felt very suicidal and have made suicidal acts and survived have felt very differently the next day. Frequently people who have survived suicide attempts have ended up physically disabled or even brain-damaged. Suicide is not an experiment.

Some other conditions to note

Several other conditions may affect people with AS and we mention them briefly for the sake of completeness.

ATTENTION DEFICIT HYPERACTIVITY DISORDER (ADHD)

Many young people with AS also have attention deficit hyperactivity disorder (ADHD). This is a disorder where there are problems with applying attention and sustaining attention to tasks. In addition, non completion of tasks, impairment of organizational skills, impulsivity and sometimes hyperactivity are often noticed. In people whose symptoms are severe enough to meet diagnostic criteria, treatment with psychostimulant drugs is well worthwhile. The main medication used is called methylphenidate (also known by the names Ritalin or Concerta). This medication reduces distractibility, hyperactivity and impulsivity and increases attention.

MANIC DEPRESSIVE ILLNESS

This is an illness where episodes of severe depression or mania, or both, occur. It is an illness affecting 1 per cent of the general population. It can be treated by psychiatrists with mood stabilizing drugs which are generally effective. Manic depression causes rapid mood swings between extraordinary highs, when life is exaggeratedly marvellous, and very deep lows, when everything is hopeless. This oscillation between abnormal elation and extremely severe depression is what gives the disorder its name. It can be treated with mood stabilizing drugs such as lithium.

SCHIZOPHRENIA

In the past, a small number of adults with AS have been misdiagnosed with schizophrenia. This has occurred due to lack of knowledge about the nature of AS. The clinician will have been unaware of the effects of AS on how people think, feel, communicate and behave. A psychiatrist might ask a person with AS if they hear voices of people who are not present. The person may answer yes but in fact he or she is referring to voices that could be heard in the next room. Therefore the person is not experiencing hallucinations. This type of response, in addition to the verbal and nonverbal communication deficits and other symptoms of AS, may be misleading to professionals unfamiliar with the condition.

Managing stress effectively

It is important to look after your own mental health. Here are some general self-care measures which will help strengthen your reserves in coping with stress. Regular exercise has a positive effect on your mood. Physical exercise releases endorphins in your brain which make you feel good. Even small amounts of exercise make a difference. Exercise helps to reduce feelings of stress and anxiety. Try to make exercise a part of your everyday life. For instance, get up half an hour earlier and go for a walk. Use the stairs instead of the lift or escalator. Go to the gym or go swimming a few times a week. In addition try to maintain a regular routine with the following.

- Get active and keep fit.

- Practise relaxation exercises every day. You could try yoga, tai chi and progressive muscle relaxation.

- Do something you enjoy every day.

- Remember to think about what you are good at, and say something positive to yourself every day.

- Try to do something positive for yourself every day. Try to say or do something positive for someone else every day. Think and act positively.

Recommendations for thinking ahead: one year from now

Starting college is a daunting experience. If you are prone to developing anxiety or depression symptoms, you need a number of mental health measures in place to help prevent problems from getting out of control or recurring. If you are experiencing a lot of difficulties with your social relationships, there is a lot you can do to help yourself. There are a number of general mental health pointers that will help you enjoy your life in college more. These repeat some of the advice given in earlier parts of the book, but they are so important that they are worth repeating.

1. Practise daily stress management strategies including relaxation strategies. Keep a daily diary of your moods.

2. Get to know the student support service when you start at college, or beforehand if possible. Find out who the student counsellor is and how you can access him or her. Foreknowledge again. After you start college it would be a good idea to contact the student counsellor a few times so they get to know you a little. Then if you are feeling bad or develop any difficulties you can arrange to meet them to discuss your problems.

3. If there is a support group on campus for people with AS, find out about it and go along to their meetings.

4. Attend a social skills group for people with AS if there is one available in your area.

If you follow through on the recommendations in this chapter, reflect back on your situation a year from now and notice the difference. Keep your electronic diary up to date. Yes, it is a pain at times, but weekly reviews will show you just how much you have experienced during the week and how you have reacted.

Increasingly college environments are becoming more supportive. Use their resources wisely, but do use them. Always remember that you have the intellectual skills to succeed, but you need to look after your mental well-being while travelling the path to academic success.

9 Establishing an AS Support Group

Ideally an AS support group will already exist on campus. Many colleges are fostering development of self-help support groups and if your college is far sighted you will have access to one on campus. An existing support group may well operate as a college student society rather than under the umbrella of the student support services. You may find the recommendations in this book useful in your support group.

Support groups may serve two purposes. First, a support group may double as a social skills group which is managed by the student counselling services, but that would be unusual. Social skills groups will have a large therapeutic input from student services. They will be managed by the experts from the counselling services. If there is not a campus-based programme, then contact the local branch of your national Asperger association to see if there is one nearby. We would expect the student counsellor to have this information in any event. Second, a support group will act as a friendship society to help people with AS meet each other and exchange information. The main business of a support group is to foster these activities. A support group tends to be 'owner' managed (run by its members) with often no official input from the college. There is nothing to prevent a support group offering social skills classes and advice, and in fact most will do this at some level informally. However, social skills groups in contrast operate like formal classes or tutorials. People go to them to cover specific social skills lessons. They are very definitely learning contexts designed to follow a social skills curriculum with structured goals. So in your own mind draw a sharp line distinguishing between social skills groups in terms of aims, and support groups in terms of structure. Both aim to offer support and advice on a variety of communication issues, but they package their objectives differently.

There are lots of support groups in existence addressing the needs of people throughout society. The most common ones cater for people with alcohol, drug and marital problems and by and large will be of little relevance to students with AS. Others cater for students with specific medical diagnoses. Support groups are not treatment groups. This is important to grasp. However, they have a valuable role in sustaining people who are taking courses of treatment. They can help with treatment by encouraging a member of the group to stay the course and by providing feedback from other members. For example, a social skills group (which is a type of treatment programme) may last for 12 weeks with as many as three two-hour classes each week. Many classes will involve role play. If you were on such a course from time to time you might find the schedule demanding and the role play stressful and exhausting. You might go through periods of being downhearted due to your performance. In fact you may get so downhearted that you might consider leaving the course altogether. It is at this point that a support group can be very useful. Other members will offer you encouragement and the benefit of their experiences with the same social skills programme. Knowing that other people have an understanding of your self-doubt and frustration can help you overcome the challenges and complete the course.

The dos and don'ts of a student society

If a support group already exists, you will not want to set up a rival group. Join the existing one and learn to enjoy being in it. Over time you will also learn how to make appropriate contributions to enhance the 'mission' of the support group. Since support groups are owner managed each member has a responsibility to keep the group functioning. A group will wither away unless there is regular attendance. Every support group has a collection of similar housekeeping tasks that members must be willing to do for the group to survive. When we mention 'you' we mean 'you plus a few collaborators'. A student society cannot be formed by just one person, obviously. However, if you are driving the formation of the society, you will be the leader in any initiative.

In what follows we outline several issues that will arise if you are planning to set up an AS support group in college, and also maintain that group. Points about the latter are more relevant to existing groups. We have a few recommendations for setting up a support group. One recommendation is to consider defining your support group as a regular college society with open membership, rather than a group only open to those diagnosed with AS. An informal group is by definition not an official college society. Colleges have clear guidelines for funding college societies and your proposed group could do better financially by declaring itself as a college society. You can still call it a group, by the way, but the official college sanction is usually financially beneficial. Investigate the financial pros and cons of one society identity over another before committing yourself (and your supporters) to a particular choice. We are back to foreknowledge and planning again.

Are there similar societies?

Before deciding that an AS support group should be established, find out if there are any existing college societies or informal groups fulfilling this role. The student counselling service should know this. In a very large college, there are many small societies and informal groups that meet regularly but hardly publicize their existence. You may come across a friendship society or a society specifically for those in their first year in college that will be of use to you. Yet unless they have an AS-oriented outlook, the social benefits, while good, may be less than you would like.

Assuming that there is a group, ascertain whether it meets as an official college society or an informal one. If you are a member of a college society, you will have access to rooms, facilities and funds for social occasions. If it meets as an informal group, this may indicate that the college has decided against granting it college society status. This will not affect you in any personal sense, but the group will have less funds and more restricted access to resources as a result.

Colleges may not be equally enthusiastic about having an official AS support group. We know of one college that refused official college society status to the group. The college argued that such a society could be seen as promoting 'illness'. As a result the group had very limited access to meeting rooms as well as photocopying and printing facilities. When all activities are being managed on a voluntary basis, such restrictions can handicap the development of a group.

Clear objectives

If you have decided that a new AS support group is required as an official college society, or you have decided to 'convert' an existing support group, then you will need to state its objectives clearly. If the national AS association has a local chapter, it may be able to assist you. Certainly you should solicit a letter of support from it. The memorandum of agreement defines the main objectives and activities of the society. Usually the memorandum has some legal status and colleges are keen that the memorandum follows a prescribed format. You can access this through the college society office or your students' union club. It is best to work closely with the college society officer when drawing up a memorandum as he or she will have a better idea of what type of memorandum profile is most likely to be acceptable to the college authorities.

A typical support group objective is: *the promotion of the social integration of students with AS*. This is adequate, but if you want to sell the idea to the college you could consider expanding it as follows: *the promotion of the social integration of students with AS to improve their academic performance*. In the first example, the students gain from the society, but in the second both the students and the college gain from the existence of the society. You may be required to state that the society will also admit students with a research interest in AS.

You can add many other objectives, of course, but our advice is to be conservative and curb any enthusiasm for producing exhaustive lists of objectives. Ask the student counsellor to review any list of objectives before submitting one to the college society officer.

Definite demand

By definition a group or a society must have more than one member in order to function. A college is unlikely to sanction the formation of a new society that has less then a set number of members. The actual number may vary depending on the college. Assessing the demand for a support group is not trivial. Student support services will have a good estimate of how many with AS are in your college, but you and your collaborators may have to survey sections of the student population to get an accurate estimate of how many would join your group. If you are involved with a social skills group, you can estimate how many from that would be interested in your new group. It is important to take time over the survey lest any questions arise about its accuracy.

Prepare yourself for some disappointment however. You are likely to have overestimated the potential number of members. Moreover, not everyone that in your view should join will join. Also avoid estimates that included 'undiagnosed students with AS'. The business of a support group is to support those who are diagnosed, not to diagnose others. Avoid conflating these two roles, otherwise the college authorities will not look favourably on your proposal.

Drafting a proposal

Your proposal will consist of a brief statement outlining the purposes of the group, what activities it will engage in, how many members it is likely to attract, how you plan to attract members, how it intends to fund itself and what contribution it will make to college life. The memorandum of agreement will capture the purposes and objectives. A separate document, usually called the articles of association, is required to describe how the group will manage its activities. The articles describe the committee structure of the group, the quorum for the group and how its meetings are to be conducted. In addition, the articles describe procedures for electing the society's officers (the people who will run it). Normally a member of the academic staff will act as the society's patron. A chairperson (often called an auditor), secretary and treasurer will be elected by the society's members. Depending on the college, a society may be expected to produce a separate constitution of rules governing all of its activities. However, the articles of association are usually sufficient.

Colleges will have certain requirements that a society must meet, and these must be included in the articles. The college society officer will advise on the relevant details. You will have to decide whether a facilitator is required when considering the composition of the society's committee. A facilitator could be the student counsellor or a sympathetic member of the academic staff. A support group should manage its own affairs, but a facilitator may help resolve disputes between people and generally ensure that one person's wishes do not dominate the society's activity schedule. You may need to consider having two facilitators should one not be available for meetings. Depending on resources, you might consider having an external expert on AS to advise on matters occasionally. Before nominating staff members as facilitators within the proposal, discuss it with them. It is sensible to nominate staff who have an understanding of AS.

Once your proposal is completed and all the details have been checked with the college society officer, it will be put before a board in the college for consideration. At this point you wait for a decision.

Liaison with college services

When defining the activities of the society it is also worthwhile involving the counselling services and getting the benefit of their experience. They will check that the proposed activities are achievable within the college context. There must be no hint of any likely interference with academic studies.

To aid the presentation of the proposal, ask for letters of support from the student counselling services. The college authorities will be more reassured once they learn that the proposal has the support of the counselling services. In the proposal you will have to explain how you plan to attract members. The counselling services can help answer that question. For all kinds of legal reasons, it is very important to avoid any suggestion that your society will engage in its own diagnosis of students.

If you do not receive support from the counselling services, making the case to the college for the proposed society will be very difficult, if not impossible. It is best to explore proposal options with the counselling services early on in the planning process.

Making the case formally

If your proposal is sufficiently researched and argued, then there will be no requirement to elaborate any further. However, if there is a concern about any aspect of your proposal, you and your proposed committee may be invited to meet several senior figures in the college for a discussion. It is crucial that this discussion, which is really you explaining aspects of the proposal, goes smoothly. It will help your case if the student counsellor and your chosen facilitator can be in attendance. If they cannot attend, you will have to fend the questions as best you can.

Any student would find this situation nerve-racking. Make sure you greet the assembled people respectfully. Then ask whether you could briefly explain what AS is, and why you are motivated to establish a group and seek college support. If you have prepared well, you will have rehearsed your opening position statements. Ask the student counsellor to time your delivery. You are not delivering a lecture. Remember not to interrupt when being questioned and do not become angry. If you cannot answer a question there and then, respond with something like: *I am glad you raised that issue. I cannot give you a satisfactory answer now, but I will come back to you with an answer in the next few days if that is acceptable?*

At the end of the discussion ask the college representatives (1) if they have any more questions or whether everything been clarified to their satisfaction, and (2) when they will inform you of their decision.

Membership, money and management

A college society is expected to keep an accurate record of its registered members. Members are expected to pay an annual fee. Most colleges will give an additional allowance to the society depending on its size. Every society is required to keep accurate records of income and expenditure. Generally the treasurer manages the society's funds, and money is only spent with the agreement of the academic patron (though arrangements may vary from college to college). Money management is an important responsibility and it is essential that all expenditure is properly receipted and noted in the society's accounts. Membership fees vary, but you will need to decide on a fee that students are willing to pay.

Most expenditure is on refreshments after meetings, costs for having guest speakers, and printing/photocopying costs. The annual general meeting of the society combines the election of new officers with a party atmosphere so you will need to set more money aside for this meeting than routine ones. Until the society is established, the committee should involve the facilitator in making any major expenditure decisions.

Acceptance is only half the battle

Student societies do not run themselves. A small dedicated number of people, usually the committee, work hard at keeping the society visible and attracting members and visiting speakers. With a support group the demand for visiting speakers will be light. A support group will focus on helping members relate their positive and negative experiences, and how best they can be supported in dealing with stress.

Having a society endorsed by the college, or even an informal group, is no guarantee of success. All those months of painstaking work that went into establishing the group will be ineffective unless a reasonable membership is developed.

Meetings and motivation

The reality of student societies is that one or two people usually put in most of the work to keep their society afloat. This requires holding regular meetings with an agenda. A facilitator is often useful as a referee to ensure that appropriate turn taking occurs. A short weekly 'discussion topic' agenda is helpful for focusing each meeting and motivating attendance. Topics should be drawn from problematical interaction contexts, and members should have the opportunity to suggest topics for discussion. Topics should be meaningful within the everyday context of college life. Useful topics could include, for instance, the library borrowing procedures, the new canteen layout, the tutor's language on course X, etc.

A good topic is one that focuses on problems that are seemingly ordinary and routine in student life. Discussions about the latest holographic technology, the Big Bang theory and so forth are too academic and should be discouraged. Limiting meetings to three topics each time is a good idea. Try to put closure on the discussion of a topic, rather than have it 'dog' the agenda for several weeks and months. A facilitator can help here during the initial establishing period of the society. Likewise, if a member is clearly depressed the facilitator may be best at spotting it and also the best one to persuade the member to make an appointment with the student counsellor.

It is important to provide refreshments for people after each meeting. Someone has to organize this and agree to do so reliably. Do not treat this responsibility as trivial. People will not be motivated to return if there is not even a cup of coffee at the end of each meeting. Usually coffee, tea and some soft drinks are appropriate. You will learn over time how much of each is required. However, you should always maintain a stock of soft drinks in case coffee or tea run out. Unless a special meeting has been held, convenient snack food is acceptable. If you have invited a speaker to your meeting, perhaps a well-known expert on AS, and you anticipate a bigger meeting than usual, you will need to increase the refreshments. In theory, asking people to notify you if they plan to attend is an excellent strategy as it allows you to decide on exact quantities. In practice, it works at best unevenly. You will need to develop your judgement over time about what works best. Refreshments help people unwind after discussions. As a rule avoid consuming alcohol unless at a formal dinner, perhaps with a prestigious invited speaker.

People with AS may prefer to 'meet' by email first before attending on-campus meetings. You may want to design a website with chatroom facilities as a means to attract new members and motivate existing ones to attend meetings. However, maintaining a website requires time so it is best to share responsibility with other committee members. Use email to send out notices of meetings and always send out reminders at least five days before each meeting.

Motivating people to attend meetings can be very frustrating. Many people with AS will be very uncertain about what to expect. Some will be very put off by the idea of group social contact. There are no convenient answers to these issues. You will have to persevere and try email as an introduction. One word of warning, however, to you and your committee: do not neglect your academic commitments while doing all of this work.

Activity schedules

Activities should be well planned and kept to a reasonable duration (no more than two hours until the group members get to know one another). Activities that force people to talk to each other for hours at a time are unlikely to be constructive. Too many activities are worse than too few as they may increase rather than reduce social anxieties.

What most people want from a support group is support. They are there to share experiences, explore solutions and make friends. Every meeting has to allow some discussion of topics of interest to members. Short excursions are useful but their frequency should be discussed with the facilitator and the group. Asking people what they would like to do is also recommended, but that does not commit you to pursuing every suggestion. Trips to cinemas, art galleries and museums allow very little chance for genuine communication. It is far better to take trips to a shopping centre to facilitate people buying clothes or music CDs. Meals in restaurants with ethnic food can be a mixed success unless people are prepared to be flexible around their food choices. Theme parks are good places to visit. Social outings should be fun. The group should be prepared for at least one really different annual excursion, e.g. a day spent at an equestrian school, rafting, or on a working farm.

Career choices should be explored through a support group. This could involve asking the career guidance services to host a workshop outlining career choices. Representatives from a selection of AS-friendly companies could be invited to explain employment policies and recount experiences. External national AS chapters may help with the costs of such a workshop and also advise on speakers. Successful graduates with AS may be persuaded to give the group the benefit of their experiences from time to time. All of these activities help members focus on the positive career outcomes after graduation.

Involving other student societies

Organizing joint activities with other student societies may help cut costs in certain instances. If your group is keen to have an expert on AS give a lecture, then it makes sense to see if other college societies will share the costs. A psychology society might be interested, for example, in jointly hosting the speaker. Joint activities could be planned with a range of societies to help keep down costs. The question is whether your group would be willing to experiment.

You may also find that other typical students are willing to help organize events and generally help you out. If your group is willing, you might try out a few typical students as facilitators. They could be useful peer models.

Feedback

If you have very high expectations of your group, be prepared for a letdown. Do not expect overnight success and popularity. Your group may start off with half-a-dozen or so members and move either up or down over time. Even when you satisfy the needs of the vast majority in the group, the numbers may remain stubbornly stuck below your estimate.

Collect feedback from members of the group after each college term if at all possible. This will help the committee assess whether the group is moving in a useful direction or whether a rethinking of its purposes is necessary. Anonymous feedback collected from web-hosted forms is more likely to tell you something useful. Studying feedback can be immensely frustrating as often all the work that has been done is ignored and the one or two small glitches are brought into sharp focus. Try to accept the feedback graciously and avoid being drawn into rows with members over comments they may attach. The facilitator could also help you assess the value of the feedback.

Rejection and alternatives

If the college decides that your group will not be recognized as an official college society, you need to consider whether it can be sustained as an informal group. It may still be possible to operate as a group affiliated to another college society (a psychology society being the obvious choice), but the other society may not be keen on an arrangement that dilutes its resources.

Every member of the student body must be eligible to join a college society. In practice this means that every student has the option of joining hordes of societies. Your proposal for a college society could be rejected on the grounds of exclusivity, the implication being that only those with AS are welcome. This is a thorny problem since you probably want only those with AS in your group. You could redefine the group as a society dedicated to research into AS, but this will mean allowing typical students and postgraduate researchers in as members. The cost of the latter move may be the collapse of the vital support component. Colleges vary widely in how they assess support group applications and though we would like it to be otherwise, it is a matter for negotiation at individual college level.

Developing a group outside formal structures

If you choose to operate an informal support group you may encounter problems accessing college rooms for meetings. However, the student support services should help you out and provide a regular meeting place. Whether you will be able to advertise your meetings on official college society noticeboards is another issue for assessment.

The use of official noticeboards for society announcements is established in many colleges. Notices not on the official boards may be removed, and the offending societies could be fined. If you are not an official society, you cannot be fined of course, but you could lose the use of whatever meagre resources are being provided by the student support services. Presumably you will be able to announce your meetings on the support services noticeboards however.

We know of one instance where an informal support group was only allowed use of official society noticeboards once their posters had been passed by the college ethics committee. Clearly this is an unusual situation, but it does highlight the need to work within the established traditions and procedures of one's own college. Students with AS will be immensely enthusiastic in getting their group sanctioned. This is all the more reason to ensure that you are meeting college requirements for society sanction along the way. There are no simple answers. Over time, as the informal group proves that it is a responsible group, it may be possible for it to be converted into a sanctioned college society. The main thing is not to become impatient. Focus on the good work you are doing, rather than on what might have been.

Caveats

There are several strict rules to observe whether you are managing a college society or an informal group. First, if you are in charge of money, be absolutely honest in all your dealings. Any slippage in standards could be disastrous for your social standing. Second, having a mature typical person, preferably from student services, as facilitator will help keep the group focused on support issues. The facilitator will also help manage turn-taking difficulties and ensure that everyone gets heard. Third, many support groups collapse due to personality conflicts among the main initiators. This is another reason to have a facilitator. Finally, do not despair if your membership turnout is low. Many of the other students with AS may not share your enthusiasm and are not ready to move beyond email exchanges yet. All you can do is your best.

Recommendations

In this chapter we have looked at some planning issues that will need to be addressed if you plan to establish an Asperger support group. Not every college will be equally favourable in its assessment of proposals. Your group may end up operating as an informal group under the umbrella of the student services for a few years. There is nothing inherently wrong with this arrangement. AS support groups are not a new phenomenon in regular society, and many colleges are beginning to accept the need to resource greater numbers of student-managed support groups.

In the final analysis, the main focus must always be on what you can do with what you have, rather than regretting not having something more. Topics for discussion should be meaningful. They should be drawn from the everyday lived experience of your student members. You will continue to motivate students to attend if their problems with the banal and the mundane are acknowledged.

10 Inspirational AS Thinkers and Scientists

An awareness of the valuable positive features of AS has been growing over the past two decades. Researchers have noted a variety of outstanding historical thinkers and scientists who appear to have had symptoms of AS. This is leading to an examination of the impact of autistic spectrum disorders on the growth of scientific knowledge. Since all of these people have passed away, can we reasonably claim they had AS? Any post-mortem psychiatric diagnosis must have a degree of uncertainty in its conclusions. The patient is not around for an interview. Despite drawing comfort from the rule that one cannot libel the dead, one has to be as scrupulous as possible in examining their lives. However, combining what the individuals wrote about themselves, their behaviours and areas of interest, and other contemporaries' reports of the same features, we can reach some reasonable conclusions. We do not say: *Yes, he had AS. No doubt about that.* Nevertheless we can say: *Yes, he had very pronounced AS traits, but he seemed to cope quite well overall.* In other words, a lot of what we know about the individual is consistent with what we know about how people with AS live their lives. We know that there are many highly successful people with undiagnosed AS, particularly in academic pursuits. So it should come as no great surprise that there have been individuals of out-standing talent with AS.

The other point of interest, and inspiration, is that these great thinkers found satisfaction in a variety of areas. The examples in this chapter are drawn from architecture, art, mathematics, music, physics, politics and philosophy.

Traditional association with gifted thinkers

Traditionally, the gifted child has been precocious and independent minded. This was the child that spoke his or her mind, and usually spoke in a manner beyond their years. The child who was different, but more than different – this was the child who was singular. The gifted thinker allies a capacity for redoing things until reaching perfection, with a single-minded pursuit of interests. Inventive and creative, the gifted thinker is a problem solver rather than a problem begetter; the 'little professor' whose appetite for knowledge, coupled with a few eccentric-ities, make him or her a formidable genius. In the classroom the gifted child intrigues both peers and teachers. Is this the scientist or thinker who one day will push back the frontiers of knowledge?

Isaac Newton and Wolfgang Amadeus Mozart were both gifted children with different passions. Newton achieved great success and influence in his lifetime, but Mozart struggled to make a living. Both men were geniuses, and almost certainly both had AS. If we look closely at the lives of other famous people from history, we find that quite a few of them probably had AS. Some of these people were so talented and creative that they are regarded, quite rightly, as geniuses. They have made great contri-butions to human life and technological progress.

In science and mathematics, some of the key developments have been achieved by persons with AS traits: Isaac Newton, Albert Einstein and Paul Dirac. Einstein is particularly interesting. He had great difficulties with conventional schooling and was considered a mediocre college student. It was only when he had time to develop his own passion that he flourished. In philosophy we have Spinoza, Kant and, in the twentieth century, Wittgenstein, and probably Quine. In architecture we have the astonishing work of Gaudi in Barcelona. So complex were his designs that his last work is still being finished 80 years after his death. Though we do not cover them here, we mention in passing that in politics we have the great father of American liberty, Thomas Jefferson, and the leading Irish statesman of the twentieth century, Eamon de Valera. All these individuals have had a large influence on the world. In other fields, the list of highly accomplished people with Asperger syndrome continues. The world would certainly be a less interesting place without imaginative writers such as Jonathan Swift, Lewis Carroll and Hans Christian Andersen; artists such as Vincent van Gogh and Andy Warhol; and composers such as Erik Satie and Bela Bartók.

Playing to AS strengths

The strengths of AS are those associated with great minds:

- a passionate commitment to an idea

- insight and originality in tackling problems

- tremendous capacity to work to a routine, so essential in any advanced intellectual inquiry

- dogged pursuit of perfection in their chosen areas

- a willingness to forgo opulence and excessive materialism in pursuit of their ideals.

As we read through these traits, these strengths, can we doubt that AS has played a large part in defining the scientific outlook?

Of course not everyone with AS will become a great scientist or thinker. This must be acknowledged. However, it is likely that if you are a high achiever academically and have found an area of passionate interest, then you are more likely to make significant progress.

> Intellectually able + AS + Area of passionate interest = Academic success

This rule says that you can have a first-class mind but be a second-class researcher unless you find an area of interest that will become your passion. It is a simple rule. Being bright is not the equivalent of being bright and focused. What separates the academic success stories with AS from the ordinary tales is the matter of focus. We mentioned in Chapter 3 that learning to focus on academic tasks is a critical activity to monitor throughout your time in college. It is easy to become distracted and pursue tangential issues. For rare people, these tangents may become highways leading to great and marvellous discoveries. These are rare cases and it is important to remember that.

Focus, curiosity and desire to understand

Let us take a brief look at some features of AS before going on to consider the achievements of people in science, art, literature and philosophy. Persons with AS can have an enormous capacity for work, and for channelling their energy and attention in a particular direction. They are very persistent and they don't give up easily when they meet obstacles. Successful inventors show many features characteristic of persons with AS, including exceptional analytic ability, mechanical ability, perseverance and capacity for observation, particularly of details.

One inventor who combined tremendous curiosity with an intense desire to understand was Nikola Tesla (1856–1943), the physicist who discovered many of the possibilities of electrical technology. Tesla almost certainly had AS. His innovations were so important to efficient electricity generation that it would be hard to imagine the modern industrial world without them. When he was at college, Tesla suggested to his physics professor that a particular direct-current apparatus would be improved by switching to alternating current. The professor dismissed it as a preposterous idea, but Tesla refused to accept his judgement. He persisted with his experiments. Years later, as he was walking in a city park with a friend, quite suddenly the solution came to him. Alternating current was born. Tesla is a good example of the combination of doggedness and inspiration that has served many inventors and scientists well.

Openness to new ideas

People with AS are less influenced by their environment than others and often do not have preconceived ideas about a particular theory or experiment. History shows us that many have enormous capacity for originality, and do not allow themselves to be smothered by fashionable theories. Many people with AS are almost certainly iconoclasts – people who reject popular beliefs and conventional wisdom. Attraction to original thinking and developing explanations from first principles are common features among thinkers with AS. They like to work things out for themselves. Clearly, there is a potential conflict between openness to new ideas and a fondness for existing rules, and this conflict might have different outcomes in different people's lives. Persons with AS may adhere to rules that they see as fundamental while disregarding rules that they suspect of being arbitrary or limited.

Einstein, for example, was able to revolutionize how we think about the universe, but he was implacably opposed to the micro-world suggested by quantum theory. Likewise, Newton, one of the greatest thinkers and original experimentalists in recorded history, was embroiled in a series of bitter arguments with his scientific contemporaries for most of his life. Newton, despite his innovative genius, was completely intolerant of dissent.

In the sections that follow we will look in more detail at several famous people with AS traits.

Music and mathematics

A number of great composers have had AS traits. They were true musical innovators. Their greatness lies in introducing new forms of music and orchestration. Mozart (1756–91), who was without doubt one of the very greatest of all time, also devoted considerable energies to disputes with rivals. Mozart sometimes behaved naively in social company. He was a poor judge of other people and his mismanagement of money was legendary. Despite these deficits, he was a supremely brilliant composer.

In the last century both Bela Bartók (1881–1945) and Erik Satie (1866–1925) stand out as innovative composers. Both profoundly influenced twentieth-century music, and both had pronounced AS traits. Bartók was obsessed with cataloguing the folk songs of his region. Eventually he produced a huge multivolume catalogue of 7000 assorted folk songs. These songs, however, never made a direct appearance in Bartók's own work, though he borrowed some melodic properties. His later string quartets are often compared favourably to those of Beethoven. Bartók, like Mozart, was less successful in his lifetime than his talent deserved.

His relative failure to capitalize on his acheivements was due to his diffi-culties in managing social and professional relationships.

The French composer Satie created a new influence within French music and rejected the classic trend in French music of his time. Satie, like many innovators with AS, was a determined iconoclast.

Unsurprisingly, mathematics has had its fair share of innovators with AS. We have already mentioned the giants, Newton and Einstein, who were first-rank mathematicians. Almost certainly Galois (1811–32), the inventor of group theory, had AS. He is probably among the most colour-ful, but ultimately tragic thinkers with AS. Galois had difficulties in school from an early age. His respect for authority was largely nonexis-tent throughout his short rakish life. The leading French academy rejected his early mathematical papers as incomprehensible. He had few friends and was a poor judge of character. Legend has it that he wrote his famous paper on the principles of group theory on the night before he died in a duel.

Science

Isaac Newton (1642–1727) is perhaps the most famous person with AS. He is regarded as one of the most important thinkers in recorded history. He was the founding father of modern science. His mathematical creativ-ity produced the infinitesimal calculus, which has been so profoundly important to mathematical and physical modelling. Newton was a work-aholic with an intense capacity to focus on experimentation. He often went without food or sleep when exploring a problem. Unlike Mozart and Bartók, Newton was also financially successful in the wider world. He became President of the Royal Society. In his later years he was appointed Master of the Royal Mint which he promptly reorganized. Newton had a fondness for ritual and occult matters. Strange as it may seem, Newton devoted more time to alchemy than any of his other pursuits.

Albert Einstein (1879–1955) had very pronounced AS traits. He was original and single minded but not particularly attached to conventional schooling. Unlike Newton, Einstein had to struggle to establish his scien-tific and mathematical theories. After he left college he spent time as a patents clerk while developing relativity theory at night. It was by no means obvious that he would be successful, but he persisted with his work despite the scepticism of colleagues. As we know, Einstein's relativistic view of the universe gradually replaced the Newtonian model. Both Newton and Einstein represent the supreme heights of scientific achievement.

Other scientists with AS traits include Gregor Mendel (1822–84) and Charles Darwin (1809–82), two hugely important trailblazers in the fields of genetics and evolution. Both made good use of their AS aptitude for intense focus and repetitive observations. Both were meticulous notetakers and amassed volumes of diaries containing field observations. Mendel was an Austrian monk who discovered the basic laws of genetic inheritance by means of experiments with pea plants in his monastery garden. His work is the foundation for modern genetic theory. He was an obsessive experimentalist and is reckoned to have examined more than 300,000 individual peas in his lifetime, along with tens of thousands of plants. Such perseverance is staggering, but it was essential to test his ideas about genetic inheritance.

Darwin likewise showed an astonishing experimental stamina. He is reckoned to have spent at least eight years meticulously studying small barnacles under a microscope. Coincidentally, both Newton and Darwin only published their main scientific achievements years after they had first documented them. In both cases, they published partly due to fears that others would publish similar results.

Art and architecture

Famous artists who arguably had AS include Vincent van Gogh (1853–90), L.S. Lowry (1887–1976) and Andy Warhol (1928–87) – three very different characters, all of whom produced highly original work and avoided being influenced by others (showing a typical need for independence and control). The Dutch painter Van Gogh was one of the great artists of the nineteenth century. An unusual and tormented man, who famously cut off most of one of his ears, he committed suicide at the age of 37. Throughout Van Gogh's adult life there appears to have been a tension between the solitude that he embraced and the loneliness that plagued him. He managed to produce wonderful works of art that change hands for astronomical sums today, but unfortunately his problems with social relationships meant that his life was not generally a happy one.

The Manchester artist Lowry was an enigmatic man completely devoted to his painting of almost childlike interpretations of industrial society. Regarded as unusual and eccentric by his peers, the style of his work was wholly original. The subjects consisted mainly of industrial or urban scenes from the north of England. Human figures are little more than stick figures in his paintings. There is no doubt that he was an original painter and a genius.

Andy Warhol was the pioneer and leading exponent of pop art, and an influential avant-garde filmmaker. He is heavily associated with cultural upheavals of the 1960s. His typical AS fondness for repetition and routine found its artistic outlet in the mechanical, machine-like nature of the screen printing process. Romanticism was foreign to him. His art was defined by the mechanical production principles.

Antonio Gaudi (1852–1926) was one of the most original and idiosyncratic architects of the last century. Gaudi's architecture is visible throughout Barcelona. In his youth he was considered an average architect. Gradually he persuaded less than a handful of wealthy visionary patrons to give him commissions. Gaudi was a superb visionary thinker. He developed most of his designs through experimenting with 3D models. To compensate for his lack of formal mathematical training in structural engineering, Gaudi hung his models upside down as part of his structural analysis. Like many other autistic people, Gaudi was fascinated by curved forms. He was extremely fond of ritual and religiosity. His last building project, the Sagrada Familia, is perhaps two centuries away from completion. Regarded by his peers as uncommunicative, he was a reserved and committed thinker.

Literature

Three giants of literature who showed strong signs of AS were Jonathan Swift (1667–1745), Lewis Carroll (1832–98) and Hans Christian Andersen (1805–75). All three made their name with original, robust and imaginative work incorporating strong elements of fantasy. (It is not true, as sometimes stated, that people with autism spectrum disorders lack imagination.) The Danish author Hans Christian Andersen has a secure place among the world's great storytellers. He wrote many plays, poems, travel books and novels. His lasting fame has been as a writer for children, with stories such as 'The Ugly Duckling', 'The Emperor's New Clothes' and 'The Tin Soldier'. Many of his stories have autistic themes.

Lewis Carroll (his real name was Charles Dodgson) was an enigmatic English clergyman and mathematics professor. He was renowned as being both socially awkward and socially reserved. He appears to have preferred the company of children over adults. The phenomenal success of the children's classics *Alice's Adventures in Wonderland* and *Through the Looking Glass* made him a household name. It is noteworthy that Alice's main difficulties are in understanding the motives and intentions of the other characters. She is constantly tripped up by language difficulties.

This theme of cultural otherness and alienation also dominates much of the work of Jonathan Swift. He was an Irish clergyman and a major author, propagandist, polemicist and pamphleteer in his day. His best-known work is *Gulliver's Travels*. Swift's difficulties with the church authorities are well known, and his grasp of social niceties was poor. His clerical career never prospered as a result.

Philosophy

Among the great philosophers of relatively modern times that arguably meet the criteria for AS are Spinoza (1632–77), Kant (1724–1804), Ludwig Wittgenstein (1889–1951) and William Van Orman Quine (1908–2000). It is interesting that both Spinoza and Wittgenstein appeared to become less autistic and more philosophically and socially flexible in their forties. This mellowing of AS is not uncommon.

For Spinoza (at least in his early days), efficient reasoning was the yardstick for drawing conclusions to all aspects of human concern, including emotion. The root of human problems was an inability to reason properly. Spinoza offers a solution to problems of life in that he expects each person to reason things out for him or herself. The emphasis on the exercise of reason as the means to a less ambiguous existence is a common theme among philosophers with AS traits.

For instance, Kant, the great eighteenth-century theoretician of reason, was aloof and autonomous. He advocated self-control as one of the highest virtues. Hypochondria and sensitivity to noise persisted throughout his life – traits also found in Wittgenstein. He was a solitary man, uninterested in small talk, but with an astonishing capacity for work.

Wittgenstein was arguably the greatest philosopher of the twentieth century. The focus of much of his research was in areas that he had difficulties with himself: language and logic. His achievements were colossal in many areas; for example, he produced great philosophy, was a brilliant engineer, an architect and a decorated soldier, as well as a man who survived and coped with severe depression for most of his life. Wittgenstein's early work was characterized by an extreme egocentrism and the 'picture theory of meaning'. It is significant that a number of autistic writers have mentioned 'picturing' situations in helping them understand social reality. In his later work, he adopted a more socially aware and less logical view of communication. This work laid the foundation for 'ordinary language' philosophy where he spoke about 'language games'.

The American philosopher and logician Quine was heavily influenced by Wittgenstein and, like him, concentrated on understanding language. He was especially preoccupied with trying to explain how the exchange of meaning between people can occur. Again, we see dominant AS themes come to the fore.

Review and further reading

From the above, it is clear that people with AS have made enormous contributions to many aspects of life, often to the level of genius, and that they are a 'mixed bag' (allowing for the fact that they are almost exclusively male). If there were more space, many others could be included, for example, in the field of politics (Thomas Jefferson, Eamon de Valera), military life (Viscount Montgomery, Stonewall Jackson) and aviation (Charles Lindbergh). There is no reason for people with AS or other autism spectrum disorders to feel excluded or inadequate. There are many inspirational role models.

Irrespective of AS, several great biographies of leading physicists are found in Cropper (2001). Some of the most famous thinkers with presumed AS, including Newton, Einstein and Bartók, are covered by Ledgin (2002). Newton is also addressed by Fitzgerald (1999) and

Baron-Cohen (2003). Spinoza's understanding of the emotions has been examined from several perspectives (Damasio 2003; Fitzgerald 2001). Wittgenstein's presumed AS has been commented upon extensively (Fitzgerald 2000; Gillberg 2002). This literature is set to grow, and over the next decade we will learn more about the importance of AS in art, culture and science.

11 Life After College

As you come near to completing your first degree in college, a number of serious questions about your future career will need your attention. If you have fallen into an inheritance, these questions may have little financial relevance to you. However, the majority of graduates with AS will have to work for their living. You may have to look for a job after graduation or you may decide that further training is in your best interests. Continuing in the college environment suits many students with AS. Postgraduate studies allow them to pursue their special interests and open up exciting career possibilities. You may move to a different college. Others may be tired of college and want to change to a less socially demanding environment. Some will take jobs where few interactions with others occur and those that do occur are highly structured.

You may also need to consider the future of an existing relationship. If you have to move county, state or country, should you try to maintain the relationship, and if so how? If not, are there any issues you need to consider? Life after college brings a considerable number of choices, but it also brings greater measures of adult responsibility.

Career choices

After college you will be more independent, which means you will increasingly rely on your own communication skills to help you through problem situations. As an adult you will need to interact with other adults, especially if you are looking for employment or promotion within a job.

You should consider whether you need to improve (or learn) interviewing skills. An interview is a self-presentation exercise. It allows you to present the best aspects of yourself to the interviewing panel. Consequently learning to communicate within an interview is a very useful skill. Career guidance units routinely offer interviewing skills classes. Also many private companies offer interview training and analysis. You can choose either one or both options depending on your resources. We recommend, however, that the student counsellor briefs the trainers on AS in advance.

In theory the range of opportunities open to graduates with AS is equal to that of typical students. In practice certain occupations are more likely to provoke anxiety and stress than others. Academic jobs are probably most suited to those with AS. In fact any job that can grant you time out to pursue your own interests, with controllable social contact, is likely to be a good choice. Research jobs in the corporate sector are also a realistic option.

Jobs that involve high levels of interaction with the public, such as in sales and marketing, can be very wearisome. One could argue that successful salespeople are good at reading the nonverbal behaviour of their clients. Nevertheless, there are always exceptions and you should not rule out any job. It is doubtful whether counselling jobs are really suitable for people with AS. One could be a good, perhaps even excellent, research psychologist, without necessarily being a good counsellor. Counselling requires good 'people skills' and good empathy skills. It is probably best kept as a second-rank choice by someone with AS.

A final point to consider in any career choice is whether you will require continuing support in that career. In college you will have had the benefit of high-quality access to support services. You will also have been in the company of peers, many of whom may have been very supportive and understanding. These supports will not be available in a typical corporate working environment. The transition can be very stressful. You should reflect seriously on whether you need to disclose about AS to your employer.

We know of one young graduate who took a job in a video production company. He worked in the technical department. Each evening he went home at 5.30 pm precisely. The other employees thought he was slightly eccentric but were fond of him. The company began losing business and to become more competitive projects had to be completed more quickly. This meant staff staying late on occasions, usually without much notice, though time off was given as a reward. The young graduate with AS had great difficulty adjusting to this change in routine. Eventually one of his parents contacted the employer and explained the implications of AS. The employer decided that the best way to deal with any problem was to notify the employee as much in advance as he could that late working would be required. Once the potential changes were known in advance, the employee was content to stay for late working.

Stephen Shore recounts how he lost his first accounting job after a few months because the personnel officer judged that he was not fitting in, and may have failed to disclose an underlying disability before joining the company (Shore 2003, p.112). Fortunately, he recovered from this setback and secured much more rewarding employment. If you do disclose after taking up the job, your employer may be concerned that the disclosure was not made earlier. There are few convenient answers. Your national AS organization may have an insight into how best to proceed in these circumstances. Your counsellor can also help in exploring options. Remember, people with AS can be better than average in certain careers.

Importance of career guidance

Getting the right type of career guidance is important in helping you realistically to assess your employment options. Check whether the people offering career guidance actually know anything about AS. If they need additional information or a lot of information, ask the student counsellor to advise them. This is very important. You cannot be sure that student support services and career guidance share the same information about your interests and preferences.

If you have been a high achiever academically, you will have many employment choices. However, just because you are qualified for certain jobs, this does not in itself guarantee that these are suitable for someone with AS. In the worst case you may take on a job that becomes over-whelmingly stressful very quickly. In many cases employees with AS will leave and seek out less stressful positions. Often these new positions are below the ability level of the individual. Work closely with career guidance to establish a profile of a job before applying for it. Plan this exploration carefully. Reassure yourself that you can function effectively in the position before accepting it. Foreknowledge and planning are crucial to making the right choice.

One way to pre-empt difficulty is to work with the career guidance unit in your college in selecting employers that are friendly to AS gradu-ates. This is an ideal outcome but such employers are not abundant. Student counselling services may have a list of graduates with AS that are successfully employed in the locality. Ideally, as we mentioned in Chapter 9, career guidance and your local support group should invite several of these successful people to talk about their job, how they planned it, what routines they have and what problems they encounter.

The transition from college to the workplace is challenging. New people and new routines have to be accommodated. A high degree of adaptability is required. If you have worked in temporary jobs while in college, then you will be better prepared for full-time employment. If you have very little employment experience outside of college, then employ-ment off campus may come as a shock. Ideally, temporary work place-ments should be possible before committing to a job. In reality that is rarely practical, but ask career guidance if even a half-day placement is possible. Many IT courses have work placement modules which give students realistic work experience. Between three and six months will be spent off campus working. While the placement may not be with the company that will eventually employ you, nevertheless the experience is very useful.

If this option is not available, career guidance can organize day trips to companies. These visits will give you a 'feel' for the activity in each company, and also a chance to assess the environment for comfort and noise. Career choices must be considered carefully. Few employers will offer levels of support comparable to what you receive as a student. So choose wisely.

Using strengths

In your dealings with career guidance, the best outcome is employment that allows you to develop your interests and make a positive contribution in your job. Traditionally, many graduates with AS have come from engineering, mathematics, computer science and physics. These areas are very important to the economy of industrialized nations. Your contribution can have a real impact on the future.

The universities naturally capitalize on the strengths of people with AS by providing research opportunities. Of all the options open to graduates with AS, the development of an academic career should be seriously considered. One's interest and commitment to a subject, coupled with perseverance, make research very attractive. Laboratory-based work in medical and pharmaceutical settings is equally interesting and makes effective use of intellectual strengths.

Outside of direct academic research, employment based on record keeping or bookkeeping also leans on the strengths of AS. A library requires staff that have a good sense of order, neatness and fastidious attention to detail. Bookkeeping needs people who are capable of applying rules consistently, and have a fondness for neatness and detail.

Each person will have a variety of strengths and weaknesses. Career guidance should help you make a list of these. List only strengths that you have, and not those you would like to have. Acknowledging one's weaknesses is sometimes difficult, but in the matter of assessing employment suitability it is vital.

Relationship choices

If you have had a steady boyfriend or girlfriend during college, graduation is often a 'crunch point' in the relationship. Many graduates leave the locality and move to other colleges and employment far away. The question that often arises is whether to ask your partner to accompany you. There is no simple answer. A sensible piece of advice is to settle into your new environment before making any commitments. You may find that the change in environment has made continuation of the relationship impossible. Perhaps you have realized that you need all your energy to focus on settling into your new role. Of course, you may wish your partner to be with you and that is an equally valid decision.

If you are in a steady relationship or marriage, perhaps a legal agreement about property rights may need to be considered at some point. Financial security is important in relationships. If you have not already considered pensions, life insurance and mortgages, you soon will be.

Any future plans?

Have some plans for the future in mind. They will guide your choices and help frame your expectations of future events more realistically. Ask yourself a hard question such as: *Where do I want to be in my career in five years?* An even harder question to answer is: *Where do I want my personal relationships to be in five years' time?*

Future planning has to be accepted as tentative and speculative. Intermediate goals along the way may not be realized, but there is something to be said for at least laying down yearly plans and reviewing performance at the end of each year.

The issue of expectations

We commonly expect major changes in our lives and outlook after graduation. Mostly there are gradual changes. The importance of planning your daily and weekly routines should not be set aside. College is in fact quite structured and life outside may be a lot more unstructured. You may have very reasonable expectations of your employment, other people, public service, and so forth that are not realized. This can be annoying. If you have been relying on the student counsellor to provide support, you may now have to engage a private therapist.

Surprisingly, you may also experience a sense of loss after graduation. Leaving your college signifies a move away from familiarity, friends and acquaintances. Having mixed feelings is quite common. However, it is better to view change not as a setback but as a new beginning, a new learning point for the future. You may find an AS support group in your locality that will help you settle into your new environment.

Stay in touch with career guidance for the first year after graduation. You may want to be notified of other jobs. Career guidance will also be grateful for feedback from you as to whether the job has lived up to your expectations.

Marriage and family

Marriage is a big responsibility and should be approached slowly and carefully. Not everyone wishes to marry but many couples who are cohabiting satisfactorily will eventually marry, partly out of respect for tradition and partly from legal obligations deriving from property and children's rights. Valuable insights into an AS marriage are given in Slater-Walker and Slater-Walker (2002). If you are planning to marry, spend some time reading their book and identify where possible points of conflict exist in your own relationship.

Financial budgeting of your income is even more important when married. Various loans and mortgages will need to be negotiated and all of your borrowing power is dictated by your income (or joint income if both partners are working). This is why starting with the right career guidance advice is so important.

If you have children or are planning to have children, then the proximity of a home to churches, synagogues, schools, shopping centres, and so on needs assessment. As a potential or recent graduate all of these responsibilities may seem years away, but forward planning will pay dividends later.

Recommendations

The main recommendations in this chapter are to use career guidance services wisely in your choice of job. Accumulate as much advance knowledge as possible on potential future employers. Devise a policy on disclosing (or not disclosing) about AS with advice from the student counsellor, your therapist and the local branch of any national AS organization.

Do not lose touch with local support groups after graduation, and adopt some form of forward planning to help you structure your future. Marriage and family life are such big commitments that they require much preparation, patience and planning. There are few AS-specific employment guides. Although it is not graduate focused, Meyer (2001) is worth consulting on the challenges of the general workplace.

Once you have chosen a suitable career path, with time, patience and some luck you will be as successful as anyone else. As the history of ideas shows us, many of those with AS can have a great and enviable future ahead of them.

APPENDIX 1 Gillberg's Diagnostic Criteria for AS

Christopher Gillberg's diagnostic criteria are closely based on Hans Asperger's original diagnostic categories (Gillberg 2002). We include them as a handy reference.

1. Social impairment (extreme egocentricity) (at least two of the following):

    (a) Difficulties interacting with peers

    (b) Indifference to peer contacts

    (c) Difficulties interpreting social cues

    (d) Socially and emotionally inappropriate behaviour.

2. Narrow interest (at least one of the following):

    (a) Exclusion of other activities

    (b) Repetitive adherence

    (c) More rote than meaning.

3. Compulsive need for introducing routines and interests (at least one of the following):

    (a) Which affect every aspect of the individual's everyday life

    (b) Which affect others.

4. Speech and language peculiarities (at least three of the following):

    (a) Delayed speech development

    (b) Superficially perfect expressive language

    (c) Formal pedantic language

    (d) Odd prosody, peculiar voice characteristics

    (e) Impairment of comprehension, including misinterpretation of literal/implied meanings.

5. Nonverbal communication problems (at least one of the following):

    (a) Limited use of gestures

    (b) Clumsy/gauche body language

    (c) Limited facial expression

    (d) Inappropriate facial expression

    (e) Peculiar, stiff gaze.

6. Motor clumsiness:

    Poor performance in neurodevelopmental test.

© 2002 Cambridge University Press

APPENDIX 2 Useful Websites

There are so many websites that, rather than offend various agencies by their omission, we have adopted a very minimal listing. Use search engines to locate other sites. However, before doing that, look up links to national organizations at: www.autism-resources.com

The authors have a website to support social skills training of students with AS in college: www.aspergergroup.org. Remember to download the latest Flash player from www.macromedia.com

The Irish Asperger society Aspire is at: www.aspire-irl.com

Almost every country will have a variety of websites supporting people with autistic spectrum disorders. The UK National Autism Society maintains an excellent website: www.nas.org.uk

An Asperger site based in the UK is: www.as-if.org.uk

The US has many useful links but you should begin with: www.asperger.org

Some research-oriented charity sites are: www.cureautismnow.org and www.naar.org

And remember, browse carefully.

References

Attwood, T. (1998) *Asperger's Syndrome: A Guide for Parents and Professionals.* London: Jessica Kingsley Publishers.

Baron-Cohen, S. (2003) *The Essential Difference: Men, Women and the Extreme Male Brain.* Harmondsworth: Penguin.

Cropper, W.H. (2001) *Great Physicists: The Life and Times of Leading Physicists from Galileo to Hawking.* Oxford: Oxford University Press.

Damasio, A. (2003) *Looking for Spinoza: Joy, Sorrow and the Feeling Brain.* Orlando, FL: Harcourt.

Eggins, S. and Slade, D. (1997) *Analysing Casual Conversation.* London: Continuum.

Ekman, P. (2003) *Emotions Revealed: Recognizing Faces and Feelings to Improve Communication and Emotional Life.* New York: Times Books Henry Holt and Company.

Fitzgerald, M. (1999) 'Did Isaac Newton have Asperger syndrome?' *European Journal of Child and Adolescent Psychiatry 8,24.*

Fitzgerald, M. (2000) 'Did Ludwig Wittgenstein have Asperger syndrome?' *European Journal of Child and Adolescent Psychiatry 9,* 61–65.

Fitzgerald, M. (2001) 'Was Spinoza autistic?' *Philosophers Magazine 14 (spring),* 15–16.

Gerland, G. (1997) *A Real Person: Life on the Outside.* London: Souvenir Press.

Gillberg, C. (2002) *A Guide to Asperger Syndrome.* Cambridge: Cambridge University Press.

Grandin, T. (1996) *Thinking in Pictures and Other Reports from My Life with Autism.* New York: Vintage.

Grandin, T. and Scariano, M. (1986) *Emergence: Labeled Autistic.* New York: Warner.

Holliday Willey, L. (1999) *Pretending to be Normal.* London: Jessica Kingsley Publishers.

Jackson, L. (2002) *Freaks, Geeks and Asperger Syndrome: A User Guide to Adolescence.* London: Jessica Kingsley Publishers.

Lawson, W. (2003) *Build Your Own Life: A Self-help Guide for Individuals with Asperger Syndrome.* London: Jessica Kingsley Publishers.

Ledgin, N. (2002) *Asperger's and Self-esteem: Insight and Hope through Famous Role Models.* Arlington, TX: Future Horizons.

Meyer, R.N. (2001) *Asperger Syndrome Employment Workbook: An Employment Workbook for Adults with Asperger Syndrome.* London: Jessica Kingsley Publishers.

Ozonoff, S., Dawson, G., *et al.* (2002) *A Parent's Guide to Asperger Syndrome and High Functioning Autism: How to Meet the Challenges and Help Your Child Thrive.* New York: Guilford Press.

Robertson, I. (2000) *Mind Sculpture: Unleashing Your Brain's Potential.* London: Bantam Press.

Sacks, O. (1995) *An Anthropologist on Mars.* London: Picador.

Shore, S. (2003) *Beyond the Wall: Personal Experiences with Autism and Asperger Syndrome.* Shawnee Mission, KS: Autism Asperger Publishing.

Slater-Walker, G. and Slater-Walker, C. (2002) *An Asperger Marriage.* London: Jessica Kingsley Publishers.

Index